# Bloom's Modern Critical Interpretations

*Bloom's Modern Critical Interpretations*

# Homer's
# *The Odyssey*
## *Updated Edition*

*Edited and with an introduction by*
# Harold Bloom
Sterling Professor of the Humanities
Yale University

BLOOM'S
LITERARY CRITICISM
*An imprint of Infobase Publishing*

**Library of Congress Cataloging-in-Publication Data**
Homer's The Odyssey / [edited by] Harold Bloom. -- Updated ed.
    p. cm. -- (Bloom's Modern critical interpretations)
  Includes bibliographical references and index.
  ISBN 0-7910-9425-1 (hardcover)
  1. Homer. Odyssey. 2. Epic poetry, Greek--History and criticism. 3. Odysseus (Greek mythology) in literature. I. Bloom, Harold. II. Title. III. Series.
  PA4167.H66 2007b
  883'.01--dc22                          2006035201

Contributing Editor: Pamela Loos

Cover designed by Ben Peterson

Cover photo: The Granger Collection, New York

Printed in the United States of America

Bang EJB 10 9 8 7 6 5 4 3 2 1

This book is printed on acid-free paper.

# Contents

# *Editor's Note*

The Introduction sees Odysseus as The Great Survivor, admirable but inspiring little affection in the reader.

Charles Segal meditates upon ritualistic strands in Odysseus' homecoming, while Margalit Finkelberg finds "endurance" to be the new mode of heroism in the *Odyssey*.

The narratives of wandering center S. Douglas Olson's essay, after which Lillian Eileen Doherty contrasts female and male modes of storytelling in the poem.

In a Feminist reading, Helene P. Foley argues for Penelope as *Odyssey*'s moral center, while Frederick Ahl and Hanna M. Roisman consider the opposite homecomings of Odysseus and of Agamemnon.

Penelope, in Nancy Felson-Rubin's view, is judged to be a highly complex moral character, after which Stephen V. Tracy outlines the elegant inter-structures of the *Odyssey*.

Bruce Louden seeks out Kalypso's function in the plot, while the role of Proteus is given prominence by Mark Buchan.

In this volume's final essay, Richard Heitman sums up Penelope's centrality in the plot.

HAROLD BLOOM

# Introduction

The *Odyssey*, though a clear sequel to the *Iliad*, is an immensely different poem in the experience of all readers. If one author wrote both, then the change from the *Iliad* to the *Odyssey* is as great as the difference between *War and Peace* and *Anna Karenina*, or between *Paradise Lost* and *Paradise Regained*. Such comparisons suggest a darkening of vision in Homer, as in Tolstoy or Milton, but of course the movement from *Iliad* to *Odyssey* is from tragic to comic, from epic to romance, from the rage of Achilles against mortality to the prudence of Odysseus in recovering wife, son, father, home, and kingdom. The *Iliad*, in fierce agon with the Bible, has set our standards for sublimity, but the *Odyssey* has been the more fecund work, particularly in modern literature. Joyce did not write a novel called *Achilles*, nor did Pound and Stevens devote poems to the hero of the *Iliad*. Like Dante and Tennyson before them, they became obsessed with Ulysses, whose quest for home contrasts oddly with the role of anti-Aeneas assigned to him by Dante and, more uneasily, by Tennyson.

A permanent mystery of the contrast between *Iliad* and *Odyssey* is that the *Iliad* seems much farther away from us, though it has less of the fantastic or the fabulous than the *Odyssey*. Achilles is a remote Sublime, whereas Odysseus is the complete man of Joyce's vision, coping with the everyday. Realistic description of marvels is the romance formula of the *Odyssey* and seems very different from the tragic world in which Achilles and

Hector strive to be the best. A literary critic who is not a classicist, and with indifferent Greek, nevertheless takes away from both epics an overwhelming sense of the unity of very separate designs in the immense consciousness of a comprehensive poet coming very late in a tradition. Samuel Johnson, my critical hero, darkly judged every Western poet coming after Homer to be belated. It is a productive irony that Johnson seems to me correct as to the *Iliad*, but that the *Odyssey* overwhelmingly strikes me as the epic of belatedness, the song of things-in-their-farewell.

We cannot envision Achilles existing in the day-to-day world of the *Odyssey*, which cannot accommodate so single-minded a hero. You go west, to the Islands of the Dead, to find the great Achilles or the frustrated spirit of Ajax, doomed always to be the second best. The Odysseus of Homer, superbly unlike the anti-Aeneas of Dante and Tennyson, is the true prototype of Aeneas, but Virgil's priggish moralist is an involuntary travesty of the hero of the Odyssey. Poor Aeneas actually must carry the emperor Augustus on his back, while Odysseus is free of ideology, unless the desire to reclaim what was once your own is to be considered a politics of the spirit.

Achilles, as critics note, is somewhat childlike, but Odysseus has had to put away childish things and lives in a world where you can freeze to death, as well as be devoured by one-eyed monsters. Self-control, a virtue alien to Achilles, is hardly a poetic quality as such and in Odysseus seems unallied to any system of morality. Americans justly find in Homer's later hero the first pragmatist, unimpressed by differences that do not make a difference. Existence, for the necessarily cunning Odysseus, is a vast obstacle course that has kept you away from home for a full decade and that will exercise you for a second decade as you voyage back. When you get there, your largest ordeal begins, since a slaughter in your own home, even with yourself as shrewd slaughterer, is an altogether more daunting prospect than even the most ferocious battling upon the windy plain of Troy.

Joyce's Ulysses, the humane though masochistic Poldy, is the most amiable personage in all literature, despite the absurd moralizings against him of Modernist critics. Homer's Odysseus is a very dangerous figure, whom we admire and respect but do not love. He is a great survivor, the one man who will stay afloat when all his shipmates drown. You would not want to be in one boat with him then, but there is no one you would rather read or hear about, because survival is the best of all stories. Stories exist to defer death, and Odysseus is a grand evader of mortality, unlike the tragic Achilles, who rages against being only half a god, yet who is pragmatically doom-eager. The agon of Achilles, the best of the Achaeans, is thus of a different order than the sensible ecstasy of Odysseus, who fights only when he must

CHARLES SEGAL

# Transition and Ritual in Odysseus' Return

Passage, transition, change: this phenomenon is the most familiar of human life and also the most difficult to comprehend. It is no wonder that this theme, in one form or another, is one of the central concerns of Greek philosophy, from Heraclitus and Parmenides to Plato and Aristotle. In placing at the center of the *Odyssey* the hero's passage from the marvels of Phaeacia to Ithacan reality and probability, Homer sets out in high relief, for the first time in European literature, the sense of the inexhaustible mystery of the changes of state or being, outward and inward, that constitute human life.[1]

The universal fact of change in human life is symbolized in the *Odyssey*, as throughout European literature, by the journey itself.[2] Yet Homer's hero, unlike Dante's or Tennyson's Ulysses, does not simply travel in search of new experiences. His journey is a return. Thus in the first four books we are anchored in the world of his human past, Ithaca and the Greek mainland, before we are allowed to follow Odysseus over distant seas. We are first shown the past that is to be regained and the threatened order that is to be restored.

In most societies, changes of state are marked by rituals that define change, visibly confront its reality, and orient the individual in the new world he or she has entered. Such rituals, or rites de passage, follow a more or less

From *Singers, Heroes, and Gods in the* Odyssey: 65–84 © 1994 by Cornell University.

constant pattern and show three major phases. These consist, according to Arnold van Gennep, of *rites of separation*, *rites of transition*, and *rites of incorporation*.[3] This division is useful for analyzing Odysseus' return. The journey between Troy and Ogygia constitutes a gradual *separation* from his Trojan warrior past (compare the widespread concern for the desanctification of the returning warrior most familiar, perhaps, from the Roman practices of lustration). The sojourn with the Phaeacians is a primarily *transitional* situation, succeeding the total suspension from "reality" on Ogygia and preceding the reentrance into Ithaca. The Ithacan adventures are mostly concerned with his *reincorporation* into the society he left behind and fittingly culminate in a reenactment of marriage. The analogies should not be pressed, and there is a certain overlapping, inevitably, between these ritual functions and the different stages of Odysseus' journey. Yet both the schema of the ritual and the structure of the poem share a common perception of a fundamental experience in human life.

The poem's transitional situations are reinforced by a number of recurrent themes or motifs that are well known in almost every mythic journey: the crossing of water, the changing of clothes, the sharing of food. Such themes in their various repetitions throughout the work gain a deepening significance, an effect that is totally consistent with the nature of oral epic, which proceeds in terms of repeated themes or groups of themes—contracted, expanded, or elaborated, as the poet requires.[4] The verbal repetition of the particular formula or formulas involved in such motifs often underlines the thematic repetition.[5] Indeed, the Homeric oral formulaic style itself almost ritualizes such actions by presenting them as fixed and stylized into a set pattern. These formulas provide a familiar and constant background for the newness that Odysseus is ever encountering in the exotic world of his adventures.

There is a latent tension between the formulaic language of the *Odyssey* on the one hand and the richness of the hero's experiences and the fabulousness of the poem's far-flung geography on the other. The very forces that were causing the loosening of the severer structure and style of the *Iliad* may also have contributed to the poem's interest in the primitive reaches of mythic lore behind elements such as Ogygia, Circe, the Cyclops, and the Phaeacians. The *Odyssey*'s greater openness of style, by comparison with the *Iliad*—for which Cedric Whitman, among others, has suggested analogies with the Proto-Attic style in pottery—leaves it receptive to the strange, shadowy figures of the preheroic past and to those primitive strata of myth and ritual that have so intrigued scholars such as J. A. K. Thomson, Gertrude Levy, and Gabriel Germain. These ritual elements should be considered in close connection with folktale and with the common

Mediterranean (and Bronze Age) storehouse of fable and legend. The blending of these common Aegean elements with the formal, demanding qualities of the Greek epic hexameter makes the *Odyssey* a poem that, like its hero, straddles two worlds, whereas the *Iliad* plants itself gigantically and immovably in one.

Underlying the themes of transition is a mythical pattern fundamental to the epic of quest, namely, the cyclic alternation of life and death; the rediscovery of life after a period of sterility, darkness, and imprisonment; and the ultimate victory of life over death, of order over disorder. This kind of epic, of which *Gilgamesh* is the prototype, embodies the experience, to quote Levy, "of loss and segregation, the temptations of love and fear, the vision of death and the return of the hero to the starting point, changed by the knowledge and acceptance of defeat."[6] The *Odyssey*, though undoubtedly based on such a mythic pattern, transcends it by turning its significance away from the originally ritually enacted death and rebirth of cosmic divinities to the realities and possibilities of human action and human nature. Yet beneath the human-centered action the underlying mythic structure still makes itself felt and gives the poem what Northrop Frye calls the "encyclopedic range" of high epic, an inclusiveness that embraces the totality of human experience.[7]

I define "ritual" in this context as a regularly performed action carried out in a stylized manner to indicate a significant contact with supernatural powers that are felt to embody essential and mysterious features of our existence. Some of these transitional situations in the poem may dimly echo actual transitional rituals of a remote past. I am not concerned with survivals of actual rituals but rather with the literary function of situations of transition in the poem as a work of art. Even in this limited sense, the ritual elements open into the realm of the sacred and the numinous and thus add an important dimension to the poem's meaning. For a society such as Homer's, the sacred and the profane are still closely united, and the division between a person's physical and spiritual life is much less clear than in modern Europe or America.

We can follow the unfolding of the return through an examination of recurrent motifs that involve or accompany transition. Those that I shall consider are sleep, the bath, purification, and the threshold. All, as will appear, are associated with the mystery of passage between worlds, and all belong to the realm of experience where known and unknown cross. Only two, purification and the bath, can properly be said to be of a ritual nature. The other two, sleep and the threshold, can be described simply as themes of significant transition. All four, however, reflect important stages of the return, the hero's gradual reclaiming of all that is his own.

## SLEEP

Sleep is perhaps the most obvious means of transition between the real and unreal worlds. Odysseus' return from the Phaeacians is an awakening out of a sleep "likest to death" (13.80). Like any passage or change of state, sleep is ambiguous. It can be like death or it can restore to new life. On his wanderings in the fantasy world, Odysseus is wary of sleep. As he sails from Calypso's island, Ogygia (5.271), he is the man of alert wakefulness who has learned not to trust sleep. When he has yielded to it, it has brought disaster, as on the voyage from Aeolus' island (10.31–55) or on Thrinacia (12.38). It is only when he arrives on Scheria, the Phaeacians' homeland, that sleep becomes positive and restorative. At first he resists it, as he did earlier in the wanderings, fearing wild animals (5.470–73); but the olive thicket saves him, and Athena "poured sleep upon his eyes, that she might ease him soon of his toilsome weariness" (5.491–93). The next night he sleeps in Alcinous' palace in perfect security, "on the well-bored bed, under the resounding portico" (7.345). As he emerges from the fantasy world, or at least from its more dangerous aspects, he can yield to sleep in safety. On his last voyage, when his struggles with the sea are over, he sleeps on the Phaeacians' ship, though they pay dearly for the effortlessness and safety of his passage (see 13.134–87). His reawakening (13.187), however, is a return to consciousness and to life.[8]

Sleep frames Odysseus' entire return. On Scheria, the bridge between the fantasy world and reality, he sleeps on arrival and departs in sleep. Later, in the repetition of his Phaeacian adventures to Penelope, the theme of sleep frames his tale. His account to her is introduced thus: "And she took pleasure in hearing, nor did any sleep fall upon her lids until he had related everything" (23.308–9). His tale ends: "This was the last tale he spoke of when sweet sleep that looses the limbs came upon him, loosing the cares of his heart" (23.342–43).

Hermes, bringing the message that sets in motion Odysseus' return from Ogygia, carries "the wand with which he charms the eyes of whomever he wishes and awakens them, in turn, when sleeping" (5.47–48). He then reappears as escort of the dead with the same wand (and almost the same two lines) immediately after the reunion of Odysseus and Penelope at the beginning of book 24. Hermes and the dead suitors mark the threatening complement to the life Odysseus has regained. As the god of both sleep and awakening, Hermes unites in himself the poles of failure and success, dream and reality. We may compare his function of guiding Priam through the limbo between the two camps in *Iliad* 24. On the one hand, Hermes is connected with sleep, dormancy, death—Odysseus' state during his "concealment" on Calypso's island. On the other hand, the god makes possible the hero's conquest over a powerful enchantress: he shows Odysseus how to overcome Circe. It is fittingly Hermes and his wand that appear at the beginning and end of the journey. Through him the magical potency of sleep marks the initial stages and the final fulfillment of the hero's return.

These passages and the recurrence of Hermes and his wand at the two ends of the journey home make the entire return appear under a great metaphor of sleeping and awakening. Part of Odysseus sleeps and rests until Athena begins to promote the awakening into the real world. On the divine level, she is the real motive force behind the return; she initiates it, unlike Hermes, who is only an agent, a mechanism fulfilling that which has already been set into motion by the will of the gods. Athena, too, is often the dispenser of sleep in the *Odyssey*, and there is perhaps a deeper connection between her other functions in the poem and her ministrations of sleep. It is perhaps because she is the divine force most clearly behind the return that she controls the mechanism of sleeping and waking, knowing when withdrawal and stillness are necessary and when, the process of recovery and integration complete, the mind may again awaken to the light of reality. Sleep marks a kind of moral awakening as well, for in the closing episode of the poem, the herald Medon wakes up just in time to explain to the enraged parents and relatives of the slain suitors that Odysseus acted with the assistance of the gods (24.439–49, especially 439f.: "Medon and the divine singer approached from the hall of Odysseus since sleep left them").

Sleep has a special importance for Penelope. She, indeed, is more frequently associated with sleep than is anyone else in the *Odyssey*. Her sleep often follows grief and weeping. It is a constant reminder of the emptiness of her bed and, hence, perhaps a retiring back into herself until Odysseus comes. Athena, as the ministrant of sleep for her, may be associated with her trust in the return of her husband and her full identity as the wife of Odysseus. Her sleep, therefore, as a communion with that trust through the goddess who is contriving her husband's return, is often restorative and soothing (see 4.839–40, 18.187).

Conversely, sleep is also a sign of her reduced life and the static condition of her world without Odysseus. In her sleep she is acted on by Athena, as in the two passages just cited. Sleep, however, is not a means of change and passage for her in the same way that it is for Odysseus (as in books 6 and 13). Crucial events occur while she sleeps, such as Telemachus' departure for the mainland at the end of book 4 and especially the slaying of the suitors. In the latter case, in fact, she says she has never slept so soundly since Odysseus left for Troy (23.18–19). Her sleep during the struggle with the suitors has some analogies with Odysseus' landing on

Ithaca: she awakens (or rather is, to her displeasure, awakened, 23.15–17) to find reality changed, to be told of the fulfillment of the hoped for return; and like Odysseus in book 13, she cannot recognize the truth until later. For her, however, sleep is more correctly a sign of the suspended condition of her life as she waits in quiet endurance and hope rather than the direct renewal of strength for positive action of her own. Her task is to hold out in hope, and sleep keeps her fresh for the time when the return is accomplished.

Her sleep, as a communion with her past, also keeps fresh the beauty that Odysseus knew before the war. In the deep sleep that precedes her tempting of the suitors in book 18, Athena carefully enhances her beauty (187–96). With the return of her beauty of past years comes also the resurgence of her longing for her husband. Here her recollection of Odysseus' departure is keenest, and she relates at length his parting words of twenty years before (257–70). Penelope not only reports at great length—which she never does elsewhere—an intimate moment with her long-absent husband but also does so at the very time when she is coaxing gifts from her wooers. It is more interesting still that Odysseus, present in disguise, should be pleased (281–83). It is as if her sleep and Athena's ministrations have reawakened in her a more vivid sense of the past, through which Odysseus recognizes in truth the wife he left behind. He knows, as the suitors do not, that "her mind is eager for other things" (283).

This unexpected flashback of Penelope's into the past also brings an ironical foreshadowing of the near future wherein the past will in fact be restored. The desire that Penelope arouses in the suitors is described with the metaphor of "loosing their knees" ("There were their limbs loosed, and they were made spellbound with desire in their hearts," 18. 212). The phrase refers not only to erotic desire but also to death or to the sinking despair at the fear of death. Telemachus echoes the phrase in this sinister sense shortly afterward, praying that the vanquished Irus' fate might be extended to the suitors ("and the limbs of each would have been loosed," 18.238). The same metaphor describes the suitors' reaction when Odysseus prepares to turn the deadly bow on them ("Thereupon were their knees and hearts loosed," 22. 68).[9] There are other ironic foreshadowings here in book 18, as when the suitors "die with laughter" (100). It has sometimes been suggested that from this point on there is operating within Penelope an intuitive or subconscious recognition of her disguised husband that prepares her for the "real" recognition in book 23.[10] If so, it is again sleep that creates the setting for this prerecognition, serving as the essential mediator between past and future, illuminating past happiness with the stark light of present longing.

Penelope's sleep in book 18, like Odysseus' in book 13, is compared with death: "I wish that chaste Artemis would send so soft a death" (18.201–2). Sleep, death, and change form a related cluster of motifs in the return but differ in their significance for Odysseus and Penelope. Her sleep after Telemachus' assertion of his authority over the bow (21.354–58) and during the slaughter does, in fact, mark a crucial passage, but one of which she remains oblivious until later. As a woman in a patriarchal society, Penelope lacks Odysseus' freedom and initiative; and so the transitions for her are veiled in sleep. Unlike Odysseus, she does not even know that a transition is being made. Yet for her, as for Odysseus in book 13, sleep marks a communion, through a kind of death, with her suspended status as wife and queen and precedes its vital awakening into life.

## THE BATH

The bath is a long-established sign of welcome (see Gen. 18:4) and mark of accepting a stranger into a new environment. It indicates to the newcomer a point of crucial entrance, and washing by water probably retains a certain ritual significance as the ceremony for this tradition. It is also obviously connected with birth and hence rebirth. Like other transitional situations, the bath has an essential ambiguity. It is physically pleasant (cf. the Phaeacians' pleasure in warm baths, 8.249) yet involves a potentially dangerous exposure. This latter aspect of the bath is familiar from the post-Homeric version of the return of Odysseus' less fortunate companion, Agamemnon. Through the bath changes can also occur, both in appearance (as frequently in the *Odyssey*) and in mood.

Here too the formulas underline the ritual element involved, for, as one would expect, similar formulas are used in nearly all the bathing scenes. There is, of course, a great deal of variety, but practically the same pair of lines occurs near the beginning of each instance of bathing ("X washed Y and anointed him with oil and put a beautiful cloak around him").[11]

Like sleep, the bath, through its outward function as a sign of welcome, can emphasize the danger of the passage to a new situation. Such is the bath Helen gave Odysseus at Troy when he entered the city in disguise (4.242–56). A bath may also be only partially accepted. Thus Circe has Odysseus bathed as a sign of her acceptance of him and his successful passage through the danger of her enchantments (10.348–53). Her bath has all the sensuous accompaniments that a bath by Circe should have (see especially 359–60, 362–63), including the four maidservants born "from springs and groves and from sacred rivers" (350–51). But still all this "pleased not" Odysseus' heart (173), and his grief for his companions disturbs the usual smooth flow of formulaic motifs. Here the purely physical restorative powers of the bath do not operate on the man who seeks a restoration of another kind. When the companions are changed back, however, all are bathed (449–51) and happily spend an entire year with her.

There is even a figurative bathing in a situation of dangerous passage in 12.237, where the seething of Charybdis is compared to water boiling in a caldron (*lebês*). In the next book, however, though seven years later, the Phaeacians in 13.13 make the friendly gift of a tripod and caldron, the implements regularly associated with bathing. The Phaeacians, too, are addicted to the comfort of warm baths (8.249).[12]

Two instances of bathing are of especial interest, that on Scheria in book 6 and Odysseus' bath by his nurse in book 19. In the first passage Odysseus, for the only time in the poem, is bathed in "the flowing streams of a river" (6.216), the "beautifully flowing river" that saved him from the sea and the rocks (5.441–44). The sweet waters succeed the "salt water";[13] and Odysseus' washing off of the "salt seawater" (6.219, 225–26) marks his return to safety, the end of his duel with the sea and Poseidon. Yet he refuses to let Nausicaa's maids bathe him, out of reluctance to be seen nude by "fair-tressed maidens" (220–22), especially after the ravages of the sea ("he appeared frightful to them, all befouled by the sea," 137). His refusal is perfectly in keeping with the situation: he shows a tactful delicacy of feeling in not offending the young girls on whom his salvation depends. Yet such an attitude toward nudity is unusual in the epic.[14] Odysseus' refusal, then, may be more than embarrassment. It may indicate also his hesitation to be drawn into his new environment more than is necessary, bathing being the sign of welcome and acceptance. When he was luxuriously bathed by Circe, after all, he spent a whole year. Now, ready for his return to Ithaca, he wishes to keep his distance from new involvements. Hence he bathes alone and thus keeps outside of the gaiety, youthful beauty, and carefree energy of the Phaeacian girls. He is bathed later by Arete's servants only when he is assured of his return (8.449–57).

The bathing by Eurycleia in book 19 (343–507) is, like the first Phaeacian washing, a ritual that is not fully or perfectly performed. Again Odysseus holds back, permitting himself to be washed solely by an old servant, "who has endured in her heart such things as even I have endured" (347). His refusal to let himself be washed by the younger servants, as in the Nausicaa episode, marks his insistence on reentering his world only under the sign of the suffering and aging that have become integral parts of him. Thus he seeks out the servant with whom he has the greatest bond of suffering (see 360, 374, and 378). The bath here has a double function: both ritual entrance and the means of revealing identity.

When Eurycleia drops the basin with a loud clang as her hand touches the scar (19.467–70), she spontaneously interrupts the proper ritual and thus inadvertently reveals the ambiguity of Odysseus' position—what should be a welcoming and safe gesture, the bathing of the master in his own house, is, in fact, fraught with danger. The reentrance is a perilous one and accordingly so indicated. Correspondingly, the revelation of his identity would be dangerous, as Odysseus firmly points out to his nurse (479–90). When Odysseus has overcome the danger, the familiar formula recurs ("she washed him and anointed him richly with oil," 505), but with the added details that Odysseus draws his stool closer to the fire to warm himself and "covered up the scar with his rags" (506f.).

This scene of bathing, by far the longest in the poem, recalls a corresponding situation of danger from which Odysseus escaped triumphantly: his bathing by Helen in Troy (4.252–56). The similarity is bitterly paradoxical, for on Ithaca he is now as much in the house of his enemies as he was at Troy. The clang of the basin may also serve as an evil omen for the suitors (like the clanging of the pitcher in 18.397), for the ritual of the bath marks Odysseus' official "entrance" into the life of the palace.

Odysseus' final bath in book 23 seals the fulfillment of his return and immediately precedes his recognition by Penelope (152–65). Here at last he is bathed openly in his own house without mishap and no longer, as in book 19, as a stranger. Athena, directress of his return to himself, enhances his beauty in lines repeated from the similar scene at his arrival in Scheria (23.157–62 = 6.230–35). Thus the beginnings of his return are brought full circle with its completion. Both crucial entrances are marked by a welcoming ceremony and divine aid. Washed up from the sea on Scheria, however, and among strangers, Odysseus bathed himself alone, in a river; here, on Ithaca, he is washed by his housekeeper, Eurynome, not merely under the shelter of a regular human dwelling but in his own house as well. After isolation, wandering, and exposure to the elemental forces of a mysterious world, he is now ensconced in the stability and safety of a reestablished social order. Athena presides over both scenes as the constant element. She reveals in the grizzled warrior the young husband who left twenty years before. The decisive recognition through the trial of the bed can thus follow immediately thereafter (23.171–208). The supernaturally enhanced beauty of the bathed Odysseus both in book 6 and in book 23 carries associations of nuptial imagery, the radiance of the newly married couple.[15] In book 23, however, the "wedding" is fully appropriate and figuratively takes place soon after, when the old nurse, Eurynome, leads the couple into their chamber, carrying the torch, just as in the nuptial ceremony (289–96).[16]

Finally, in book 24, the bathing of Laertes marks the extension of the process of rebirth and rejuvenation brought about by Odysseus (365–71). This passage also shows how the formulaic style reinforces the ritual repetition. The formulas used of Laertes here repeat those used in the bathing and miraculous enhancing of Odysseus' stature in the preceding book: "She made him larger and stouter to look upon than before," 24.369; and "larger and stouter to look upon," 23.157. The same formula, naturally, also introduces both bathing episodes:

> Then a Sikel maidservant washed and anointed with oil great-hearted Laertes in his own house.
> (24.365–66)

> Then Eurynome the housekeeper washed and anointed with oil great-hearted Odysseus in his own house.
> (23.153–54)

For both men, this bath marks a return to their rightful position of authority in "their own house." Both recover a lost vitality as father and king. The archetypal pattern of the restoration of the dead or maimed king is operative, in a sense, for Laertes as well as for Odysseus. Odysseus, to be sure, is now king (see, e.g., 24.501: "Odysseus led them"); yet Laertes performs a kingly action, as of old, in being the first to strike down his enemy (24.520ff.).[17] Odysseus' reentrance into the fullness of his past life, with its human ties, also re-creates those lives that wait on his; and they, too, are washed of their previous sufferings and prepared to resume a fullness of existence that had been lost.

## PURIFICATION

The bathing episodes can be seen as a ritual cleansing as well. But it is fire that replaces water as the purifying element in the crucial transition after the killing of the suitors and their accomplices (22.481–94). Odysseus refuses Eurycleia's offer to exchange his rags for more decent garb and insists on first purging the house with fire and sulphur: "Let there first of all [*prôtiston*] be fire in my halls" (24.491). It is perhaps felt that only the violence of fire, by a kind of homoeopathy, is sufficient to cleanse away the destructive aspects of the return that culminate in the suitors' death. Indeed, the thoroughness of this purgation—the only one of its kind in the *Odyssey*—is possibly the poet's indication that he recognizes and wishes to mitigate the brutality involved in the suitors' slaughter, the maids' execution, and the mutilation of Melanthius.

For Odysseus, too, fire is the final exorcism of the violence of the past years. Now leaving behind the war and the destructive monsters of the journey home, he must nevertheless reenter his house as he left it, a warrior, under the sign of violence—the blood-spattered lion and the purifying fire. Odysseus as a blood-splattered lion at the end of the slaughter is the image that Eurycleia reports to Penelope at the beginning of the following book: "You would have been warmed in spirit," she tells her just-awakened queen, "to have seen him splattered with blood and gore, like a lion" (23.47f.). The lion image evokes again the Iliadic world that the hero has been so long in leaving. At the same time, it is natural for the elderly servant to see in Odysseus the terrible warrior who has made good his return. She sees the outward, grim, one might say official aspect of Odysseus. The warrior, too, though speaking kindly words, was Penelope's last picture of her husband, as it recurred to her mind in book 18. But in the final recognition between them, she will look deeper into the past for another image: "For we have signs," she says, "hidden, which we alone know, apart from others" (23.109f.).

The fire at the end of book 22, ordered by the returned master from the faithful servant, helps make the palace his own again and rids it of the intrusive influences of the past. Only gradually, however, will Odysseus undergo the stepping-down process to become once more the familiar husband and "gentle father." He is curt and imperious in rejecting the clothes Eurycleia offers (485–91) and perhaps implicitly rejects also the bath that would naturally accompany such a change of raiment. The other participants in the slaughter wash immediately after the deed and the execution of the delinquent maids: "Then washing off their hands and feet they went to Odysseus in the house, and the deed was accomplished" (478–79). It is at this point that Odysseus calls for sulphur and fire. There is no bath for him until line 154 of book 23, immediately before the recognition near the bed. For him, the destructive, purifying force of fire precedes restorative waters at this point of crucial transition. It is only *after* this purgation that he is ready to reassume the positive elements in his life, to shed his rags (23.155), claim the living bed (23.181–206), and appear again as Penelope's husband.

This purification of the past parallels and completes another loss by fire and sulphur in the past, the blasting of his ship by Zeus' lightning off Thrinacia at the end of book 12: "The ship was filled with sulphur, and the companions fell from the ship" (417; cf. also Odysseus' tale to Eumaeus, 14.305–15). Ship and companions, the unstable remnants of his Trojan past, are purged before the hero undergoes the total isolation of Ogygia. This purgation is necessary and implicit in the preceding adventures, wherein Odysseus moves further and further from the heroic world into experiences of an increasingly private nature (Circe, the Sirens, the visions in Hades, Calypso). This sulphurous fire leaves Odysseus totally alone, cut off from his remaining human ties, "suspended" (12.432–36) over the abyss, surrounded by death. It also marks the transition to his greatest point of isolation, the seven years with the goddess Calypso, who would complete his separation from the mortal world and make him, like herself, immortal.

The sulphur and fire in his halls, however, mark the end of his isolation and the return to his full human position. He himself commands that the sulphur be brought: he is again in a world that he can understand and control, and in it he has reestablished his rightful authority. With the return of the legitimate king, order is restored and disorder purged. In book 12 the purgation is followed by loss and death; in book 22, by recovery and life. Both have been necessary, and the second naturally succeeds the first; but both also constitute a purgation of the forces that prevent the full return.

Odysseus' successful purgation through blood and fire contrasts with a bloody death of a different outcome, the murder of Agamemnon, as the victim describes it in Hades. The blood of the murdered king "seethed upon the ground" (11.420).[18] The contrast between Agamemnon's return and that of Odysseus is not only between death and life, failure and success, but also between pollution and purification. The parallel is pointed up by the repetition of this half-line about the bloody ground in the slaughter of the suitors (11.420 = 22.309); and the half-line occurs but once more in Homer, when the suitors describe their death to Agamemnon in Hades (24.185 = 22.309). There is a significant inversion of the theme in this repetition, for it was first Agamemnon who described to Odysseus the "seething" of his own (and his companions') blood (11.420); it is now Odysseus' vengeful shedding of blood that is described to him (24.185).

The parallels are part of a carefully developed antithesis between the two returns. Both Agamemnon and the suitors are slaughtered at a banquet, amid tables and feasting. The death of Agamemnon, however, is a sinister, perverted ritual. He is, as it were, "sacrificed" like an ox ("as one would kill an ox at the trough," 11.411 = 4.535, and cf. Aegisthus' sacrifices, 3.273–75). Agamemnon fails at his point of crucial transition as Odysseus succeeds at his. Both returns at their completion contain ritual elements involving fire and sacrifice. In Agamemnon's return this significant entrance and the ritual motifs accompanying it have their full measure of potential destructiveness. For him these purgative and ritual associations bring only defilement and pollution. For Odysseus, the "seething" blood and sulphurous fire are succeeded by water and the restorative, cleansing bath.

## THE THRESHOLD

Because it marks the passage between known and unknown, the crossing of the threshold is, like bathing or the receiving of guests, a significant, danger-fraught act. Even in today's industrialized and rationalized societies, the threshold retains its symbolic value as a critical transitional point, safeguarded by magical representations or good-luck charms. It is but one example of the many dangerous entrances or guarded gates to be encountered in every epic journey into the unknown, from *Gilgamesh* on. The threshold in the *Odyssey* serves as the human, comprehensible counterpart to such mysterious entrances as the double-portalled "misty cave" on Ithaca in book 13, the crucial juncture between worlds.

At the beginning of the human action in the poem, when Athena sets in motion Odysseus' return and Telemachus' journey, she appears to the latter "on the threshold of the court" (1.104) as he is thinking of his father's return and the expulsion of the suitors. Inviting her within the house is the initial sign of his new spirit of manly independence that will now take him to the courts of the heroes on the mainland.

In Odysseus' journey the threshold is more involved with dangerous and supernatural elements. The Cyclops' great stone bars his threshold (9.242) and makes the passage out one of the greatest tests of Odysseus' wit and courage. In his entrance into and passage out of the Phaeacian kingdom, the crossing of thresholds receives special attention. Alcinous' threshold, like Aeolus' palace, is of bronze, and Odysseus approaches it with anxious thoughts (7.82–83), to be succeeded by wonder (see 7.134), until he crosses it to find the Phaeacians engaged in pious libations (7.135–38).

For the Phaeacians as well as for Odysseus, this entrance produces a tense situation, for the treatment of a stranger is always a delicate and dangerous matter. Coming from the unknown and potentially hostile outside, he must somehow be incorporated into the familiar, made *philos*, a part of what is "friendly" and so part of "one's own" normal reality (the double meaning of Homeric *philos*). For Odysseus, there is also his accumulated experience of other ways, not all friendly, in which a stranger may be treated. Thus at this point of crucial transition, the Phaeacians' remarkable silence emphasizes the tension and the in-between state of Odysseus (7.154). The tension is resolved and the full entrance effected by a succession of ritual acts. Echenaos breaks the silence with the suggestion of a libation to Zeus "who attends suppliants worthy of respect" (7.165). Then King Alcinous takes Odysseus by the hand (a significant establishment of physical contact: cf. 3.36–39) and seats him on a "bright chair" in the place of his own son, Laodamas (7.167–70). Odysseus is then washed (172–74); a table is set, and a common meal, shared (175–77).

The due libation to Zeus "who attends suppliants worthy of respect" (181 = 165) is then carried out (179–81). Here, not only the ritual acts themselves but also the familiar formulas by which they are described strike a reassuring note and mark the successful completion of an important stage in the return.

When Odysseus is about to leave Phaeacia and make the final crossing of waters back to the mortal world, the threshold once more underlines the significant passage. His last conversation among the Phaeacians is with Arete, their queen: "'Fare you well, O Queen, all the time until old age and death come which come upon men. But I depart. Do you in this house take joy in children and people and Alcinous the king!' So saying, over *the threshold he crossed*, noble Odysseus" (13.59–63). He then boards the swift ship and embarks for Ithaca, his mind fully turned, in this conversation, toward the human world he is about to reenter.

Later, on Ithaca, Odysseus approaches his palace disguised as a beggar and actually sits on "the ash-wood threshold within the doors" (17.337–40). He now occupies in squalor the very point of entrance to what he has so long sought. Later, in 20.258, Telemachus seats Odysseus further inside, "by the stone threshold," but still just barely within his house. Then, in the contest of the bow, Telemachus tries it at the threshold (21.124), whereas Odysseus, in slaying the suitors, shoots from his seat to the door (21.420–23). He thus not only demonstrates his masterful ease with the bow but also establishes his rightful position inside the palace. Finally, at the beginning of the slaughter, Odysseus "lept upon the great threshold" (22.2), and later "the four stand upon the threshold, but within the house are many men and noble" (22.203–4). Here, the proper place of inner and outer is again reversed, and the rightful possessor must for the last time make good his claim and establish his identity through a dangerous passage. Here, also, the transition to a new condition is underlined by a throwing aside of clothing: Odysseus throws off his rags (22.1) to reveal himself to the suitors and leaps on the threshold.

Afterward, when Penelope is informed, she wonders "whether she should address her dear husband from a distance or stand beside him and kiss his head and take his hands." She then "crosses over the stone threshold" and sits "opposite Odysseus" (23.86–89). These lines also recall Odysseus' significant entrance among the Phaeacians in the seventh book, where he hesitates before crossing the threshold (7.82–83 = 23.85–86). The description of Penelope sitting "in the light of the fire" (23.89) also recalls Arete sitting by the fire in that scene of book 7 (cf. 7.153–54; also 6.305).[19] There, Odysseus supplicated the Phaeacian queen directly after crossing the threshold into Alcinous' hall and then sat himself "on the hearth by the fire" (7.153–54).[20] A striking combination of transitional themes thus connects the two episodes: in both, the hero confronts a queen, and in both, hesitation at the threshold is combined with sitting by the fire. Here, too, the beginnings of the return in the emergence from fairyland are joined to its completion on Ithaca. Now, however, Penelope rather than Odysseus initiates the crucial passage back to reclaim what has been lost. After the man has won his way back by his strength and endurance and by the constant exercise of his will and reason, the final movement of acceptance, the spontaneous rekindling of the intimate tie between them, is left to the woman. She will test the man who has been the tester on so many other occasions.

The return of Odysseus has been described above in terms of a reawakening. It appears also as a rebirth. The theme of bathing, as suggested earlier, has obvious connections with birth and rebirth. Occurring at points of significant entrance, it naturally accompanies the exchange of age and debility for youth and freshness. One of the most crucial entrances makes the connection explicit. The nurse who bathes Odysseus in book 19 is an obvious maternal figure, and she vividly remembers the actual birth of Odysseus and his naming by his grandfather (19.399–409, and cf. especially 400, "newborn child," and 482–83, "Why do you wish to destroy me, my nurse? For you yourself nursed me at your breast").[21]

Birth and death, then, the most mysterious passages of human life, underlie the overall rhythm of the return and oscillate ambiguously in it in a kind of contrapuntal movement. To obtain passage back to mortal life, Odysseus must visit the land of the dead. The knowledge of his own death gained from this visit is present to him even at the moment of the joyful reclaiming of his human life and his spouse: "O wife, we have not yet come to the limit of our trials, but afterward there will be still measureless toil, much and difficult," he begins (23.248), and goes on to tell her, reluctantly, of Teiresias' prophecy of his death (263–84). Earlier, Odysseus regarded his Phaeacian landing as a rebirth and thanked Nausicaa for "giving him life" (8.468). It is fitting that the fresh princess should be the restorer of life to the exhausted warrior; yet his sleep on the ship that brings him back to the mortal world and fulfills the Phaeacians' promise is "most like to death" (13.80). In the same contrapuntal fashion, the dead suitors are paraded off by Hermes, "leader of souls" (*psuchagôgos* or *psuchopompos*) as the grim counterpart to Odysseus' successful return to full "life."

Odysseus' rebirth is also a source of life for those who waited: son, wife, and father. It is a rebirth for Odysseus' line as well, marked in the joyful utterance of Laertes, himself rejuvenated after his bath (24.365–82), when he sees "son and grandson striving concerning excellence" (24.515). The renewal of Odysseus' life is here fulfilled in terms beyond himself; and he stands in the middle as the link between generations, between past and future. This rebirth is transferred also into moral and social terms at the very end of the *Odyssey*: the interference of the gods ends the cycle of strife and assures "wealth and peace in abundance," as Zeus had promised Athena (24.486). The poem thus ends with the order of Zeus with which it began; and the promised restoration of the land comes with the return of the rightful king and "gentle father," as foreshadowed in Odysseus' first words with Penelope on his return, when he addresses her, disguised as a beggar, in the darkened halls:

> My lady, never a man in the wide world
> should have a fault to find with you. Your name
> has gone out under heaven like the sweet
> honor of some god-fearing king, who rules
> in equity over the strong: his black lands bear
> both wheat and barley, fruit trees laden bright,
> new lambs at lambing time—and the deep sea
> gives great hauls of fish by his good strategy,
> so that his folk fare well.
>     (19.107–14; Fitzgerald's translation)

Though Penelope and Odysseus have not yet explicitly recognized each other, they meet here both as the individual characters they are and as the archetypal king and queen, the partners in a sacred marriage. In terms of Frye's "encyclopedic range" of epic, their union symbolizes the ever-renewed fertility of the earth and the fruitful harmony between society and cosmos.

These ritual elements not only imply this larger dimension of meaning but also point to an artistic function behind a basic component of the poem's style: the ritualizing quality of the repeated formulas. Through the repetition of the verbal formulas, the recurrent acts of sleep, bathing, entrance, and departure stand out in a suggestive ritual character, with the overtones of meaning carried by that ritual character for a society such as Homer's. One may regard this cooperation of matter and style as a happy by-product of Homeric language. Yet there may be an inner congruence between the material and the style, a congruence that grows out of the culture itself and its means of apprehending and ordering the world. The outwardly inflexible demands of the oral style, in other words, seem to suit the ritual modes of thought that doubtless helped to create the style in the first place. These are modes of thought in which recurrent cycles of loss and regeneration, alienation and rediscovery, and death and rebirth are celebrated as the fundamental facts of existence and form an organic link between human life and the natural world. Such cyclical patterns are both metaphor and reality;

and the ritual patterns discussed here help unite the two, for ritual itself partakes of both play and seriousness, both imaginary projection and realistic confrontation.

The very fabric of Homer's language, then, presents the expected, reenacted situations that make up the return through the equally predictable, crystallized, ritualized expressions that make up the formulas. These recurrent formulaic expressions themselves intimate the steady sameness, the shared narrowness, and the richness in limitation that form the substance of that for which the hero has journeyed back to Ithaca. The contrast between the circumscribed, formulaic language of the *Odyssey* and the richly varied, brightly colored adventures it describes also reflects the poem's movement between exploration and return, between the exotic and the familiar, and between the open possibilities of the free traveler who consorts with goddesses and the accepted constraints and rewards of the land dweller who is bound to a mortal woman.

## NOTES

1. For the significance of the Phaeacian episode and the hero's reclaiming of his human identity, see above, Chapters 2 and 3.

2. For the symbolic implications of the journey in the "epic of quest," see Levy (1953) chapter 5 and passim.

3. Van Gennep (1960) 21 and passim. See also the introduction by Solon T. Kimball, vii ff.

4. For the recurrent theme in oral epic, see Lord (1960): "Each theme small or large—one might say, each formula—has around it an aura of meaning which has been put there by all the contexts in which it has occurred in the past. It is the meaning that has been given it by the tradition in its creativeness. To any given poet at any given time, this meaning involves all the occasions on which he used the theme, especially those contexts in which he uses it most frequently; it involves also all the occasions on which he has heard it used by others, particularly by those singers whom he first heard in his youth, or by great singers later by whom he was impressed. To the audience the meaning of the theme involves its own experience of it as well. The communication of this suprameaning is possible because of the community of experience of poet and audience" (148). See in general chapter 4, "The Theme," and especially 89–91 and 109 for ritual elements in recurrent epic themes; on the level of the formula rather than the theme, see Whitman (1958) chapters 1 and 6.

5. The simplest definition of the formula in Homer is a recurrent expression of fixed metrical value, such as "rosy-fingered dawn" or "so speaking he went off." I use the term "formulaic," however, somewhat more broadly here, to apply also to the repeated passages of one or more lines that describe certain standard actions, for example, bathing, eating, and the embarkation of ships. On the formula in general, see Lord (1960) chapter 3.

6. Levy (1953) 21–22.

7. Frye (1957) 218ff.

8. See above, Chapter 3, note 15.

9. Note also the similar "and their knees were loosed" in a sinister sense elsewhere in book 18, e.g., 238, 242, and 341. This mixture of the sinister and the erotic in the "loosing of the knees" is taken up later in the book in Odysseus' banter with the maids who have become paramours of the suitors. He assures them that he will be able to supply light for all, even if they wish to stay up until dawn: "They will not conquer me," or as Fitzgerald (1963) translates, "They cannot tire me out" (18.319), at which the maids laugh and glance at one another (18.320). This possible double entendre in "loosing the knees" is reflected in the twofold use of the closely related adjective *lusimelês*, "loosing the limbs," an epithet of sleep and death, on the one hand, and of love, on the other: cf. *Od.* 20.57, Hesiod *Theog.* 121 and 911, Sappho fragment 130 Lobel-Page (1955), and *Carmina Popularia* 873.3 Page (1962); also Alcman 3.61 Page (1962).

10. For discussion of Penelope's recognition of Odysseus in book 18, see Amory (1963) 100ff.; also Harsh (1950), esp. 10ff. For a different interpretation, see Else (1965) 47–50 and Russo (1982) passim, especially 11ff.

11. See 3.466–67, 4.49–50, 4.252, 6.227–28, 8.454–55, 10.364–65, 17.88–89, 23.154–55, 24.366–67.

12. For the soothing and gentle connotations of bathing, see also Pindar *Nemean* 4.4–5.

13. Note the use of the phrase "salt water" three times in close succession of Charybdis: 12.236, 240, 431. Compare also the single occurrence of the phrase "sweet water" of the safe harbor on Thrinacia (12.306). Thrinacia is, in fact, a place of shelter as long as the Sun's cattle are not harmed.

14. For the usual absence of such self-consciousness about nudity and bathing, see Stanford (1958–61), on 3.464. Germain (1954) 310ff. would explain the irregularity of this modesty by the influence of the Near East and the oriental sacral significance of nudity.

15. Note especially the allusion to the hair like hyacinth in lines 6.231 = 23.158 and Sappho's epithalamion, fragment 105c Lobel-Page (1955).

16. On this scene see below, Chapter 5.

17. Note that earlier (24.353–55), too, Laertes is the first to assess the danger of reprisal from the suitors' families.

18. The verb *thûein* (probably the same root as "Thyiad") means literally "rushed forth," "flowed," but there may also be some association with "smoke" or "steam" (cf. Latin *fumus*), which might suggest a connection with fire and purification: see Stanford (1958–61) on 11.420, Heubeck and Hoekstra (1989) on 11.420, and Caswell (1990) 52–63.

19. The theme of sitting by the fire is developed in the first meeting of Odysseus and Penelope as well. First, in 17.572 Odysseus sends word to Penelope through Eumaeus that it would be better to meet him in the evening, "seating me nearer the fire." Then, in 19.55, when Penelope comes down from her chamber, she is given a seat "by the fire." Finally, Odysseus, just before she addresses him and immediately after his bath by Eurycleia, draws his stool "closer to the fire" (19.506). The theme of meeting by the fire thus prepares for and is duly completed by the final meeting "by the fire" in book 23.

20. For this scene as a situation of ritual rebirth, see Newton (1984) 8–9.

21. The connection between Eurycleia's bathing of Odysseus and the theme of birth is stressed by Baudouin (1957) 45ff., who would go so far as to regard the scar as a "signe de naissance."

MARGALIT FINKELBERG

# Odysseus and the Genus 'Hero'

T he *Iliad* proceeds from an idea of hero[1] which is pure and simple: a hero is one who prizes honour and glory above life itself and dies on the battlefield in the prime of life.[2] Indeed, in spite of what Achilles says at a bitter moment of the choice between a short and glorious life and a long and obscure one, his actual choice is made when, warned by Thetis that Hector's death is only a prelude to his own, he prefers to kill Hector and die himself rather than leave Patroclus unavenged.[3] Hector behaves in a similar way: having chosen honour over life, he remains outside the walls of Troy to meet his death at Achilles' hands.[4] Hundreds of minor Iliadic warriors make the same choice in a less spectacular way, by the very fact that they volunteered to come to Troy in order to win glory in war. This is true both of young Simoeisios, who came to Troy even before he had time to take a wife, and fell 'like a black poplar' at Ajax' hands, and of Lycaon son of Priam who, having slipped away from nearby Arisbe where he was kept in safety as a hostage, returned to the battlefield only to be taught in his last moments the bitter lesson that death is after all the inevitable conclusion to life.[5] This attitude of the Iliadic warrior is epitomized in the following words of Sarpedon to Glaucus:

> Ah, friend, if once escaped from this battle we were for ever to be ageless and immortal, neither would I fight myself in the

From *Greece & Rome* 42, no. 1 (April 1995): 1–14. © 1995 by Oxford University Press.

foremost ranks, nor would I send thee into the war that giveth
men renown, but now—for assuredly ten thousand fates of death
do every way beset us, and these no mortal may escape nor
avoid—now let us go forward, whether we shall give glory to
other men, or others to us.[6]

There can be no doubt that this is a pattern into which Odysseus of the
*Odyssey* would not fit. True, Odysseus' surviving the war was far from being
a matter of his personal choice: he did not shrink from risking his life on
the battlefield (*Il.* 11.401–13 is the best proof of this), nor did he challenge
the heroic code of behaviour by preferring long life to glorious death. It was
above all the circumstances of Odysseus' life that determined that he should
stay alive rather than die young. The fact however is that these circumstances
exposed him to a life-experience in the face of which any conventional heroic
response would have been out of place, with the result that there is no way in
which Odysseus' behaviour throughout the *Odyssey* can be accounted for as
heroic on terms of the *Iliad*. In what follows, I shall argue that the *Odyssey* not
only is aware of the fact that the situation of its hero differs essentially from
that of the heroes of the *Iliad*, but that this poem proceeds from a different
idea of hero than that found in the *Iliad*.

## I

The presence of 'unheroic' features in the character of Homeric Odysseus
was noticed long ago, and since the time of the ancient commentators it has
become habitual to gloss those features by predicating them on Odysseus'
*metis*, 'cunning', as opposed to the *bie*, 'might', of other Homeric heroes,
first and foremost Achilles.[7] There is, however, reason to believe that the
difference between the heroes of the two epics goes far beyond these two
characteristics.

   That the feature of *metis* does not exhaust the character of Homeric
Odysseus has been made clear by W. B. Stanford, who in his exemplary study
of this hero showed that 'Homer ... skillfully succeeded in distinguishing
Odysseus by slight deviations from the norm in almost every heroic
feature'.[8] The following features seem to be of special interest in this
connection:

   (a) Odysseus is the only hero who is represented, both in the *Iliad* and
in the *Odyssey*, as being concerned with food and explicitly discussing this
subject: 'If one remembers that no other hero in the *Iliad*, nor any Homeric
heroine in either poem, even uses the word for "belly" and still less discusses
its effects, it is clear that Odysseus is an untypical hero in this respect.'[9]

Moreover, it is precisely in this respect that Odysseus is directly opposed to Achilles in their debate on food in *Iliad* 19;[10]

(b) Odysseus is the only Achaean hero of importance who is described (in the *Odyssey* and in *Iliad* 10 only) as using the 'unheroic' bow rather than the spear, that standard weapon of the other heroes;

(c) Odysseus is the only Homeric hero who, in both the *Iliad* and the *Odyssey*, bears the epithet *polutlas*, 'much-enduring',[11] and who is systematically described (in the *Odyssey* only) as passing through compromise and humiliation: 'Ajax or Achilles would never have been willing to undergo some of Odysseus' experiences—his three adventures in beggar's disguise, for instance, and his ignominious escape from the Cyclops' cave by hanging under a ram's belly.'[12]

These and other features make of Odysseus a figure completely isolated in the epics, an 'untypical hero' par excellence. This is not yet to say that the Greek tradition as a whole possesses no niche in which a hero like this could be placed.

Six times in the *Odyssey* the life-experience of Odysseus is defined by the word *aethlos*.[13] Both in Homer and in Greek in general this word (*athlos* after Homer) and its cognates have two meanings: of 'athletic contest' and of 'labour', the latter being best exemplified by the labours of Heracles. The distinction between the two meanings, while clear-cut in the Homeric Lexicon of Ebeling, which discerns between *certamen, ludus* on the one hand and *aerumna, labor, contentio*, on the other, is blurred in the Liddell-Scott-Jones (LSJ) Lexicon due to the tendency to subsume all the usages of the word under the meaning 'struggle'. The fact however is that this rendering not only ignores the indisputable etymological affinity between *aethlos/athlos* and the adjective *athlios* 'wretched', 'miserable', but also fails to account for all the usages of the term in both Homer and later authors. This can be seen from the following examples.

In her lament for Hector in *Iliad* 24, Andromache describes what might happen to the young Astyanax after the fall of Troy: 'and thou, my child, shall either go with me upon a place where thou shalt toil at unseemly tasks, labouring before the face of some harsh lord etc.'[14] The LSJ translation '*struggling* or *suffering* for him' is unsatisfactory: the rendering 'struggling', issuing as it does from the attempt to reconcile the Homeric usage with the later and more widespread meaning 'contest', does not fit the context, whereas 'suffering' seems too weak a rendering in respect of the specific kind of experience involved.

This becomes clear from comparison with another verbal usage of the same root. In *Il.* 7.452–3 Poseidon complains to Zeus that the wall built by the Achaeans will make men forget the one built by Apollo and himself during their service to Laomedon: 'and men will forget the wall that I and Phoebus Apollo built with labour for the hero Laomedon.' Again, the LSJ translation '*having contended* with him' misses the point.[15] This becomes especially clear from Poseidon's words to Apollo in *Il.* 21.441–5, where the same experience is rendered by the verb θητεύω, 'to be a serf or labourer': 'Thou rememberest not all the ills that we twain alone of the gods endured at Ilios, when by ordinance of Zeus we came to proud Laomedon and served him through a year for promised recompense, and he laid on us his commands.' These instances go well with the *Odyssey*'s definition of Heracles' labours as pronounced by Heracles himself 'I was the son of Zeus Kronion, yet had I trouble beyond measure, for I was subdued unto a man far worse than I, and he enjoined on me hard labours.'[16] In so far as there is a struggle here, this is a struggle for survival, and in so far as there is suffering, this is suffering involving humiliation. As was shown by Gregory Nagy, the underlying semantic affinity between *aethlos* 'contest' and *aethlos* 'labour' is at its clearest in Pindar:

> In the inherited diction of praise poetry, what an athlete undergoes in his pursuit of victory is denoted by *ponos*, 'ordeal', also called *kamatos*, and these very same words apply also to the life-and-death struggle of heroes with their enemies, man and beast alike. There is a parallel situation with the partial synonym *aethlos* (*athlos*), from which *athletes*, 'athlete', is derived: besides meaning 'contest', *aethlos* also means 'ordeal' and is applicable both to the athletic event of the athlete in the present and to the life-and-death struggle of the hero in the past.[17]

The only other individual hero besides Odysseus to whom the term *aethlos* is consistently applied in the epics is Heracles. Note indeed that of the fifteen epic usages of *aethlos* and its cognates meaning 'labour' as registered by Ebeling, six, as already said, relate to the life-experience of Odysseus, and five to that of Heracles.[18] Consider now that, seen in the perspective of Iliadic heroism, Heracles proves to be as untypical as the Odysseus of the *Odyssey*. Moreover, it can be shown that the characteristic features of this hero exactly correspond to those of Odysseus as adduced above: Heracles' attitude to food is no less prosaic than that of Odysseus (cf. Heracles the glutton and drunkard of the Attic scene); the bow is one of his permanent attributes, and his entire life-experience proves that Heracles, who knew many compromises and was constantly exposed to humiliation (see his service to Eurystheus and his being a slave of the Lydian queen Omphale), was as 'much-enduring' as Odysseus.[19]

The encounter of Odysseus and Heracles in the Underworld shows that it is not mere chance that these two are the only individual heroes characterized in the epics through the word *aethlos*. As A. Heubeck put it, 'the descent into Hades is deliberately mentioned as an example of the ἄεθλοι; it is a deed which both heroes have in common and the most dangerous enterprise undertaken by either.'[20] Consider especially the words with which Heracles greets Odysseus on their meeting in the Underworld:

> 'Son of Laertes, of the seed of Zeus, Odysseus of many devices:
> ah! wretched one, dost thou too lead such a life of evil doom, as
> I endured beneath the rays of the sun?'[21]

There can be little doubt that this address with its emphatic 'and you too' was deliberately cast as a 'formal' recognition of Odysseus as a hero of the same type as Heracles himself.

Thus not only Odysseus but even Heracles, who is of course a 'hero' par excellence, cannot pass for one by the standards of the *Iliad*. Consider now that after all Heracles is only the most prominent representative of an entire category of such heroes of Greek tradition who, like Perseus, Bellerophon, Jason, Theseus, and others, are mostly conspicuous by the labours they performed; some of them, as, for example, Theseus, also underwent the ultimate experience of a *katabasis*. None of the heroes of this group died on the battlefield. This prompts the question as to the grounds on which one was recognized as a hero.

## II

In so far as the Homeric usage is not taken into account, the main criteria on the basis of which a hero is identified in modern scholarship are those of the cult. A hero receives honours similar to those paid to the chthonic deities: the colour of the victims is black, they are offered at night and are slaughtered throat downward (and not upward, as for the Olympians), the liquids are poured into a trench, or low altar, ἐσχάρα, etc.[22] According to the widely accepted classification introduced by L. R. Farnell, among those who received these honours the following sub-groups can be discerned: 'heroes of divine or daimonic origin' (such as Trophonius, Linus, Ino-Leucothea); 'sacral heroes' (Aineias, Iphigeneia, Amphiaraüs, Melampous); 'functional heroes', whose names are in fact nothing more than appellative epithets; and also Heracles, the Dioscuroi, Asclepius, each of whom is taken as a category in his own right; the heroes of the Homeric epics; and, finally, historical figures who became objects of a hero-cult.[23]

It is difficult to see what common feature could possibly be shared by all these heterogeneous figures to turn them into a clearly defined class. It is not surprising, therefore, that the only attempt to arrive at a definition accounting for all the cases of Greek heroism is, to my knowledge, Walter Burkert's remark that 'it is some extraordinary quality that makes the hero; something unpredictable and uncanny is left behind and is always present'; whereas the *Oxford Classical Dictionary* defines the hero-cult as 'the worship, as being superhuman, of noteworthy dead men and women, real or imaginary, normally at their actual or supposed tombs'.[24]

It seems, however, that the ancients knew better. That they did possess a coherent concept of heroism can be seen, for example, from Diodorus Siculus, according to whom 'it is an excellent thing ... to receive in exchange for mortal labours an immortal fame. In the case of Heracles, for instance, it is generally agreed that during the whole time which he spent among men he submitted to great and continuous labours and perils willingly, in order that he might confer benefits upon the race of men and thereby gain immortality; and likewise in the case of other great and good men, some have attained to heroic honours and others to honours equal to the divine ...'[25] On other occasions Diodorus mentions Perseus' war against the Gorgons as his greatest labour, the labours of Jason who, 'since he observed that of the men of former times Perseus and certain others had gained glory which was held in everlasting remembrance from the campaigns which they had waged in foreign lands and the hazard attending the labours they had performed, he was eager to follow the examples they had set', and Heracles again, who 'by his own labours had brought under cultivation the inhabited world'.[26]

Late and Hellenistic as it is, Diodorus' evidence deserves serious attention, because it highlights in a clear and concise form the elements which are dispersed in earlier sources. Thus, the idea that toil and suffering bring with them the highest reward is found also in such utterances of Pindar as 'if there is some happiness (*olbos*) among men, it does not seem to have come without effort', or 'But without hard toil, few have won the kind of victory that sheds a light upon their lifetime for all the deeds they accomplished'.[27] The heroes whose *aethloi* are most celebrated by Pindar are the same as those mentioned by Diodorus—Heracles, Jason, Perseus.[28] In Sophocles' *Trachiniae* and *Philoctetes* Heracles is represented as one who laboured for the benefit of all Greece and whose toil qualified him for divine status.[29] That the enduring of labours was seen as inseparable from the hero's mission follows also from the fact that Socrates is presented in Plato's Apology as describing his own mission in terms of labours: 'I have to describe to you my wanderings, similar to those of one who endures labours....'[30] In his description of the Sicyonian cult of Adrastus, Herodotus supplies what seems to be our only direct evidence that the idea of labours and the hero-cult might have been felt to be mutually connected: 'Besides other things, the Sicyonians used to honour Adrastus with tragic choruses on account of his sufferings.'[31] However, Sophocles' *Oedipus at Colonus* gives us a vivid description of how a man whose only achievement is the immense suffering which he endured in the course of his long life eventually becomes a blessed hero,[32] and the evidence provided by the *Trachiniae* and the *Philoctetes* regarding Heracles eventually amounts to much the same.

This is not yet to say that the hero-cult provided the only context in which the idea of the life of labours as resulting in the highest reward could be applied. Thus, in his famous moral allegory the fifth-century philosopher Prodicus set hardship and toil endured for a good cause as a precondition of the highest happiness. In much the same vein as Diodorus' characterization of the hero four centuries later, Prodicus makes Heracles choose the labours of Virtue over the pleasures of Vice: 'Of the good and beautiful things, nothing is given by gods to men without labour and effort, but if you wish to placate the gods, you must serve the gods; if you desire to be loved by your friends, you must be a benefactor to your friends; if you are eager to be honoured by a state, you must serve the state, and if you wish to be admired by the whole of Greece for your virtue, you should try to be a benefactor of Greece.'[33] Although Virtue's words are addressed to Heracles, the parable itself was obviously meant to apply to every man, so that 'the most blessed happiness' proposed by Prodicus as a reward for the life of labours need not necessarily imply the kind of reward earned by Heracles himself.[34] Characteristically, the divine status achieved by Heracles is usually designated by the same words, *olbos* and *olbios*, as the happiness achieved in this life.[35]

In view of Odysseus' specific experiences in the *Odyssey*, there is nothing extraordinary about the fact that the term 'labour', *aethlos*, bearing as it does the connotations of toil and suffering, should be associated from time to time with the poem's hero. Yet, the range of the term's application to him demonstrates beyond doubt that Odysseus' association with *aethloi* was deliberate. Consider first the following lines of the prooemium: 'But when now the year had come in the course of the seasons, wherein the gods had ordained that he should return home to Ithaca, not even there was he quit of labours, not even among his own.'[36] Since at this point in the story Odysseus is with Calypso on Ogygia after he had lost all his companions, and since Phaeacia is the only remaining stop on his way to Ithaca, there can be no doubt that, while the former labours suggested by this line may well refer to Odysseus' adventures at sea, by speaking of the 'labours' in store for Odysseus the poet meant the latter's experience as a beggar in his own home.[37] This is not to say, of course, that Odysseus' wanderings are not

regarded in the same way. Consider indeed Odysseus' words to Penelope in
*Od.* 23.350–3: 'Lady, already we have enough of labours, thou and I; thou,
in weeping here, and longing for my troublous return, I, while Zeus and the
other gods bound me fast in pain, despite my yearning after home, away from
my own country.' And this is not all. In *Odyssey* 4 the term *aethlos* extends
over Odysseus' experience during the war itself, both generally, as in 4.170,
and particularly, in Helen's reminiscence of how Odysseus penetrated Troy
disguised as a beggar (4.241).

Thus, all of Odysseus' experience, from his fighting at Troy to his
return to Ithaca, is consistently described in the poem as falling into the
sphere of *aethloi*. But it is *Odyssey* 23 that is especially illuminating. The war is
over, and so also the wanderings, and even the struggle to reestablish himself
in his own home is behind the hero of the *Odyssey*. But what does Odysseus
say to Penelope immediately upon their happy reunion?

> 'Lady, we have not yet come to the issue of all our labours; but
> still there will be toil unmeasured, long and difficult, that I must
> needs bring to a full end.'[38]

The *aethlos* meant this time is Odysseus' future journey with an oar
on his shoulder to the country of men who 'know not the sea, nor eat meat
savoured with salt', predicted to him by Teiresias in the Underworld. The
difference between this labour and the others lies first of all in the fact that
Odysseus' last labour is not only self-imposed but also, in the vein of Heracles'
civilizing mission, purports to serve the common good. Above all, however,
the last labour of Odysseus is remarkable in that it is regarded as a crowning
achievement in his life, an achievement which, in accordance with the view of
labours outlined above, will guarantee him the appropriate reward. Indeed,
according to the prophecy of Teiresias, only upon accomplishing this mission
will Odysseus be able to return home, where he will live happily and die of
old age: 'And from the sea shall thine own death come, the gentlest death
that may be, which shall end thee foredone with smooth old age, and the
folk shall dwell happily around thee.'[39] This promise seems to be a clear
indication of the fact that the *Odyssey* is not only aware of the popular notion
of heroism as outlined above but also deliberately models its hero to fit into
this notion.

## III

Why is Achilles, doomed as he was to die young, never described by
Homer in terms of labours? Metrically, Odysseus and Achilles are twins, so

that nothing would prevent the poet from creating the expression πολύτλας δῖος Ἀχιλλεύς. Consider now the remarkable fact, paid due attention by Walter Burkert, that 'it is the exception, not the rule, for those who fall in battle to receive heroic honours'.[40] This goes well with the archaic Greek practice, reflected in Herodotus' story of Tellus the Athenian, that the highest honour paid to an individual for a glorious death on the battlefield was public burial on the place of the battle.[41] Consider also that Alexander, born warrior and admirer of Achilles as he was, insisted on conceiving of his conquests in terms of labours and, consciously modelling his own achievements on those of Heracles, regarded them as a necessary precondition of his future deification.[42]

It seems significant in this connection that more often than not early death was treated in popular Greek thought as a kind of blessing. To quote Theognis, 'blessed, fortunate, and blissful is he who goes down to the dark house of Hades without having experienced labours.'[43] According to Mimnermus, the fates of death, keres, hold two lots of men, one of 'hateful old age' and the other of death; it is better to die young and thus to avoid the suffering which will come sooner or later, because 'there is no one to whom Zeus would not give many sorrows'.[44] The story of Cleobis and Biton, on whom Hera bestowed early death as a special divine blessing, bears witness to the popularity of this idea.[45]

This attitude to early death is more easily understood when seen against the popular belief according to which human life is nothing but a long series of ups and downs. One need not go so far as Pindar, Herodotus, and Sophocles to illustrate this view. Take, for example, the Homeric parable of the jars of Zeus put in the mouth of Achilles in *Iliad* 24, which begins with the words: 'this is the lot the gods have spun for miserable men, that they should live in pain.'[46] There are only two kinds of gifts that Zeus can bestow on mortal men: either evil mixed with good or evil unmixed, so that the life in which evil is mixed with good should be recognized as a normal one. Suffering therefore should be accepted as a necessary component of human life, and it is characteristic that the life-stories of two old men, Priam and Peleus, are adduced to illustrate this thesis.[47]

This is not yet to say that man should try to escape suffering by committing suicide or should accept his lot passively, without trying to make something of his life. Thus, the Heracles of Euripides, whose involuntary murder of his own wife and children caused him to consider suicide, eventually arrives at the conclusion that this would be the act of a coward, because 'the man who cannot bear up under the blows of fortune would not be able to bear up under the weapon of a man either'.[48] The Heracles of Bacchylides comments on the sad life story of Meleager told to him in the

Underworld in a similar vein: 'For mortals it would be best not to be born nor to look at the light of the sun. But those who grieve about this cannot act, and so one must talk about what can be done.'[49] True, life is full of toil and suffering, but man should be able not only to endure but also to transform this toil and suffering into a supreme achievement. 'To make of this suffering a glorious life'—these words of the deified Heracles of Sophocles, addressed to his friend Philoctetes when the latter is sunk in the agony of despair, sum up everything the heroic life is about.[50]

Undoubtedly, this is the kind of life of which the Homeric Odysseus can be an example. As distinct from the Iliadic hero, who sets an example of how one ought to die, all Odysseus' life-experience demonstrates how one ought to live. Earthy and prosaic as he is, Odysseus manages to pass through all the tests that life puts before him: to contrive the escape from the Cyclops' cave, to abstain from eating the flesh of the sacred cattle of Helios, and to endure the crowning humiliation of living as a beggar in his own house. Moreover, it is not unreasonable to suppose that Odysseus was able to overcome everything life had in store for him not in spite of being earthy and prosaic but because of these qualities, for to be earthy and prosaic (a feature, we should remember, shared by Heracles) is after all nothing else than being human. Much as has been written of the choice of Achilles, one should not forget that Odysseus too had to make a choice. Yet, as distinct from Achilles whose choice is between early death and long life, Odysseus chooses between human life and immortality, offered to him by Calypso. In full conformity with popular Greek ethics, Odysseus is represented as contented with his lot and preferring to immortality his own life even if it is a life of toil and suffering.[51] In this, he proves as exemplary a hero as only a Greek hero can be.[52]

We saw that Mimnermus made provision for two fates of death (keres)— that of early death and that of death in old age. Now in the Iliad Achilles too had two keres of his own, one of early death in battle accompanied by everlasting glory, the other of the peaceful but inglorious death of old age, and eventually chose the former (see n. 3 above). This is, however, not the kind of choice Achilles is prepared to repeat in the Odyssey. On meeting the ghost of Achilles in the Underworld, Odysseus proclaims that, as distinct from himself, whose life is full of sorrows, Achilles is the most blessed of men, for even when still alive he was honoured by the Achaeans 'equally to gods' and after his death he holds a princely position among the dead. Achilles' answer is illuminating:

> Nay, speak not comfortably to me of death, oh great Odysseus.
> Rather would I live on ground as the hireling of another, with a

landless man who had no great livelihood, than bear sway among
all the dead that be departed.[53]

The verb θητεύω, 'to be a serf or labourer', used by Achilles here, is
the same that designates the labours Poseidon and Apollo endured while
serving the Trojan king Laomedon. As we saw above, this verb can function
as a synonym of ἀθλεύω, 'to labour' proper; note also that the motif of
serving one's inferior is closely connected with the idea of labours in
general and the labours of Heracles in particular (see Section I). This seems
to indicate that Achilles' choice in the Underworld is not, as is usually
supposed, a choice between heroic death and unheroic life but one between
two kinds of heroism.[54] While the Achilles of the *Iliad*, in conformity with
the ethos of this poem, chooses early death in battle and the everlasting
glory by which it is accompanied, the Achilles of the *Odyssey* prefers the life
of labours.

To be sure, neither the *Iliad* nor the *Odyssey* make any provision
whatever for the kind of immortality suggested by the hero-cult.[55] This
is not yet to say that the ideas associated with this phenomenon were
unfamiliar to Homer. Indeed, if the present interpretation of the *Odyssey*'s
evidence is correct, there seems reason to suppose that the idea that the life
of labours must needs be crowned with an appropriate reward, characteristic
as it is of the popular Greek attitude to the phenomenon of hero-worship,
is at least as early as the Homeric *Odyssey*. This is not necessarily to say that
this idea had been there from the very beginning of the *Odyssey* tradition:
the alternate epithet *polumetis*, 'of many devices', is no less frequently
applied to Odysseus than the epithet *polutlas*, 'much-enduring', not to
mention the fact that not all of Odysseus' adventures would readily fit
the pattern of labours.[56] What is important, however, is that this is the
overall interpretation to which these adventures were eventually subsumed
in our *Odyssey*, and we have seen that this interpretation is consistent in
that it spreads over all of Odysseus' life-experience, while his meetings
with Achilles and Heracles in the Underworld were obviously designed to
deliver the same message.

To sum up, either Homeric poem offers its own version of heroism. In
the *Iliad* being a hero amounts to readiness to meet death on the battlefield:[57]
the sense in which the words 'heroism' and 'hero' are used today ultimately
descends from this concept. According to the *Odyssey* a hero is one who is
prepared to go through life enduring toil and suffering. Whatever the reasons
for this difference,[58] there can be no doubt that it is the *Odyssey*'s version of
heroism that conforms to the popular Greek attitude to the phenomenon of
hero-worship.

NOTES

* An early version of this paper was read in May 1991 at a colloquium held at the Hebrew University of Jerusalem in honour of Ra'anana Meridor. I have much pleasure in dedicating it to her.

1. The Greek word 'hero' can designate either people of the remote past who lived up to the time of the Trojan War and whose deeds are celebrated in the epic songs, or people who became the object of cult after their deaths; the latter category also includes those who lived in historical times. The religious aspect of the word 'hero' is completely alien to the Homeric epic, either because the formative stage of the Greek epic tradition preceded the development of the phenomenon of the hero-cult or because for some reason or another this tradition preferred to ignore this phenomenon. See further M. L. West, *Hesiod, Works and Days* (Oxford, 1978), pp. 370ff. and G. Nagy, *The Best of the Achaeans* (Baltimore and London, 1979), pp. 114ff.

2. See J. Griffin, *Homer on Life and Death* (Oxford, 1980), pp. 81ff.; S. L. Schein, *The Mortal Hero* (Berkeley, 1984), pp. 67ff.; M. W. Edwards, *Homer, Poet of the Iliad* (Baltimore and London, 1987), pp. 149ff.

3. *Il.* 9.406–20; 18.94–126. Cf. Pl. *Symp.* 179e: 'after learning from his mother that if he slew Hector he should die, while if he spared him he should end his days at home in the fullness of his years, he made the braver choice and went to rescue his lover Patroclus, avenged his death, and so died...' (tr. M. Joyce). Cf. also *Ap.* 28c-d.

4. *Il.* 22.90–130; cf. 6.440–65.

5. Simoeisios *Il.* 4.473–89; Lycaon *Il.* 21.34–114.

6. *Il.* 12.322–8; cf. also 6.487–9; Callin. 1.8–13. The English quotations from the *Iliad* are given in the translation by Andrew Lang, Walter Leaf, and Ernest Myers, and those from the *Odyssey* in the translation by S. H. Butcher and Andrew Lang; a few slight changes have been introduced for the sake of terminological uniformity.

7. See further Nagy (above n. 1), pp. 42ff.

8. *The Ulysses Theme* (Oxford, 1963), p. 66.

9. Ibid., p. 69.

10. *Il.* 19.154–83; 198–237.

11. As part of the formula πολύτλας δῖος Ὀδυσσεύς; the meaning of the epithet ταλασίφρονος, which appears with the genitive of Odysseus' name, amounts to much the same. Note that Stanford (above n. 8), p. 74, is mistaken in claiming that the epithet 'much-enduring' is also applied to Nestor.

12. Stanford, loc. cit.; cf. also J. Griffin, *Homer, the Odyssey* (Cambridge, 1987), pp. 93ff.

13. *Od.* 1.18; 4.170, 241; 23.248, 261, 350.

14. *Il.* 24.732–4.

15. The same tendency can be seen in the translation of πολλά περ ἀθλήσαντα at *Il.* 15.30, relating to Heracles, as '*having gone through many straggles*': see LSJ s.v. ἀθλέω.

16. *Od.* 11.620–2.

17. G. Nagy, 'Early Greek Views of Poets and Poetry' in G. A. Kennedy (ed.), *The Cambridge History of Literary Criticism* (Cambridge, 1989), p. 12; cf. id. (below n. 28), pp. 136ff. This double use of the word *aethlos* can already be seen in the presentation of the chariot race in the pseudo-Hesiodean *Shield of Heracles*; see vv. 310–11: 'So they [the charioteers] were engaged in an unending toil, and the end with victory came never to them, and the contest was ever unwon' (tr. H. G. Evelyn-White).

18. *Il.* 8.363; 15.30; 19.133; *Od.* 11.622, 624; cf. *H.Hom.* 15.8; Hes. *Th.* 951. Of the remaining four, two relate to the participants of the Trojan War *en masse* (*Il.* 3.162; *Od.*

3.262), one to the work done by Poseidon and Apollo in the service of Laomedon the king of Troy (*Il.* 7.453), and one to the possible future of the child Astyanax (*Il.* 24.734).

19. Cf. *H. Ham.* 15.6 (of Heracles), 'he himself did many deeds of violence, and endured many'.

20. In A. Heubeck and A. Hoekstra (edd.), *A Commentary on Homer's Odyssey* II (Oxford, 1989), p. 116 (on 11.623–4); cf. G. K. Galinsky, *The Herakles Theme* (Oxford, 1972), pp. 132f.

21. *Od.* 11.617–19.

22. See, e.g., E. Rohde, *Psyche* 1 (Tübingen, 1921), pp. 148ff.; W. K. C. Guthrie, *The Greeks and their Gods* (Boston, 1954), pp. 221ff.

23. *Greek Hero Cults* (Oxford, 1921), p. 19.

24. *Greek Religion* (Cambridge, Mass., 1985), p. 208; *OCD* s.v. 'hero-cult'.

25. Diod. Sic. 1.2.4; cf. 4.1.4–6.

26. Perseus 3.52.4; Jason 4.40.2; Heracles 5.8.5; cf. 4.11.1.

27. *Pyth.* 12.28–9 and 01.10.22–3.

28. See esp. *Isthm.* 6.48 (Heracles); *Pyth.* 4.220, 165 (Jason); cf. Pyth. 10.29ff. (Perseus); cf. also Bac–chyl. 9.8; 13.55–7. See further G. Nagy, *Pindar's Homer* (Baltimore and London, 1990), p. 138.

29. Soph. *Trach.* 1011–13 and *Phil.* 1419–20. Cf. Eur. *H.F.* 1252; cf. 1309–10.

30. *Ap.* 22a6–7.

31. Hdt. 5.67.5.

32. See especially *O.C.* 563–64, Theseus' recognition of the labours of Oedipus as being of the same kind as those endured by himself.

33. Prodicus B 2.28 DK (=Xen. *Mem.* 2.1.28).

34. Ibid. 33.11–12. Cf. Galinsky (above n. 20), p. 103.

35. Cf., e.g., Hes. *Th.* 954–5; cf. also Pind. *Nem.* 1.68–75; Soph. *Phil.* 1418–22.

36. *Od.* 1.16–19.

37. This was the interpretation preferred by Aristarchus; for a different assessment of these lines see S. West in A. Heubeck, S. West, and J. B. Hainsworth (edd.), *A Commentary on Homer's Odyssey* I (Oxford, 1988), p. 74 ad locum.

38. *Od.* 23.248–50.

39. *Od.* 11.134–7; cf. 23.281–4.

40. Burkert (above n. 24), pp. 207 and 431 n. 50; cf. West (above n. 1), p. 370. Characteristically, all the examples of the worship of those who fell in battle adduced by Burkert relate to collective rather than individual worship, such as that of those who fell at Marathon, at Plataea, or the Persian Wars in general: this seems to be in accordance with the Homeric practice of applying the term *aethlos* to the participants of the Trojan War in general rather than to the individuals who fell in this war (see n. 18 above).

41. Hdt. 1.30.3–4. See further D. Asheri, *Erodoto. Le Storie* 1 (Fondazione Lorenzo Valla, 1988), p. 284 ad locum.

42. Art. *Anab.* 5.26; cf. also 4.15; 4.29; 5.25 (twice); 5.29; 6.24.

43. Theog. 1013–14.

44. Mimn. 2.15–16; cf. Theog. 767–8; Soph. *O.C.* 1224–38.

45. See Hdt. 1.31; cf. 7.46.3–4.

46. *Il.* 24.525–6; cf. *Od.* 18.130–42.

47. Note that the epithet *polutletos*, 'much-suffering', which comes very close to Odysseus' epithet *polutlas*, is applied in the *Odyssey* to old men in general; see *Od.* 11.38.

48. Eur. *HE* 1349–60; cf. 1347–8.

49. Bacchyl. 5.150–2.

50. *Phil.* 1422.

51. *Od.* 5.202–24; 7.254–8; 23.333–7; cf. 9.25–36.

52. Characteristically, it was Odysseus who, again together with Heracles, was adopted as an exemplary figure in the vein of Prodicus' exegesis by the fifth-century philosopher Antisthenes and later by both the Cynics and the Stoics. The reasons why these two were chosen as a philosophers' ideal lie in their self-restraint, endurance of hardships, disregard for indignities and humiliation, and in their readiness to serve the common good. See Stanford (above n. 8), pp. 96ff. and 121ff.

53. *Od.* 11.481–91.

54. Cf. Griffin (above n. 12), pp 95f.: 'We must hear in this scene the retort of the *Odyssey* to the glamorous and passionate heroism of the *Iliad*; they would sing a very different tune, the poet suggests, when they really faced the facts of death. The heroism of the survivor is not such a small thing.'

55. There is good reason to suppose that *Od.* 11.602–4, commenting on the emergence of Heracles among the ghosts of the Underworld to the effect that this is only a 'phantom' whereas Heracles himself dwells with the gods (cf. Hes. *Th.* 954–5; frr. 25.26–33; 229.6–13), is an interpolation. On this passage and the apotheosis of Heracles in general see M. L. West, *The Hesiodic Catalogue of Women* (Oxford, 1985), pp. 130, 134, 169.

56. On an interesting attempt to reconcile Odysseus' cunning with his endurance by interpreting these two qualities in terms of the development of character see R. B. Rutherford, *JHS* 106 (1986), 145ff.

57. It is doubtful whether Hesiod's account of the race of heroes as found in *Work and Days* reflects a belief different to that found in the *Iliad*. According to Hesiod, while the people of the golden and the silver races were transformed after death into spirits (*daimones*), the people of the race of heroes, which embraced all those who fought at Thebes and Troy, either died in battle or were transferred to the Isles of the Blessed: see *Op.* 166–73. Whatever the idea of immortality enshrined in the myth of the Isles of the Blessed (on this subject see especially West [above n. 37], p. 227), it is clear from Hesiod that it does not concern those who fell in war; see further West (above n. 1), pp. 192 (on line 166) and 186 (on line 141).

58. As is generally recognized, the *Iliad* and the *Odyssey* substantially differ from each other in their treatment of the religious and moral issues. This difference is alternately approached either in terms of historical development or in those of the social or genre standing of both poems. On the discussion see, e.g., Guthrie (above n. 22), pp. 117 ff., H. Lloyd Jones, *The Justice of Zeus* (Berkeley, 1983), pp. 27ff.

S. DOUGLAS OLSON

# *The Wanderings*

When Odysseus washes up on the Scherian coast at v.441–57, he has lost his ships, his men, his share of the treasure from Troy and even the clothes off his back. What he has not lost is his reputation (e.g. i.344; iii.126–9; iv.240–89, 816), and over the course of the next seven Books he gradually establishes his identity among these strange and vaguely threatening people.[1] He does so in a very deliberate way, first by carefully controlling the stories by means of which he is introduced to his new hosts and then by offering them what turns out to be a highly tendentious account of his adventures since the fall of Troy (ix.39–xii.450). His goal is to respond to a very specific set of problems posed by his appearance and thus to suggest that things are not what they might seem to be. The poet himself, meanwhile, uses the tales of the Wanderings to answer long-standing questions about the character of his hero's return and to make a series of more general points about how men act in groups and how they must be governed as a consequence. On all its various level, therefore, κλέος here is once again not only and perhaps not even principally a reflection of the world, but instead an active intervention in it and an attempt to reach beyond its incoherent and confusing surface to the truth which allegedly lurks within.

Two strands of narrative intent must be separated from the very first here. Many modern critics have been tempted to see in the stories in Books

From *Blood and Iron: Stories and Storytelling in Homer's* Odyssey: 43–64 © 1995 by E.J. Brill.

ix–xii a process of character development, as Odysseus evolves from the headstrong and hybristic pirate of the attack on the Kikonians (ix.39–61) and the encounter with Polyphemos (ix.170–542) into the allegedly wiser and somewhat wilier man who arrives alone on the Scherian shore.[2] Although Homer remains in overall control of his story, however, the Wanderings are not straightforward narrative like (e.g.) the bulk of Books vii and viii. Instead, Odysseus is telling a retrospective tale to an audience which holds his future in its hands. He must offer them some explanation of how he spent the preceding nine years and of why he has arrived in their country friendless, shipless and utterly impoverished. In all other ways he is free to shape his tale as he will, however, and his apology therefore cannot be read as a simple documentary source for his past, and any 'development' which took place in him over the course of it would have to be understood as in the first instance a product of his own intentions as a narrator.[3] Perhaps even more to the point, Odysseus says nothing in his story to the effect that he is different now than he once was, and there is no difficulty in understanding him throughout it as a brilliant but entirely static character: wily, dangerous, virile, resourceful, a clever and instinctive liar, bold almost (but not quite) to a fault and deeply concerned for his men and his own reputation. The point of these stories must accordingly be sought elsewhere than in character development (a concept which, I will argue in more detail in the following chapter, is largely foreign to the storytelling style of the *Odyssey*-poet) and preferably in themes and concerns signalled explicitly in the text. Nor are these far to seek. Homer's own interests are apparent already in the first ten lines of the epic, which are insistent on the fact that a central concern of this tale of Odysseus must be the fate of the men who accompanied him on his journeys but did not make their way back to Ithaca (i.5–9). For a great hero to return from abroad without his companions, after all, raises a series of potentially very embarrassing questions (cf. xxiv.426–8): how can it be that he has failed to protect those who were so obviously dependent on him? is it not possible, perhaps even likely, that he is responsible for their destruction? and how did he manage to get away alive when all of them were lost? The 'recklessness' by means of which the poet claims the comrades were destroyed (i.7–9) is immediately echoed in Zeus' tale of Aigisthos (esp. i.35–43) and then again in the outrages of the Suitors on Ithaca (esp. i.8–9 parallel to i.108). All the same, the Muse declines the poet's express invitation to begin 'from somewhere in these things' (i.10), i.e. with the Wanderings (cf. i.1–9), and tells instead of Telemachos' journeys (Books i–iv) and of his father's escape from Kalypso and arrival among the Phaeacians (Books v–viii). She (and Homer) thus leave the obviously very pressing problem of the companions aside for the moment, but simultaneously conspire to put the stories of the

general Achaian departure from Troy (iii.130–83) and Odysseus' escape from
Ogygia (v.55–vi.2) out of the way well before Book ix begins. The hero for
his part, meanwhile, disposes of the question of how he came to be trapped
with Kalypso relatively early on (vii.244–57; cf. xii.450–3) and then arranges
to have the sack of Troy described by Demodokos just before giving up his
name (viii.474–520). When he at last offers his apology, therefore, he is free
to begin after the war is over (cf. ix.37–8) and to conclude with the disastrous
departure from Thrinakia (xii.399–450). Indeed, the narrative focus which
results is of a piece with his conduct throughout the previous two days.

When Odysseus first approaches Nausikaa on the Scherian coast,
he is careful to characterize himself not as the isolated wanderer he might
otherwise appear to be, but as a great if anonymous leader of men, fallen on
hard times (vi.164–5). So too when he responds to Arete's initial suspicious
questions about his identity (vii.237–9), he conceals everything significant
about his past before his capture by Kalypso except the fact that he once had
comrades who have perished (vii.241–97, esp. 251).[4] Although he does not
yet give up his name, therefore; Odysseus also does not allow his basic social
status to be underestimated, and over the course of the next day the fact that
he is indeed someone to be reckoned with becomes gradually apparent: he
is handsome and powerful (viii.18–23, 186–240) and quick to anger when
provoked (viii.165–85), but also gracious and well-spoken when that is more
appropriate (viii.382–4, 413–5).

The name 'Odysseus' is mentioned for the first time on Scheria in a
song sung by Demodokos during the first feast in Book viii, describing a
quarrel which arose between the Ithacan hero and Achilleus at a banquet and
caused Agamemnon to rejoice (viii.73–82). Demodokos' song contributes to
the larger structure of Homer's poem by prefiguring Odysseus' confrontation
with Euryalos a little later on (viii.158–85) and by suggesting an underlying
opposition between βία on the one hand and μῆτις on the other.[5] At the same
time, however, it is entirely appropriate to its immediate narrative context.
Phaeacian society is marked by an intense interest in inter-male competition
(esp. viii.100–3, 109–30, 145–8; cf. viii.370–1) and a strong tendency toward
quarrelling and verbal aggression (esp. vii.16–7, 30–3; viii.158–64), if not by
genuinely heroic achievements in either area (cf. viii.186–253). The local
bard thus naturally presents the great heroes of the Trojan War as masculine
arguers and competitors par excellence, while the joy Agamemnon feels at
their confrontation is openly reflected in the pleasure the Phaeacian men
take in listening to this tale at another, somewhat less turbulent, although not
necessarily less significant sacrifice and feast (viii.90–1).[6] Although Odysseus
clearly recognizes himself in what he hears (viii.83–6), however, he does not
seize this obvious opportunity to reveal his identity to his hosts. Instead,

he waits all through the day until a second great meal in Alkinoos' palace, at the end of which he asks Demodokos in a very flattering (viii.487–91) and manipulative (viii.496–8) manner to sing of his own role in filling the Wooden Horse with men and bringing it within the Trojan citadel (viii.492–5). Naturally this is not the simple call for information and entertainment it must appear to Odysseus' fellow-banqueters to be. He has been promised transport home this very evening (vii.317–23; cf. viii.31, 444–5), after all, and cannot help but know he must identify himself momentarily if he is to obtain it (cf. viii.28–30, 550–6).[7] He is thus on the very edge of having to give up his name and thus his story, and his request to hear of the Wooden Horse works to put the war at Troy in the narrative past (contrast viii.81–2), setting the stage for a fresh and compelling tale which his hosts cannot have heard before (cf. i.241–2) and which ought therefore to win the most favorable reception possible from them (cf. i.351–2).[8] In addition and even more important, the topic the hero suggests to Demodokos represents a subtle effort to control who it is he will soon be revealed to be, by replacing the singer's earlier image of Odysseus the quarreler and competitor (esp. viii.75–7), all too convincingly confirmed by events that morning on Scheria (esp. viii.165–79, 201–33), with a picture of the wily and successful leader of men (esp. viii.494–5).[9] Unfortunately, this essentially positive image, which Odysseus has been cultivating for himself ever since his initial meeting with Nausikaa on the beach (vi.164–5; cf. vii.251), brings with it its own peculiar set of problems and questions: if he is the great and brilliant commander of the Trojan War, who once had hundreds of troops behind him and must have received a substantial share of the booty when the city was sacked, how is it that he has come here alone and in such wretched circumstances? This is the problem Homer posed at the very beginning of his poem (i.5–9) and also the central concern of Odysseus' tale of his Wanderings.[10]

Demodokos' final song depicted Odysseus as the great military hero of the victory at Troy, and the abbreviated tale of the sack of Ismaros with which the Wanderings begin (ix.39–42) seems designed in part to evoke that image again and thus associate the narrator ever more closely with the famous warrior the Phaeacians thought they knew only through, his κλέος.[11] There is no sign in the text that Odysseus sees this attack as in any way reprehensible or as a mistake *per se*; the Kikonians were Trojan allies (cf. ii.846–7; xvii.73) and this is therefore simply heroic business as usual. What is instead important is that here for the first time he came into conflict with his men.[12] In an initial example of the odd prescience which he claims characterized him again in the Kyklops-story a little later (ix.213–5), Odysseus says that he himself was for fleeing immediately once the city had been taken but that his companions—'greatly foolish' (cf. i.8)—refused to be persuaded (ix.43–4). A drunken feast ensued on the beach (ix.15–6) and the Kikonians used the opportunity to rally their forces (ix.47–50), attacking at dawn the next day and routing their enemies, killing six men out of every ship (ix.51–61).

Odysseus thus begins the story of his return from Troy by presenting the other Ithacan sailors as fools who refused to listen to his good advice and instead gave in to their own misguided appetites, bringing destruction upon themselves as a result. He was in one sense their leader, in that he could argue, urge and even order them to do what he considered best. All the same, he had no formal or enforceable authority over them and could not compel them to do anything if they opposed him *en masse* (ix.43–4). After this telling initial catastrophe, he reports, he took special care to see that the men who died were remembered, and his crews seem to have acquiesced in this (ix.64–6; n.b. μοι). So too in the land of the Lotos-Eaters to which they were driven next (ix.83–104), he was able first to order three men to go off as scouts (ix.88–90) and then to force them back to the boat when they ate the lotos and tie them down there despite their protests (ix.98–9). He was only able to save the situation in this way, however, because his other companions responded readily to his command to embark and row away out of fear of losing their homecoming (ix.100–4). The social roots and larger implications of the tensions between him and his crew come into considerably sharper focus in the story of Polyphemos which follows (ix.106–542).[13]

Odysseus puts a strong and consistent spin on the narrative from the very first here, aggressively defending himself against an implied charge of having brought about the death of six of his comrades by his own recklessness (cf. x.435–7). He begins by characterizing the Kyklopes generally as lawless and overbearing (ix.106), and Polyphemos in particular first as someone who knew ἀθεμίστια and scarcely resembled a man (ix.188–91) and then a little later on, in another odd, allegedly prescient flash transparently designed to shape his audience's understanding of what follows, as a savage unaware of δίκας or θέμιστας (ix.213–5; cf. ix.428).[14] He also makes a series of sneering remarks about the limitations the Kyklopes' lack of technological sophistication and especially their inability to sail imposed upon them (esp. ix.125–30), and compares the blinding of Polyphemos specifically to boring through a ship's timber (ix.382–8) and tempering iron (ix.389–94), two advanced human abilities such 'crude and backward' creatures ought not to understand.[15] At the same time, he calls his opponent a fool outright several times, first for drinking off Maron's wine so greedily (ix.361) and then again for failing to detect the men tied underneath his animals (ix.442–3), and lays tremendous stress on his own cleverness in the encounter (ix.281–2, 316–8, 413–4, 419–24), going so far as to claim that the ram which carried him out of the monster's cave moved with dangerous slowness because it was burdened down with 'me and my close thoughts' (ix.444–5).

Part of Odysseus' purpose here is thus to present a story of his own civilized human cleverness winning out over Polyphemos' brutish folly, and so to lay claim once more and quite emphatically to the image of the master of δόλοι he has fostered for himself on Scheria (esp. viii.494–5) and with which he in fact introduces his apology (ix.19–20). If he and the majority of his men ultimately escaped the Kyklops' cave, the obvious implication is, the credit must all go to him.[16] Indeed, Odysseus is at pains throughout this story to show he did everything possible to protect and save his shipmates and took all the greatest risks himself. It was he who spoke up when Polyphemos spotted them and asked a general question about their identity (esp. ix.251–62), for example, and he who thought of turning the crude length of olive wood he found lying in the cave into a weapon (esp. ix.316–20). It was also he who took charge of all the vital steps in the operation, sharpening the point of the beam while his comrades merely smoothed down its sides (ix.325–8), firing it to make it hard (ix.328) and hiding it in the sheep-dung lying all around (ix.329–30).[17] So too he was the one who placed the beam in the fire a second time that night to grow hot (ix.375–6) and encouraged the others, knowing they might otherwise abandon the task in terror (ix.376–7), and he who took the decisive role in driving the stake into the Kyklops' eye (ix.383–4). He also invented the plan to escape the monster once it had been blinded (esp. ix.420–4), binding animals together and tying the other men beneath them (ix.427–31) but saving himself in a different and far more difficult way, clinging throughout the night by the strength of his hands alone to the belly of the ram who was naturally 'by far the best of all the sheep' (ix.431–5). In the end, he was also the last man to escape (ix.444–5) and the one in greatest danger, since the blinded Polyphemos stopped and stroked the animal beneath which he was suspended (ix.446), puzzling out loud over why it was moving so slowly (ix.447–52) and cursing his enemy Οὖτις in the bloodiest terms possible as he did so (esp. ix.458–60).[18] Once out of the cave, finally, it was Odysseus who freed the others from their bonds (ix.463) and got the crew as a whole away to safety (ix.468–72).

One basic point of this story is thus that Odysseus saved himself and his comrades from the brutish and uncivilized Polyphemos by means of his famous treachery and cleverness (esp. ix.408, 413–4). It was also his decisions which got them into trouble in the first place (ix.171–8, 224–30), however, and that fact has a decisive further influence on the character and content of his narrative. In part, this is merely a matter of shifting blame. Throughout the tale of his encounter with the Kyklops, Odysseus presents himself as a man who honors the Olympians and who accordingly believes in and supports the conventions of ξενίη.[19] He explains his initial impulse to leave the safety of Goat Island as driven by an Alkinoos-like desire (cf. viii.575–6) to find out whether these new people honored strangers and the gods (ix.174–6), for example, and pauses in his story on the way up to Polyphemos' cave to tell how he and his men spared Apollo's priest when they sacked the city of the Kikonians and were given gifts in return (ix.197–205).[20] So too the specific reason he supplies for his fateful decision to wait to meet Polyphemos face-to-face is the hope of getting ξείνια from him (ix.229), and he says he capped his initial appeal to the monster for mercy with an insistence on his rights as a guest and suppliant and on the claims of the gods in general and Ζεὺς ξείνιος in particular (ix.266–71). The lawless, reckless, savage (cf. ix.106, 189, 215) Kyklops, on the other hand, declared at once that he cared nothing for the Olympians who had given him so many good things (ix.273–8; cf. ix.107–11), and went on to prove this by preparing two of his visitors for dinner (ix.288–91), an action whose utterly uncivilized character Odysseus underlines by comparing him to a mountain-bred lion (ix.292–3). Odysseus also says he chided his enemy for his shortsighted neglect of hospitality as he got him drunk (ix.349–52), but received in reply only another brutal and disgusting parody of decent behavior: his guest-gift would be to be eaten last of his companions (ix.369–70). As a result, the hero declared himself the vengeance of Zeus incarnate as he sailed away, and insisted he had acted specifically in defence of the rights of ξενίη (ix.477–9). His story falls apart at once under hostile scrutiny, of course, for he and his men consistently played the part not of guests but of pirates or burglars (esp. ix.216–8, 224–7, 231–2), and if they were foolish enough to wait for the master of the house they had invaded to return, one might easily argue, they deserved whatever punishment they got.[21] Much more important than reading so aggressively against the text, however, is recognizing the point Odysseus wishes to make: although he did miscalculate by staying in the cave (ix.228–30), it was only because he failed to realize that anyone could be as outrageous and impious as Polyphemos, who is the person genuinely at fault for everything which happened and thus for the death of the six men.[22] At the same time, the issue of guest-gifts serves to highlight the social divisions which existed between Odysseus and his crew and ultimately brought disaster upon them.

Although Odysseus could not force the other Ithacan sailors to do his will when they opposed him as a group (cf, ix.43–6), they did offer him a reasonable amount of obedience so long as he did not attempt to push them too far (esp. ix.88–91, 98–104). They also showed him respect in other, more concrete and quantifiable ways. When nine animals were allotted to each ship after the successful hunting on Goat Island, for example, ten were given him alone (ix.159–60), and when the Kyklops' herds were split up 'equally' among the crews, he received the ram which carried him out of the cave as an extra portion (ix.548–51).[23] These are all presented as collective decisions on the part of the other men (ix.160; ix.550–1) and appear designed to mark and affirm Odysseus' superior status among them. Maron behaved in a similar way, giving seven talents of gold, a krater of silver and twelve amphorae of wine to Odysseus individually (ix.201–5; n.b. 197, 201, 202, 203), despite the fact that it was the Ithacan warriors as a group who spared and honored him (ix.199–200); Odysseus was their leader and this was thus his natural due. These very different social expectations are at the root of the division of opinion which followed immediately upon the arrival in the land of the Kyklopes. When Odysseus and his men first came up to Polyphemos' cave, the others were for taking some of the cheese they found there back to their boat, returning for the lambs and kids and then fleeing to the island whence they had set out (ix.224–7). They could expect nothing more from the owner of this house than they had received from Maron, after all, and were accordingly predisposed to loot and run. Odysseus, on the other hand, thought he could get himself another guest-gift (ix.228–9; n.b. μοι) and somehow prevailed upon his companions to remain in the cave with him (ix.231–3). That this was a bad decision only became clear in retrospect; at the moment, an easy meal was in reach (ix.231–2) and no obvious danger threatened, and they accordingly allowed themselves to be persuaded. So too near the end of the story, when Odysseus turned about to shout at Polyphemos, his men, interested only in escape, tried to restrain him (ix.494–9). He was eager to claim the honor likely to be associated with the blinding of the monster's eye, however, and refused to be dissuaded (ix.500; cf. ix.228).[24] In this case, no-one was injured as a direct result of his decision (ix.482–3, 539–40) and he accordingly expresses no regret for it (contrast ix.228–30).[25] All the same, the same stark division of personal interests is apparent here as at the beginning of the story: unlike his men, Odysseus had an interest in and expectation of receiving specifically heroic goods such as κλέος and ξείνια, and conflicts inevitably arose when his needs and concerns came into conflict with theirs. He had no desire to bring ruin upon them, and if he somehow accidentally got them into trouble by pursuing his own interests, he did his best to get them out again and bitterly regretted whatever damage was the result.[26] Had they simply stood by him through thick and thin and trusted in his leadership, the great majority of them might have made their way back home alive in the end. Instead, they gave in once more to folly, ignored their proper place in the world and precipitated the tragedy which followed the visit to Aiolia (x.1–76).

When Odysseus and his men arrived on Aiolos' island, he reports, he alone was treated as a ψίλος by the king and engaged by him in conversation (x.14–6), and it was to him that the bag of winds intended to ensure the safe homecoming of the group as a whole was entrusted (x.19–24).[27] Odysseus was obviously acting with the common good in mind when he asked Aiolos for transport back to Ithaca (x.17–8), and even stayed awake for nine full days and nights on end holding the sheet in order that he and his comrades might get home as quickly as possible (x.28, 32–3). When he briefly fell asleep with land in sight, leaving the others to their own devices (x.29–31), disaster struck. The men had noticed the special treatment Odysseus received wherever they visited (ix.196–205; x.14–6; cf. ix.355–70) and now declared they had come to resent it (x.38–9). They also expressed disgust at returning home from war with 'empty hands' while he was bringing back 'many lovely stores of plunder' (x.40–2), and accordingly interpreted the visit to Aiolos as only the latest example of a galling general pattern: once again their leader had been treated with φιλότης and allowed to add to his reputation and (apparently) his personal wealth (cf. ix.196–205, 502–5), and once again they had been ignored. Odysseus himself ultimately takes some blame for what happened next, speaking of 'our (collective) folly' (x.27; x.79) and not just of mistakes made by his crew. His implication is not that he erred in failing to tell them why the sack was not to be opened, however, and it is not obvious that he would have been able to restrain them in any case (cf. ix.43–6). Instead, his point is simply that he should not have fallen asleep (x.31), for by allowing his companions to escape his supervision for even a brief period of time he contributed to their ruin, in that they could now do things they would not otherwise have dared and which he would never have allowed.[28] Eager to know exactly how much gold and silver he had got from Aiolos (x.35–6, 43–5) and unrestrained by his usual active oversight of their affairs, the men opened up the bag (x.46–7). There was literally nothing inside it except the guarantee of their safe homecoming (cf. x.19–24), and had they simply left well enough alone, they would have been back in their fatherland very shortly (x.29–30). By growing resentful of their leader and prying ignorantly into his affairs, however, they ruined themselves and him as well (x.47–55; cf. x.78–9), and nothing he could do thereafter to remedy the situation was of any use (x.59–77).

This unfortunate tendency on the part of the companions to ignore Odysseus' natural social superiority over them and the disastrous consequences of this tendency came to a sad initial climax in the visit to Telepyle (x.81–132). Odysseus remained sufficiently in command of his forces here to be able to select and send out three men to reconnoiter the countryside (x.100–2), just as he had done in the land of the Lotos-Eaters (ix.88–90). Although he chose to anchor his own ship outside the harbor, however, the other eleven crews ignored his lead and opted instead for the apparent calm and safety within (x.91–6). As a result, they were destroyed in a brutal and disgusting fashion (x.118–24), and only the men who were with Odysseus escaped and even then only because they responded immediately to his order to flee (x.128–32). With this disaster, the first phase of the Wanderings comes to an end. The relationship between Odysseus and his men was tense and difficult from the first, and he did accidentally send a few of them to their deaths (ix.288–91, 311, 344; x.100–16). All the same, he did the best he could for them and the stories he tells repeatedly reveal that to reject his leadership was to choose to die (esp. ix.59–61; x.121–5), just as to question the prerogatives his position brought him and thus the extent of his concern for his comrades was to risk losing one's homecoming, which amounts to the same thing (x.34–49). From this point on, the Wanderings take on a slightly different character and explore a separate but closely related set of issues. Odysseus has already hinted that the men in his ship were not entirely interchangeable by saying he chose the twelve best of them to accompany him on his visit to the Kyklops' cave (ix.195) and by adding that it was to the four he would have preferred that the lot fell on the next day to assist him in blinding the monster (ix.334). Only now, however, after a twelve-fold reduction in the overall number of sailors, do particular individuals within the crew emerge with any clarity: Polites was 'the dearest and most devoted of my companions' (x.224–5); Perimedes seems to have been particularly reliable as well (xi.23–4; xii.195–6); Elpenor was weak and something of a fool (x.552–3); Eurylochos was important and influential (x.203–5; xi.23–4; xii.195–6) but increasingly insubordinate (esp. x.429–37; xii.278–94, 339–52). At the same time, the focus of the stories shifts to the problem, already raised obliquely in the tale of Aiolos and the sack of winds, of how much a commander can and should tell his men of what he knows about their future and of what happens when they fail to follow his orders without question when he withholds such information from them.

After the ship came to land on Aiaia (x.135), Odysseus reports, it was he who put an end to two days of general exhausted mourning (x.142–3), by taking the independent initiative to spy out the countryside (x.145–7) rather than send out some of the others, as had been his practice before (ix.88–90; x.100–2). Indeed, he might actually have gone off alone to find the source of the smoke he saw in the distance (x.149–50), he declares, but decided (in another typically precise flash of intuition) that it would be 'more profitable' to give dinner to his crew and send them out instead (x.151–5).[29] When on the next day their lack of enthusiasm for the mission became apparent (x.198–201), he abandoned this plan as well and divided the men into two groups of equal size, assigning one to himself and the other to Eurylochos, and called for lots to be cast between them (x.203–6). Although he was among those initially left behind on the beach, therefore, this was a simple matter of chance (x.207–9), for he willingly accepted an equal share of the risk and had even considered carrying out the project alone.

Eurylochos was Odysseus' close relative (x.441) and thus, like him, qualified by birth to be a leader of men (x.205). He was also no fool, as he showed by suspecting from the first that Kirke's invitation was a trap and refusing to follow his comrades into her house (x.232). That he failed to keep them from acting foolishly does not necessarily reflect badly upon him (cf. ix.43–6). His behavior when he returned to the ship alone later in the day, on the other hand, was patently disgraceful. As soon as Odysseus heard what had happened to the first half of his crew, he armed himself with a sword and bow and asked to be taken back to them (x.261–3). Eurylochos refused, begging desperately to be excused, and actually suggested that they leave the other men to their fate and flee (x.264–9). Horrified panic (esp. x.246–8) was perhaps on some level an appropriate reaction to what he had seen, and his assessment of the likelihood that his kinsman would be able to return safe and unassisted to the ship with his comrades was in fact entirely accurate (x.267–8; cf. x.284–5). Odysseus nonetheless chose to head off alone into the interior to face the danger, whatever it might be, remarking by way of explanation only that 'harsh necessity is on me' (x.273–4). He could not abandon his men, and as a result, he insists, even after he had slept with Kirke and was being entertained in her halls (x.346–73) he remained unable to eat or drink until he had them with him (x.373–87; contrast x.271–3). Eurylochos, on the other hand, opposed him to his face when he came down to the beach to fetch the second half of the crew back to the house, reminding them of what had happened in the Kyklops' cave and insisting that just as the 'blind folly' of the 'rash Odysseus' destroyed some of their comrades there, so it would destroy them now (x.429–37). This very aggressive piece of storytelling amounted to a direct challenge to Odysseus' authority and the hero says he accordingly toyed with killing Eurylochos on the spot (x.438–41). Rather than letting that happen, the other men put the dissenter safely out of the way, affirmed (at least for the moment) their submission to Odysseus' authority and followed him off to the house (x.441–6). Indeed, even Eurylochos straggled along in the rear, afraid of what might otherwise be said to and about him later (x.447–8). His initial bid for power had failed and the real quality of his leadership should have been apparent (x.268–9). By safeguarding his life even as they declared their allegiance to Odysseus, however, the other members of the crew protected the political and social alternatives he represented. Had they known what would eventually come of this, they might have handled the situation somewhat differently.

Precisely what went on between Odysseus and his men on Kirke's island is never made clear. As the hero initially presents the tale, the others shared with him in a year-long round of feasts and then made a sudden request to depart (x.469–74), which he granted the moment he heard it (x.475). In his account of his conversation with Kirke that evening, on the other hand, he suggests that there was actually a quiet struggle for a long time over when they would leave Aiaia (x.485–6) and that only after the crew confronted him privately (x.471–4) and were about to go into open revolt did he act to satisfy their demands. What is more important is that from this point on Odysseus managed his men and their affairs in a consistent and aggressive fashion. Unlike Kalypso, Kirke offered no overt resistance to being abandoned by her mortal lover, but merely announced that he and his men would have to go to Hades before they could reach home (x.489–91).[30] This was heartbreaking (cf. x.496–8, 566–7) and extremely important news, but rather than sharing it with his companions at once, Odysseus simply told them they were leaving, just as they had requested (x.546–9; cf. x.472–4); only when they were ready to sail and the issue could not be avoided any longer did he inform them that their destination was the Underworld (x.562–5). This pattern, in which Odysseus knows in advance much of what is likely to happen to his men but declines to share his knowledge with them, is constantly in evidence throughout the final half of the Wanderings.[31] When the ship finally reached the Kimmerian coast, for example, he notes that the entire crew accompanied him to the spot Kirke had described (xi.20–2) and adds that Perimedes and Eurylochos actually assisted in the sacrifice (xi.23–4, 44–7). It was him alone the Dead addressed and seemed to see (e.g. xi.60, 92, 473, 617), however, and his panic which put an end to the visit (xi.633–5; cf. xi.43). So too the fact that he was later able to present Tiresias' prophecy about the hazards they would encounter to the other sailors as something of which they were unaware (xii.271–6; cf. xi.105–13) makes it clear that that interview, at least, was entirely private. Once they were back on Aiaia, moreover, Kirke congratulated the crew as a whole on their voyage and promised them detailed directions for the next stage in their journey (xii.20–7), but only after the others were asleep and she had for good measure drawn Odysseus apart (xii.32–3) did she offer specific advice about what was to come (xii.37–141). Even the song of the Sirens was reserved for Odysseus alone, with the other members of the crew required to plug their ears rather than to listen to it (xii.47–52, 166–200).[32] This difference between him and them and its political and social consequences are of decisive significance for the end of the Wanderings and indeed for the *Odyssey* as a whole.

Although he insisted the next morning that everyone in the crew should hear what Kirke had told him (xii.154–7), Odysseus actually discussed only the Sirens with them (xii.158–65) and made no mention of what was to follow (cf. xii.55–110). This is quickly shown to have been a wise decision. As soon as the sound of the Clashing Rocks and the sight of mist and water leaping up from them became apparent, Odysseus reports, his men dropped their oars in panic and the ship began to drift (xii.203–5). Given that there was no longer any wind driving them forward (xii.168–9), the direction in which they headed would have to be a matter of deliberate choice (cf. xii.56–8) and organized, energetic action; were this to fail, general ruin would be the inevitable result (cf. xii.62–8). This was accordingly no time for a popular debate on possible courses of action, and Odysseus says he resorted instead to 'honeyed words' (xii.207), recalling the apparently even more threatening encounter with the Kyklops in as favorable terms as possible (xii.209–12; contrast x.435–7) and deliberately failing to mention Skylla (xii.213–25, esp. 223). Kirke had told him that the price of getting past this monster would be six random and horrible deaths (xii.98–100), but had argued this was better than losing the entire crew to Charybdis (xii.106–10), and Odysseus himself was sure the terror already apparent in his men would drive them under their rowing-benches if they understood the situation fully (xii.224–5). For their own good, therefore, he concealed the truth from them and so doomed some of them to die. He did attempt to protect them to the extent he could by putting himself at risk, arming and stepping forward without explanation to confront Skylla face-to-face (xii.226–31).[33] Nevertheless he failed, and he says the way the monster's victims called out to him as they were dragged up and strangled was the most awful thing he witnessed during all his wanderings (xii.245–59, esp. 258–9), even worse, apparently, than seeing Polyphemos' victims dashed against the ground 'like puppy dogs' and cut up limb from limb (ix.288–93, 311, 344) or watching hundreds of others crushed by stones and speared like fish in Telepyle (x.121–4). In this case, after all, he had made a deliberate decision to let some of his men die, and yet the victims still expected him to save them. That anyone at all got away here was a consequence of the fact that the crew could still be cajoled into something approaching obedience. When the ship drew near to Thrinakia toward evening (cf. xii.291), matters became considerably more difficult.[34]

The moment he heard the sound of cows and sheep coming from the island (xii.264–6), Odysseus reports, he realized where they were and told his men not to land, invoking prophecies he had received from Tiresias and Kirke to justify his orders without specifying exactly what he knew (xii.271–6). Had they only obeyed him now, they might have made their way back home alive (cf. xi.110–1; xii.137–8). Instead, the already once rebellious (x.429–37) but apparently rehabilitated and reconciled (xi.23–4; xii.195–6) Eurylochos, whom the crew had deliberately protected after his previous bid for power (x.438–45), spoke up again, attacking what he characterized as his kinsman's failure to appreciate the needs and limitations of his men and his lack of real concern for their welfare (xii.278–90; cf. x.429–34) and proposing an apparently much more reasonable course of action (xii.291–3). Eurylochos' failings as a leader should have been obvious from his willingness to abandon his comrades on Aiaia (esp. x.268–9), but this time the crew, hungry and exhausted from their long and terrible day (xii.283, 292), applauded his words (xii.294; contrast x.441–6). Isolated and facing another general revolt (n.b. xii.297; cf. ix.43–6; x.471–4), Odysseus had no choice but to give in, extracting in return for his consent to land an oath that the men would not eat any cattle or sheep they might encounter on the island (xii.298–302).[35] One could perhaps make the case that the Wanderings might have ended differently, had the hero taken this opportunity to tell his men everything he knew about the hazards which awaited them on Thrinakia. Indeed, even after contrary winds sprang up to keep them there (xii.313–5, 325–6), he only announced again that unspecified trouble would ensue if damage were done to the animals he now identified as belonging specifically to Helios (xii.320–3). To read so aggressively against the text is once again to risk missing the point of the story for its narrator, however, and Odysseus in fact expresses no retrospective regret for any of his decisions here (contrast ix.228, 230). His men had no need for further details from him, provided that they kept their word. Only when they were once again left to their own devices (xii.333–8; cf. x.31–46), therefore, did disaster occur, as Eurylochos spoke up for a third time, offering another seemingly reasonable but in fact thoroughly misguided plan (xii.340–52; cf. x.268–9, 431–4; xii.291–3). This time Odysseus was even less to blame for the actions of his crew than he was in the story of the bag of winds, for it was the gods, he says, who put him to sleep (xii.338; contrast x.31) and his comrades had been warned explicitly in advance about what they ought not to do (xii.320–3). That they used the opportunity afforded by his absence to adopt Eurylochos' proposals and slaughter the cattle of the Sun (xii.353–65) was thus entirely their own responsibility; despite his constant, devoted efforts on their behalf (esp. xii.333–7), he was unable to save them (cf. i.5–9). Not surprisingly, their rebellious group-solidarity did not last for long. As soon as Odysseus returned to the ship, they began to quarrel and blame one another for what had happened (xii.391–2), doing their best not to be held individually responsible by him for what was obviously a reckless collective decision. All the same, the damage had been done (xii.392–3), and as soon as they put to sea Zeus destroyed them all (xii.403–19), leaving only Odysseus to be carried by the wind and waves to Ogygia (xii.420–53).

The Wanderings thus describe a series of political rather than personal developments, as Odysseus' relationship with his men slowly deteriorates and they bring about their own ruin. He did not fail his companions, he insists, and is not responsible for what happened to them; indeed, he did everything he could to save them and risked his own life over and over again in their defense. Instead, it was they who failed him by rejecting his advice and authority, thus bringing trouble upon themselves and their leader as well. When they refused to listen to him on the Ismaran beach and chose instead to feast on the wine and animals they had captured there (ix.43–6), their enemies rallied and routed them, killing six men out of every ship (ix.47–61); when they grew resentful of the warm reception and gifts Aiolos and others gave him and opened up the bag of winds (x.34–46), they were blown decisively away from their homeland (x.47–9); when eleven ships entered the harbor at Telepyle rather than anchoring outside with him (x.91–6), they were all destroyed (x.121–5); when the survivors of this first great disaster ignored his pleas and their oath as well and slaughtered the cattle of the Sun (xii.340–65), they signed their own death-warrant (xii.403–19). He was not always right and his errors cost some of his men their lives (esp. ix.224–30). In addition, he was forced from time to time to allow certain individuals to be put at risk or even to die for the common good (esp. xii.223–5).[36] In every case, however, he rescued as many of his comrades as he could, and never asked them to face a danger he was not willing to confront at least as aggressively himself (esp. ix.331–3; x.203–6, 273–4; xii.226–31). The political arrangement all this represents is not a particularly democratic one, but it could not have been, for the crew were generally incapable of saving themselves or making the hard decisions necessary from time to time if they were ever to return home. Instead, they had a leader whose duty it was to act in their best interest as well as his own, neither pandering to them nor allowing them to know more than they needed or was good for them at any particular point in time. Regardless of appearances, his decisions were always made with their good in mind or at least with the intention of doing them no harm. On occasion he was wrong or ill-informed or even momentarily reckless, but then his men were free to offer him their comments or to voice their concerns. In general, however, to submit oneself to him by mastering one's appetites in even the most tempting or difficult circumstances (esp. ix.43–4; xii.329–32), or by obeying him although his orders appeared outrageous and his motives were unclear (esp. xii.271–6) was to choose life and homecoming. To reject his commands and give in to the demands of one's belly (ix.44–6; xii.340–65)[37] or to resentment against the undeniable privileges his position brought him (x.34–46), or to second-guess his judgment and search for an apparently more accommodating commander (esp. xii.278–94), on the other hand, was to opt for disaster and death. That is what the comrades did over and over again, and in the end their foolishness ruined them and Odysseus as well. That he is now impoverished and alone ought therefore not to be held against him; the truth of the situation is in his story rather than in what seems to meet the eye. Homer as well, of course, is concerned to insist that his Odysseus did not return from his wanderings with the blood of his companions on his hands (i.5–9), and in this sense his purposes intersect neatly here with those of his hero. At the same time, the poet uses the tale told in Books ix–xii for more substantial purposes, preparing his own auditors for what is to come on Ithaca while offering a powerful initial comment on the question of how men behave (or misbehave) in groups and how they must be handled as a consequence.[38]

Odysseus has been gone from his native island for close to twenty years, leaving the other Ithacans free to act as they will. A few continue to respect his authority and keep in mind the possibility of his return and all that might involve (esp. ii.163–9, 235–8). The majority do not (esp. ii.233–4), however, and instead allow their young men to run wild, slaughtering the absent king's animals and drinking his wine (e.g. ii.55–8), foolishly convinced they will never have to account for their behavior (e.g. ii.182–3, 246–51). As the stories of the Wanderings make clear, personal and political recklessness of this sort leads directly and inevitably to disaster (esp. ix.43–61), and the fact that the king is temporarily absent from his land is very much beside the point. He will come back soon enough to interrupt the feasting (esp. xii.368–73; cf. xx.390–4; xxii.8–21), and then there will be no time or use for excuses (xii.391–3; cf. xxii.45–67). Indeed, Odysseus eventually likens the Suitors specifically to a group of men with whom he once sailed and who, he says, brought about their own ruin by their outrageous and incautious actions (xvii.425–41; cf. xxiv.426–9).[39] The punishments dealt out to the Suitors and their families at the end of the poem thus pick up themes already established in the first half of the Wanderings and illustrate again and even more emphatically the danger of ignoring a legitimate leader's authority, regardless of how safe or appealing revolt might seem to be. The behavior of the much more finely-drawn characters within Odysseus' house, on the other hand, reflects the concerns of the similarly individualized second half of the tale offered the Phaeacians, by dwelling on the need for obedience to one's natural social superiors even when one is not sure what they are up to or why. The precise and careful loyalty of Odysseus' wife, son and servants, even to commands almost two decades old and some of which now appear contrary to their own best interests (xviii.257–73; xx.209–23), after all, is vital not only to his success but to their own as well, while even the apparently most insignificant or well-intentioned acts of disobedience have the potential to bring about disaster (xxi.359–67; cf. xix.476–86). If Odysseus succeeds in his return home, his friends and followers will remain there as well (esp. xxi.213–5); if he fails, they can expect nothing but agony and exile (esp.

xix.571–2). Despite that fact, not one of his allies is allowed to know all his mind: Eumaios is kept in absolute ignorance of his lord's return until the last possible moment, as is Philoitios; Eurykleia is first brutally silenced when she learns too much (xix.467–90), and then locked away without explanation in the women's quarters before the fight in the central hall begins (xxi.380–7); Telemachos knows the Stranger's identity but not the most important aspects of his plan (esp. xx.385–6); Penelope is allowed no hint that her husband has come home until he has killed the Suitors (esp. xix.203–12). The plan as a whole thus remains with Odysseus, or perhaps with Athena and the poet, and it is not the part of anyone else to know more than he or she must. Because the obedience of these subsidiary characters is automatic and unquestioning, as that of the crew was not, all their dearest and seemingly most unlikely desires are accomplished; that they were kept ignorant and in despair was somehow entirely for their own good. So too on a more general level, Homer's story insists that despite occasional appearances to the contrary and some inevitable miscalculations, i.e. despite what would otherwise seem to be the case, traditional aristocratic leaders are (or at least once were) intensely devoted to the welfare of their subordinates (e.g. ii.233–4). Common men, on the other hand, routinely make what prove in the end to be the wrong decisions, i.e. decisions which seem perfectly sensible at the moment but run contrary to the desires of those who normally wield power over them, and miscalculate their own best interest when they try to think for themselves. This is a difficult and dangerous world, it seems, where answers are rarely easy or apparent, the pressure to surrender to what is at least allegedly wrong is almost overpowering, and the knowledge which might help make better sense of things is not widely available. Not everyone can be saved in any case. All the same, the *Odyssey* and its hero are at pains to argue that the best course of action is still to accept the guidance of those who ought by right to rule, provided that they can be found. Failing that, one is left to wait, listening to tales and hoping to learn something of value from them, which is not a particularly satisfactory solution but often the only one available. The implications of that fact are particularly apparent in Homer's treatment of the story of Telemachos, to which I turn my attention now.

## NOTES

1. On the odd and unsettling atmosphere on Scheria, see Rose (1969), with the cautions and corrections of de Vries (1977); Tebben (1991); Reece (1993) 104–7. For a more traditional view, see Segal (1962). For the location of Odysseus' tale within the poem and its consequences and implications, cf. Suerbaum (1968).

2. E.g. Bradley (1976); Rutherford (1986); Scully (1987); Friedrich (1987); (1991) 27–8.

3. For cognate approaches to the Wanderings, see Friedrich (1987a) 386–8; Most (1989); Doherty (1991a); de Jong (1992); cf. Scully (1987). A few basic elements of some of these stories are attested to by Homer or other characters in the course of the poem. Thus Zeus affirms that Odysseus blinded the Kyklops and so incurred Poseidon's wrath i.68–9), and the hero's extended captivity on and eventual escape from Kalypso's island, as well as his visit to Kirke, are both obviously 'real' enough (i.51–7; v.14–5, 30–277; viii.447–53). Since the poet gives us no further information to work with or to use as a control, however, the naive question of how much of what Odysseus tells his hosts is true must be abandoned; contrast the approach of Parry (1994).

4. On Odysseus' reticence and Alkinoos' question, see Fenik (1974) 5–60; Webber (1989).

5. On Demodokos' songs, see most recently Bliss (1968); Nagy (1979) 15–58; Edinger (1980); Braswell (1982); Newton (1987); Finkelberg (1987); Olson (1989); Brown (1989); Tebben (1991) 36–40.

6. There is a further quiet irony to this song, in that it is once again a combination of Odysseus' presence and a fateful oracle which marks the 'beginning of trouble' for the audience (viii.79–82), in this case the Phaeacians themselves, although that fact only becomes apparent later (xiii.125–87; cf. viii.564–9).

7. Cf. the observations of Roisman (1994) 5–7.

8. Demodokos seems to pay a bit more attention to the other Argives than Odysseus requested (esp. viii.516), but still tells the tale in such a way that even Menelaos is reduced to a secondary role (viii.517–8). Cf. the observations of Tebben (1991) 40; Pedrick (1992) 61–2. For Odysseus' request and its motivation, see also Harrison (1971); Dolin (1973); Roisman (1994) 5–7.

9. Note the poet's parallel strategy at viii.521–31, where Odysseus' reaction to Demodokos' song is compared to that of a woman enslaved after her husband has died fighting against invaders, thus transforming the hero into a victim whose story of abuse and ill-treatment (esp. viii.527–9) properly begins with the destruction of Troy (cf. i.1–2).

10. Schwartz (1924) 44–5, put forward a similar thesis, although very briefly and in a profoundly analytic context.

11. Note the emphatic first-person singular here: ἐγὼ πόλιν ἔπραθον (ix.40).

12. Cf. Louden (1993) 9–10.

13. On the alleged folk-tale origins of this story, see Page (1955) 1–20; Glenn (1971); and the responses of Schein (1970); and O'Sullivan (1987). For a provocative reading of the story's roots in individual psychology, see Austin (1983).

14. Were it not for Odysseus' introductory remarks characterizing the Kyklopes in a negative fashion (cf. Race [1993] 105–6), one might easily conclude these creatures lived in a pastoral paradise, relying on the generosity of the gods to furnish them with all good things (ix.107–11) and free to govern their personal affairs without interference (ix.112–5). Fortunately for the hero, his hosts have a long history of bad blood with these creatures (vi.4–6) and are thus presumably predisposed to take his criticisms of them at face-value. Mondi (1983), esp. 23–5, 31, suggests that ix.107–15 preserves "a singular and precious vestige" of a pre-Homeric poetic tradition in which the Kyklopes were rewarded with a life of blessedness in return for their assistance to Zeus in the Titanomachy (cf. Hes. *Th.* 139–41; cf, 501–6), but nothing in the language or grammar of the passage suggests it is anything other than a free-floating formular description of a Golden Age existence.

15. On the contrast with the hypercivilized Phaeacians implicit here, see Segal (1962) 33; Clay (1980) 263–4; Mondi (1983) 26–8. In fact, ix.291 rather implies Polyphemos has

a knife, and ix.319–21 clearly suggests he has an axe.

16. *Pace* Scully (1987) 402–3, who argues that Odysseus presents himself as having been genuinely careless with his men here.

17. This final detail may be intended in part as a further indication of Polyphemos' savage and uncivilized nature; contrast the manure piled carefully outside the door of Odysseus' palace for use as agricultural fertilizer (xvii.297–9; contrast ix.107–11).

18. On this passage, see Newton (1983), who stresses the odd reversal of sympathy felt as the monster is transformed for a moment into the victim of a bitter fate. Whatever pity the Kyklops' words evoke is quickly dispelled, however, by his horrible description of the vengeance he would like to take on Odysseus.

19. On the theme of guest-friendship in this story and elsewhere in Books ix–xii, see Podlecki (1961); Delasanta (1967) 53–6; Most (1989); Reece (1993) 123–43.

20. For Goat Island, see Clay (1980), with the response of Bremmer (1986).

21. On another level, therefore, the confrontation with Polyphemos sets up parallels with the situation on Ithaca and thus prepares the emotional and moral ground for Odysseus' murder of the Suitors; cf. Newton (1983).

22. That Odysseus took provisions with him in the expectation that the Kyklops would prove undercivilized (ix.212–5) means only that he was prepared for rudeness; cannibalism is a very different matter.

23. For this extra share of booty, cf. vii.9–11; xi.533–4. That the Kikonian women and other goods were divided up 'so that no-one might go cheated of his due share' (ix.41–2), therefore, does not mean that everything was divided into equal portions, but that everyone got 'what he deserved.'

24. On the significance of Odysseus' surrender of his name and the use to which Polyphemos puts it, cf. Peradotto (1990) 140–1. On the hero's consistent concern for his own self-interest, contrast Friedrich (1987).

25. Note in this connection that, at least in the way Odysseus tells the story, his men ceased to complain about his behavior once out of Polyphemos' range and actually awarded him a prize of honor upon their return to Goat Island (ix.550–1).

26. Note that Odysseus waited to shout the first time until his boat was as far away as his voice could carry (ix.473–4) and then (somewhat illogically) on the second occasion until it was out two times that far (ix.491–2). These are not the actions of a man deliberately courting disaster.

27. For Aiolia and Scheria, see Clay (1985). It must be primarily his own νόστος which Odysseus reports on here, although he certainly knows of the various quarrels, divisions and false starts following the fall of the city which Nestor describes at iii.130–64.

28. At the same time, identification of this as a 'mistake' serves in an backhanded way to emphasize Odysseus' heroic powers of endurance in staying awake longer than any ordinary man could have.

29. For Odysseus' hunting at x.156–71 in light of myths of the Actaeon type, see Roessel (1989), with the response of Birge (1993) 19–22. On Odysseus' self-presentation here, cf. Schmoll (1987); on the mythic and storytelling background to the tale, see Alexander (1991).

30. The parallel with what Kalypso tells Odysseus is nonetheless striking: to go back to Ithaca is to consent to die (esp. v.135–40, 203–10), and in each case the hero recognizes the significance of what he is told but accepts his fate nonetheless (x.215–24; x.496–502; cf. i.56–9). See also Scully (1987) 407; Crane (1988) 15–60.

31. Cf. the related remarks of Scully (1987) 411–5.

32. There are once again obvious echoes here of the situation on Aiaia: Odysseus

alone is allowed to sleep with the goddess (x.347) = listen to the captivating words of the Sirens (xii.411–50; cf. i.56–7), and his men, free from this enchantment, force him to go home despite his inclinations (x.169–75; xii.192–6).

33. As the embarrassment of the developmentalists Bradley (1976) 141, and Rutherford (1986) 152, on this point makes clear, Odysseus has apparently not learned to keep clear of such creatures from his encounter with Polyphemos.

34. For events on Thrinakia, cf. Fenik (1974) 208–32, esp. 212–5; Friedrich (1987a) 389–93; and Chapter 10.

35. For this oath as a means of saving face for Odysseus, see Friedrich (1987a) 396.

36. Note how the single death on Aiaia is presented as entirely the fault of the victim (x.552–60; cf. xi.61–5). Indeed, Odysseus' tendency to tell all these stories in a manner which reflects well on himself is nowhere more apparent than in the fact that in Book x he ignores what one would otherwise take to be his embarrassing failure to burn Elpenor immediately (cf. xi.53–4) and then in Book xi actually converts this into an example of his profound concern for his followers (esp. xi.55, 80).

37. For the reckless, shameless belly and its ability to drive men to act as they otherwise would not, cf. xii.216–8; xvii.286–9, 473–4; xviii.53–4.

38. For these connections, cf. Louden (1993).

39. For these connections, see also Friedrich (1987a) 389–93.

LILLIAN EILEEN DOHERTY

# Internal Narrators, Female and Male

The frequent portrayal of female figures as narrators in the *Odyssey* would seem to offer female audiences a more powerful subject position within the narrative hierarchy than that of listener. What is more, the *Odyssey*'s female narrators, in contrast to its ideal female listeners Arete and Penelope, include figures—Helen, Circe, the Sirens—who do not conform to the norms of female chastity and solidarity with males of the same class. Indeed, when Penelope assumes the role of narrator, she too threatens to break these norms and to assume the role of actant-subject in a story of her own.[1] I regard the epic's use of such female narrators as one of its most significant openings. At the same time, internal male narrators, and the larger frame provided by the epic narrator, serve to contain the potential of these female figures to disrupt the narrative redundancies of the *Odyssey*. Exchanges of stories between male and female characters at times suggest a form of gender rivalry like that I have noted in the responses of Arete and Alcinous to Odysseus' tale. In crucial ways, however, the narrative hierarchy of the poem reaffirms the gender hierarchy of the society it portrays.

Several of the female narrators—Circe, Calypso, and the Sirens—are portrayed as divine, while one—Helen—has a divine parent and was worshiped, albeit outside the context of the *Odyssey*, as a goddess.[2] This detail is not insignificant, for divine females were thought of as exercising

From *Siren Songs: Gender, Audiences, and Narrators in the* Odyssey: 127–160 © 1995 by the University of Michigan.

powers and privileges far beyond the reach of human women. The subject positions associated with goddesses—like those associated with male gods—thus constitute a special category. Though never fully available to a human audience, who must keep the status distinction constantly in mind, they are nonetheless similar enough to aristocratic human positions to make a certain degree of identification possible. (Indeed, were this not the case, stories about the gods could have little interest for a human audience.) That divine subject positions are further marked for gender means that they have the potential to replicate as well as to modify elements of the human gender hierarchy.[3]

The sheer number and variety of internal narratives in the *Odyssey* make the prospect of cataloging them a daunting one. On closer inspection, however, a more limited subset of these narratives offers ample evidence that the *Odyssey*'s portrayal of narrators, like its portrayal of internal audiences, is marked by gender differences. In this chapter, I examine three sets of paired internal narratives that match—and implicitly compare—female with male narrators: the tales of Helen and Menelaus at 4.235–89; Circe's and Odysseus' accounts of the Sirens, Scylla, and Charybdis in book 12; and finally the sequence of stories exchanged by Penelope and Odysseus in books 19 and 23. Although the Sirens' song is not paired with another internal narrative, I single it out for further comment because it represents the most powerful challenge of a female narrator to the determinacy of the *Odyssey* text. In each case, I have chosen narratives that overlap significant portions of the epic plot and that can also be seen as replicating that plot in its essentials. This phenomenon of replication is sometimes referred to as *mise en abyme* and is characteristic of highly reflexive texts like the *Odyssey*.[4] (That it can also be seen as characteristic of oral compositions is suggested—though not in these terms—by the work of William G. Thalmann and Bruce Louden.)[5] I conclude the chapter with a look at two other examples of *mise en abyme* within the epic: the paired tales of Odysseus and Eumaeus (both narrated by males) at 14.192–359 and 15.390–484, and the account at 19.392–466 of how Odysseus got his name and his identifying scar.[6] The latter has been read with great sensitivity by George Dimock and John Peradotto as emblematic of the ambiguities inherent in Odysseus' "identity."[7] By suggesting that the passage is focalized by the slave woman Eurycleia, however, Peradotto underestimates the androcentrism of the text and misses the ways in which it marginalizes the old nurse, even by comparison with her fellow slave, Eumaeus.[8]

For each pair of narratives, I begin by identifying thematic and structural parallels that justify the treatment of these passages as *mises en abyme*, that is, as reflexive of the epic as a whole. I then proceed to consider two sets of questions about each pair: (1) To what extent does the relationship between the paired narrators, and between the contents of their narratives, reflect larger patterns of male/female relationship in the poem as a whole? What subject positions are offered to female and male members of the implied audience? (2) When does the pairing of such accounts make for narrative redundancy, and when does it make for greater openness? How are these effects related to the placement of the accounts within the structure of the epic as a whole? The ultimate question to which these researches are directed involves the relationship between internal female narrators and the epic narrator: To what extent can such female narrators be seen as "figures of the poet"?[9] This inquiry, begun in this chapter, continues in chapters 5 and 6.

In each of the accounts I examine, except for those of Penelope in books 19 and 23 and that of Eumaeus in book 15, Odysseus (or, in the "lying tales," an alter ego he invents) remains the protagonist and must overcome, by the use of disguise and restraint or by sheer endurance, one or more trials of the kind that form the core of the *Odyssey* plot. Each of the passages I examine also resembles the entire *Odyssey* in its attention to narrative framing as a determinant of meaning: what is reported must be evaluated in light of the reporter's situation, including his or her relation to a particular internal audience. On the whole, these passages reflect the gender dynamics prevailing in the epic as a whole, where female figures are cast as helpers or opponents of the male hero; this is true not just of the narrated action but of the (internal) narration as well, since the female narrator's storytelling may itself be construed as an act either helpful or harmful to her male audience. In addition, the pairing of narratives in each of the passages I examine tends to circumscribe the female narrator: although she is allowed to speak first, her account is then undermined or superseded by that of a male narrator. Openings appear in this structure in the form of implicit contradictions or inconsistencies between accounts, which are never dispelled by the epic narrator. These lead to uncertainty about whether a given narrator is a helper or an opponent; in a few cases, minor or subordinate characters temporarily displace the hero as actant-subject. By revealing the potentially negative effects of narratives on their audiences, some of the passages I examine can also be seen as subtly undermining the narrative authority of Odysseus and even of the epic narrator. In this chapter and in chapter 5, I emphasize the containment of these disruptive elements; in chapter 6, I emphasize the possibilities for open reading that they represent.

The juxtaposed tales told by Helen and Menelaus in book 4 have an almost programmatic value because of their placement early in the epic, at a point where Odysseus has not yet been introduced as a character in his own right. As S. Douglas Olson has shown in some detail,[10] each tale casts Odysseus as a disguised protagonist whose success is jeopardized by an apparent female ally (Helen in each case) who sees through the disguise. What is more, the sequence in which the tales are presented seems to set up a choice and a warning: by trusting Helen in the first episode and revealing to her "the whole purpose of the Achaeans" (4.256), Odysseus enables her to mount the insidious attack on the Greeks in the Horse, which is recounted by Menelaus. In this second episode, Odysseus triumphs by resisting seduction and maintaining his disguise as Helen calls out to the Greeks in *their wives' voices*. Though the internal auditor for whom this story is framed is Telemachus rather than Odysseus, an implied male audience for the epic as a whole might be expected to apply the "lesson" to Odysseus' imminent homecoming; and in fact the course Odysseus chooses to follow is that of thoroughgoing concealment, even from his loyal wife.

In content, then, the paired tales of Helen and Menelaus reflect a tension implicit in male–female relationships throughout the poem: the danger (from the male's perspective) that the female, by seeming to offer hospitality and aid, will seduce and betray him.[11] On the level of narration likewise, the juxtaposition of the tales dramatizes this same tension in the relationship between female and male narrators. As Ann Bergren has noted, Helen's tale, offered as it is in conjunction with the "good drug" that suppresses grief, is itself an act of seduction.[12] In the figure of Helen, the *Odyssey* breaks the pattern I described in chapter 3 to give voice and focalizing power to a "bad" woman—one who has broken the rules of marital fidelity and gotten away with it. Despite her show of repentance and propriety (4.145, 259–64), her transgression is not altogether in the past, since she reenacts it, not only for her husband but for the younger males Telemachus and Peisistratus. (To judge by his farewell speech at 15.180–81 and his report to Penelope at 17.118–19, Telemachus is not unimpressed by Helen's performance.) Helen is successful in the role aspired to by Calypso and Circe: she keeps a male hero (Menelaus) permanently in thrall to her beauty, her drugs, and the comforts of her household. The epic narrator includes several incidents that seem designed to demonstrate Helen's superiority to Menelaus in intelligence or at least in initiative. Helen twice interrupts a floundering Menelaus, first to identify their young guest (4.116–46), and later to interpret an omen in his favor (15.166–81). As if to reinforce the portrayal of Menelaus as dependent on a superior female guide, the story of his encounter with the sea god Proteus stresses the intervention in his behalf of Proteus' daughter Eidothea (4.363–446). (Eidothea rouses him from a self-pitying torpor, gives him detailed instructions for ambushing Proteus, and even provides ambrosia to mask the stench of Proteus' seals, which Menelaus finds intolerable!) That Menelaus' dependency will be his permanent fate is suggested by Proteus' prophecy that, as son-in-law of Zeus—that is, as Helen's husband—Menelaus will enjoy eternal ease in the Elysian Plain (4.561–69).

But Helen's initiative goes beyond the provision of mere physical comforts: in telling her story of Odysseus after Menelaus has explicitly called for an end to such reminiscences (212–15), she undertakes to fashion and promulgate a revisionary *kleos* of her own. In the narrative hierarchy, this puts her on a par with the other bards portrayed in the poem and indeed with Odysseus himself, who unlike the others narrates events in which he has played a central role. The subject position offered to a female listener identifying with Helen is powerful indeed. If Helen's status is quasi-divine as a result of her parentage, her household and her roles therein are nonetheless portrayed as fully human—hence recognizable and accessible to a female listener.

Yet Helen's power is also carefully circumscribed by the structure of the epic narrative and by the terms in which it defines female *kleos*. Most obviously, her story is rebutted by that of Menelaus, which describes her as seeking to betray the Greeks at a point later in the Troy story than that at which she claims to have had a change of heart. Menelaus' tale also portrays an Odysseus who, in contrast to the Odysseus of Helen's tale, resists Helen's seduction and keeps his disguise intact. (This Odysseus also restrains and thus rescues his male companions, including Menelaus, when they are similarly tempted.)

Thus within the scene itself, Helen's revisionary tale is counterbalanced by a male narrator's version of events that subtly contradicts her own. In the broader pattern of the epic plot, moreover, Odysseus is portrayed as rejecting, not once but several times, the position of dependence on a superior female that Menelaus has accepted. Even in Ithaca, by refusing to confide in Penelope—and most pointedly by refusing a bath, which Helen says he accepted from her—Odysseus follows the model proposed by Menelaus' tale, triumphing over his enemies as a disguised "outsider," with minimal help from his wife. In the perspective of the epic plot, then, the couple Helen/Menelaus, like the temporary couples Calypso/Odysseus and Circe/Odysseus, serves as a foil for the central couple Penelope/Odysseus. Insofar as Odysseus' culminating relationship with Penelope eclipses the others, it is significant that Penelope, while exercising a degree of control over Odysseus, keeps a far stronger rein on her own erotic impulses. She is even portrayed as herself revising Helen's story (23.218–24):

> Nor would Argive Helen, daughter of Zeus, have made love with
> a foreigner, if she had known that the warlike sons of the Achaeans

were going to bring her back home to her own fatherland. Surely
a god spurred her to do the shameful deed; for before that she
did not cherish in her heart this ruinous folly, from which sorrow
first came to us also.

By identifying Helen's adultery as the cause of the Trojan War and of "our
sorrow," Penelope implies that the story has come full circle with the "happy
ending" brought about by her own fidelity. At the same time, by blaming
the gods, she denies Helen an active role in the adultery and paints her as a
"good woman" led astray.

Admittedly, the Helen of book 4 makes a similar move in her self-
portrayal as the repentant wife. Thus, while she has transgressed the code
of sexual conduct with impunity and is portrayed as exercising an unusual
degree of control over her husband, Helen is required to maintain at least a
semblance of the conventional wife's role. Even in her tale of Troy, she paints
herself as longing for her Greek husband, so that the *kleos* to which she lays
claim as bard ultimately differs from Penelope's only in its speciousness.

If the potentially powerful figure of Helen is thus circumscribed, what
openings, if any, are left to the feminist reader of book 4? To begin, the
contradictions between Helen's story and Menelaus' are left implicit; neither
the epic narrator nor the internal audience comment on them. Moreover, the
epic narrator neither confirms nor undercuts either story by allowing other
characters to relate the same events.[13] Loopholes are thus left in the pattern
of redundancy, and readers or listeners are licensed to mistrust Menelaus
as well as Helen. On the whole, however, I am inclined to take this as one
of those paradoxical openings that make the determinacy of a work more
palatable. By letting the audience detect the contradictions for themselves,
the epic narrator pays them an implicit compliment, and even puts them in
the position of seeing through and resisting Helen's seduction—as Odysseus
himself does in Menelaus' story.

More far-reaching is the opening detected by Ann Bergren, which
takes the form of a symbolic equation between the ambiguous effects of
Helen's drug and the effects of epic performance. In Bergren's words, "when
it (re)turns upon Helen, the text turns upon itself."[14] Once Helen has been
cast in the role of bard and allowed to control, even briefly, the apparatus
of epic discourse, the attempt to discredit her must raise questions about
the consistency of that discourse and about its effects on its audiences. In
particular, in the context of the *Odyssey*, an equation between a drug (even a
"good" drug), an act of seduction, and a bard's power to charm an audience
suggests that there is an inherent danger in listening to stories—and the
better told, the more dangerous the story. Audiences who perceive this

equation in book 4 may be put on their guard against subsequent internal narrators, and possibly against the epic narrator himself. Yet it is relatively easy for a male member of the audience (or an "immasculated" female one) to associate Helen's untrustworthiness with her femaleness and thus to dismiss the more deeply subversive implications of the episode. At this point, a feminist critic should insist on the possibility of an open reading, in which Helen's narrative seduction raises the specter of an analogous seduction by the epic narrator.[15]

A similar and still more radical opening can be detected in the portrayal of the Sirens as Muse-like figures whose divine status and claim to poetic authority are balanced by the accusation that they use these attributes to lure men to death. As in the case of Helen, however, this presentation of the Sirens is framed by an elaborate pattern of male–female interactions whose effect is to contain the most subversive implications of the opening. As in book 4, a female character—Circe—gives the first of a pair of accounts, and a male—Odysseus—gives the second (in fact, he gives two in quick succession).[16] Once again, there are subtle differences between the accounts, which leave the Sirens' motives somewhat ambiguous. This time, however, it is not a simple case of a male narrator undermining a female; instead, the female Circe puts Odysseus on his guard against the female Sirens, and the hero proceeds to tell how, by following Circe's advice, he was able to resist this most dangerous of female narratives.

The account of the Sirens is but one element in a crucial sequence of adventures (with the Sirens, Scylla and Charybdis, and the Oxen of the Sun) that are narrated twice: first prospectively, by Circe to Odysseus, and then retrospectively, by Odysseus himself. Circe's account is integrated into Odysseus' retrospective version, addressed to the Phaeacians, which arrangement deprives "her" account of the relative autonomy that Helen's tale of Odysseus retained. Yet the two accounts do not tally on every detail, so an element of counterpoint is maintained. Like the stories of Helen and Menelaus, moreover, the accounts of Circe and Odysseus resemble the epic plot as a whole in both content and attention to narrative context.

The content of these accounts not only resembles the epic plot but constitutes an important segment of it, including the adventure of the Oxen, singled out by Tiresias (and the epic narrator, 1.8–9) as decisive for Odysseus' homecoming. Yet while the sequence of events is subsumed by the epic plot, it can also be said to recapitulate the essential elements of that plot, which it reduces to their starkest and least realistic terms. Odysseus remains the protagonist of these adventures, which offer a reprise of the chief forms of danger he encounters throughout the poem: annihilation on the one hand; and on the other, the temptation to satisfy prematurely desires that can forestall the achievement of homecoming. Odysseus evades these dangers, here as elsewhere, by a combination of cleverness and self-restraint. On the primary level of narration, he is also using the tale of his adventures to win the help of the Phaeacians. By portraying Circe—who at first posed a threat to his *nostos*—as his staunch ally in this sequence, he models the proper response of the Phaeacians, who are to speed him on his way after an interlude of mutual fascination.[17]

In their distillation of the epic plot, the paired accounts of Circe and Odysseus also reproduce the pattern that casts female figures as either opponents or helpers of the male hero. In keeping with the elemental but fantastic form of these pivotal adventures, a number of the "female opponents"—the inanimate Planctae or "Clashing Rocks"; the sea, here referred to as Amphitrite (a feminine noun, 12.60, 97);[18] and the monstrous Scylla and Charybdis—are not even anthropomorphic.[19] Juxtaposed with these subhuman (if immortal, 12.118) females are the superhuman but equally female Sirens. With their command of epic diction and their claim to knowledge of all that happens on earth—including, more specifically, what happened at Troy (189–91)—the Sirens seem designed to evoke the Muses of epic poetry, as critics have noted.[20] Since the narrator of the *Odyssey* claims to owe his own performance to a Muse (1.1), the Sirens potentially represent a female subject position (albeit a superhuman one) of great power in the narrative hierarchy. As Pietro Pucci has argued, their song would, if allowed to continue, usurp and silence the narrative that frames it.[21] Moreover, while they address an exclusively male audience, the Sirens do not, like the Muses, speak through a male bard; they address their audience directly, as does Helen in book 4. Their portrayal, like that of Helen, thus opens up the possibility that the subject position of bard might be available to females. Insofar as this possibility subverts the gender hierarchy prevailing in the poem as a whole, it can be seen as an important opening. Yet as in Helen's case, it is also contained by being assimilated to the negative pattern of female seduction and betrayal of males.

The female opponents who feature most prominently in this portion of the epic are balanced, as they so often are elsewhere, by females willing to help the hero. Most prominent of these is Circe, but Odysseus is also told that Hera helped Jason to pass the Clashing Rocks (12.69–72) and that the only recourse in opposing Scylla is to pray to the monster's mother, Crataiis ("Powerful Force" personified, 12.112–26).[22] Circe is particularly important, not only as the narrator of the prospective account of these adventures but as a once-dangerous female opponent who has become a powerful helper. By forewarning and advising Odysseus in more detail than Tiresias has done, she ensures his survival. The fact that the opponents she warns against are predominantly female (and that Crataiis is said to oppose her own daughter in answer to a hero's prayer) fits the larger narrative pattern that isolates female subjects from one another while focusing on their ties to males.[23]

Like the tales of Helen and Menelaus in book 4, the paired accounts of Circe and Odysseus in book 12 dramatize the wider issue of male–female competition on two levels: that of story content and that of (internal) narration. At the level of narration, however, the competition in book 12 is minimized and contained by Circe's voluntary cooperation with Odysseus. As in book 4, moreover, there is an interplay between the two levels that can contribute to the characterization of an implied audience. Circe's portrayal as both highly intelligent and supportive, by tallying with the portrayal of the model listener Arete, may reinforce the appeal to the implied female audience to approve these characters' individual alliances with the hero, and to identify with the subject position of helper rather than with that of independent narrator (represented by the dangerous Sirens).[24]

In comparison to Helen's, then, the greater daring of the Sirens' challenge to the structure of poetic authority is contained by a more elaborate set of narrative checks and balances. Their song is not only contained within Odysseus' account of it; it is also discredited in advance by the account of an intelligent female (divine like themselves) who has chosen the role of ally to the hero and who resembles in this respect other exemplary females addressed by him.

Yet there remain a few openings in this thicket of redundancies. As in book 4, there are inconsistencies between the paired accounts, which are neither emphasized nor dispelled by the epic narrator. Circe's description of the Sirens' many victims mouldering on the shore of their island (12.45–46) is never confirmed in Odysseus' account, and the Sirens themselves, as quoted by Odysseus, promise their listener a homecoming in addition to the pleasure and knowledge he will gain from their song (186–88). Thus while the narrative frame casts the Sirens in the role of the hero's opponents, the confirmation of their hostility that might have been provided by Odysseus or the epic narrator is lacking. What is more, while their song is cut short—ostensibly because of its threat to the hero and to the continuation of the *Odyssey*—this very fact can enhance its evocative power. More than any other temptation, the song of these unauthorized[25] and potentially hostile Muses appeals to Odysseus; as Circe anticipates,[26] he is not able to forego the temptation altogether but arranges to mitigate its effects by having himself bound. Thus the master manipulator of words is himself portrayed as enthralled by the Sirens' song. Though Odysseus is portrayed as himself describing the encounter, in this case he has no reply to the narrative of another, no last word to mark the outcome of the contest as his victory.[27]

If the Sirens represent the most serious female challenge to the authority of the *Odyssey* narrator, Penelope comes closest to displacing Odysseus as actant-subject and chief focalizer of the epic.[28] The stories exchanged by these two characters in books 19 and 23 provide yet another set (composed of three subsets) of paired narratives by female and male narrators whose content recapitulates and advances the plot of the poem. Once again Odysseus' *kleos* is at issue, as he prepares—in disguise and dependent on a woman's help—for the battle that will secure or obliterate his homecoming. Once again the narrative framing of the stories provides a second, reflexive level on which the issues of the poem are played out, and on which the act of telling affects the meaning of what is told. But for the first time, Odysseus' centrality is in question, however briefly. As Marilyn Arthur Katz has painstakingly shown, in these books the *kleos* of Penelope threatens to take a form that will be inimical to the *kleos* of Odysseus.[29] The epic narrator has arranged it so that the pivotal decisions are made during two exchanges of stories between Penelope and Odysseus (19.104–599 and 23.166–230), in which the characters take turns not only in the roles of narrator and listener but in those of actant-subject and helper or object. Once the revenge and reunion have been accomplished, the two exchange a final pair of tales (23.300–343), from which (as Nancy Felson-Rubin has remarked),[30] the traces of alternative versions have been expunged. This final exchange, presented in indirect discourse by the epic narrator, provides a form of closure to an ambiguous narrative sequence. In particular, by recapitulating in outline the tale told to the Phaeacians, Odysseus' story at 23.310–41 contributes to his own portrayal as a reliable narrator. At the same time, by following and capping Penelope's tale, which it exceeds in length by a factor of eight, Odysseus' account has the effect of reclaiming the epic narrative for its hero. Though Penelope is mentioned and even elaborately praised in book 24,[31] she does not speak or act again after hearing this "authorized" version of Odysseus' *nostos*.

The exchange of tales in book 19 creates difficulties of interpretation that are exceptional even for the *Odyssey*. In contrast to the earlier exchanges I have discussed, the interview of Odysseus and Penelope portrays one narrator as concealing his identity while speaking of himself in the third person. At the same time, the epic narrator refuses to tell his audience whether Penelope guesses that the "beggar" is Odysseus. From Odysseus' perspective, as reported in his speeches and in narrative asides, such as lines 209–12, he remains in control of the interview: as in Menelaus' story of the Horse (4.271–84), he restrains a normal desire for the emotional satisfaction of reunion to maintain the disguise from which he will ambush his enemies. Knowing what he knows, Odysseus can even accept Penelope's proposal of the bow contest as furthering his own scheme,[32] and he gives it his approval as if it were his own idea. From Penelope's perspective, however[33]—and more importantly, from the perspective of an audience who do not know whether she has identified Odysseus—the dynamics of the interview are somewhat different. It is possible to see Penelope as Odysseus' pawn here, and thus to discount her role in the denouement. But this view forecloses the possibilities opened up by the narrator's silence—possibilities that previous patterns of male–female interaction in the poem should lead us to envision. Like Helen in book 4, and like the Sirens if we take their own words seriously, Penelope is potentially *either* opponent or helper to the hero; in addition to being the object of Odysseus' story, she is also potentially the actant-subject of a story of her own. By drawing out the period of uncertainty about these roles, the narrator not only maintains suspense but enhances the impression that Odysseus and Penelope are equals in cunning and endurance. To the extent that her power—like Odysseus'—stems from her control of words, Penelope represents a female subject position whose prerogatives overlap those of the hero and of the epic narrator. As in the cases of Helen and the Sirens, however, this genuine opening is carefully hedged about by narrative redundancies that limit its impact.

The exchange of stories between Odysseus and Penelope falls into three major subsections. In the first (19.104–599), all the stories are unfinished, the possibilities still open. The second section (23.166–230) follows the revenge and serves as the vehicle of reunion: Odysseus is tricked into telling the story of the bed, which identifies him to Penelope; and Penelope in turn reveals her fear of repeating Helen's story. In the third and final exchange (23.300–341), both stories are complete, and that of Penelope is clearly subordinated to that of Odysseus.

The first section, which is also the longest and most complex, opens with disclaimers on both sides: Penelope rejects the praise of her *kleos* by the "beggar," while he refuses to tell his own story on the grounds that grief might prompt him to behave unsuitably (19.115–22). Penelope then tells of how she put the suitors off with the weaving trick; but in contrast to the suitors' own version of this episode in book 2 (93–126), hers lays no claim to *kleos* and indeed ends with an admission that she can think of no further device (metis) by which to delay her remarriage (19.151–58). The "beggar" then gives a false account of his home and parents but almost immediately introduces Odysseus into the story, claiming to have entertained the hero on his way to Troy. These "falsehoods like truths" cause Penelope to weep tears like melting snow for "the husband sitting beside her," while Odysseus, though pitying his mourning wife, keeps his own eyes rigid as horn or iron (203–12). Penelope, not to be taken in too easily, demands details by which she may determine the truth of the story, and Odysseus, in doing so, manages to compliment her indirectly on her weaving. He also praises Odysseus to her as a man of rare stature (239–40), one whom a wife might well mourn (264–67). Then he goes on to report that Odysseus is nearing home but has gone to the oracle of Dodona to inquire whether he should return "openly or in secret" (296–99).

Up to this point, Penelope has played the part of the faithful wife whose identity is wrapped up in that of her husband; the interludes of weeping further portray her as vulnerable to Odysseus' manipulation, while he maintains the detachment of one in control. At the announcement of Odysseus' return, however, Penelope unexpectedly balks, despite the "beggar's" solemn oath to his veracity. From here to the end of book 19, her refusal to believe gives her the initiative she lacked in the first half of the scene. As Katz has shown,[34] Penelope, by her display of hospitality, resumes her full prerogatives as mistress of Odysseus' household, even as she makes plans to leave it. Almost at once, however, her initiative becomes a potential betrayal of Odysseus. The "beggar" must now refuse her offer of a bath, lest it reveal his identity prematurely (as in Helen's tale, 4.244–56); even the footbath he substitutes for it reveals him, against his will, to the old nurse Eurycleia. Not least, Penelope's decision to set the contest of the bow suggests that she is now willing to take a new husband in Odysseus' place. Here again Katz has astutely noted that Odysseus must "misread" Penelope's action to make it fit seamlessly into his own plans.[35] Throughout the second half of the scene, Penelope resolutely resists the news that Odysseus is coming home, even as she recounts a dream that ostensibly confirms the news. In her dream, she says, an eagle killed her pet geese and then announced that he was her husband, come to kill the suitors. Penelope makes a point of asking the "beggar" to interpret this dream that seems to trumpet its own interpretation. When Odysseus reiterates the obvious meaning, she rejects it yet again and insists on going ahead with the contest; once more he must adjust his interpretation to her plans ("Odysseus will be here before these men can string the bow," 585–87). If the power of narration is—at least in part—the power to inspire belief in one's audience, both Penelope's and Odysseus' narrative powers decline in the course of this scene: by its end, they claim to trust one another's friendship, but each refuses to believe what the other most solemnly affirms. Alternatively, if the emphasis is placed on the interpretive power of the listener, Penelope and Odysseus can be seen as laying equal claims to this power by resisting one another's accounts and holding out for opposed interpretations of Penelope's dream.

There is another way to read this passage, according to which Penelope has in fact divined the stranger's identity by this time and is actively collaborating with him by setting the bow contest. I agree with those who have followed this line of interpretation that not to entertain it is seriously to underestimate the skill of the poet and the metis he ascribes to Penelope.[36] I further agree with Katz and Murnaghan that to insist on this interpretation is also to "misread": neither reading can be fully supported by the text, yet both are suggested by it. This is a bona fide opening, a refusal of determinacy that requires active interpretation on the part of an audience.

Nancy Felson-Rubin is right to urge the possibility, at this stage, of seeing Penelope as a focalizer of the scenarios that are still available to her. Within the framework of the *Odyssey* as a whole, however, Penelope can only temporarily be viewed as a primary focalizer, or as actant-subject of her own story; the role of actant-subject is Odysseus', while hers must be that of object and either helper or opponent in his story. The indeterminacy involving her intentions is reduced, in this perspective, to a choice between two incompatible roles. Paradoxically, the *Odyssey* poet has chosen to portray Penelope as filling the role of helper even while resisting it: thus it is by (ostensibly) rejecting the possibility of Odysseus' return that she puts the bow into his hands. As I have shown, the *Odyssey* as a whole displays a pattern in which female characters serve as either opponents or helpers; frequently they are potentially both and must be won over to the hero's cause. Penelope's resistance to the role of helper is especially odd because her underlying loyalty to Odysseus is constantly affirmed, not only by the character but by the epic narrator as well. Thus her resistance; however suggestive of autonomy, is actually hedged in at least two ways: it is futile because it is based on a premise the audience knows to be false (that is, that Odysseus will not return), and it runs counter to her own professed desire. It does force Odysseus to compete for her hand; and in this respect it can be seen as enhancing her value as object by making her more difficult to attain. As bride/prize, Penelope represents another female subject position typical of Greek epic, one that links her not only to Helen but to Nausicaa and Pero (one of the "heroines" in the Nekuia, 11.487–97) as well. She is unusual only in arranging the contest herself. Yet here again, she proves primarily a helper by framing the contest as one that only Odysseus—or his equal—can win.

Penelope's anomalous independence is further hedged by the contrast between it and the behavior of her disloyal slaves, who actually sleep with the suitors and make little effort to conceal the fact. Katz has argued that this alternative model for Penelope's behavior in book 19—active infidelity—is "displaced" onto the disloyal slaves (especially Melantho).[37] Here again I think the class distinction between these characters and Penelope has important repercussions for the implied female audience. If, as I believe, the female listener is invited to identify with Penelope, the class differences make it easier to dismiss the slaves' behavior as obviously inappropriate to a queen. Penelope can be portrayed as contemplating remarriage but not as contemplating sexual activity outside of marriage. She hints at the latter possibility only once and very indirectly, in her decisive test of Odysseus in book 23.

This test is at the heart of a second exchange of stories between Odysseus and Penelope in book 23 (166–230), the only set in which Odysseus speaks first.[38] Odysseus usually manages to learn what others have on their minds before telling his own story,[39] but here Penelope succeeds in tricking him into showing his hand before she reveals hers. Significantly, she does so by intimating that Odysseus' bed is movable— that is, by using a symbolic equation to suggest her own infidelity.[40] Odysseus' anger at this suggestion prompts him to reveal the secret of how he built the bed, a secret Penelope accepts as proof of his identity. Here Penelope, the listener, not only elicits a particular story but interprets it (as an identity token). Yet the protagonist of this story is Odysseus: it is the account of how *he* built "his" marriage bed (23.189; cf. the use of μοι at 184 and 203). Penelope's role is to keep it for him—to see that no other *man* moves it (203–4).

Although Penelope is both narrator and focalizer of the story she tells in reply, the account she gives of her motives for resisting Odysseus does not so much portray her as a subject of the action as confirm her in the roles of object and helper. She says that a fear of deception led her to withhold herself until she was convinced the "stranger" was truly Odysseus. She goes on to present a revised version of Helen's story, which she assimilates to her own. Not even Helen, she says, would have slept with a stranger had she known the Greeks would bring her home again; some god must have prompted her to the shameful deed (23.218–23). Even at the moment of reunion, as the specter of Penelope-as-Helen is put to rest, it is evoked once more—and by Penelope herself. The effect is complex. Penelope's comments imply that one way she preserved her fidelity was by keeping before her the cautionary tale of Helen's misdeed and its aftermath. She can be seen to have internalized the standards by which Helen was judged, and to have kept herself in line not merely for love of Odysseus but also from a sense of shame and fear should Odysseus return to find her unfaithful (hence the emphasis on Helen's ignorance that her first husband would reclaim her). At the same time, however, she seeks to exonerate Helen on the grounds that she was a good woman compelled by a god. This claim again unsettles the "good woman"/"bad woman" dichotomy by suggesting that even "good women" (as in Agamemnon's tirade, 11.434 = 24.22) are subject to lapses and therefore suspect.

Thus Penelope's story at 23.209–30, though focalized by her and having herself and Helen as apparent subjects, is penetrated by the androcentric values of the culture represented in the poem. While the ascendancy of these values, even in Penelope's speeches, may seem self-evident, I think we need to remind ourselves of it with some frequency, lest we lose sight of it in our desire to affirm the strength and intelligence that the character of Penelope also undoubtedly displays. Penelope's story of herself and Helen carries added weight, moreover, because of its placement in the poem: paired with Odysseus' secret of the bed, it has the quality of an intimate confidence; coming after a sequence in which Penelope's motives have been left ambiguous, it has the effect of resolving the ambiguity in favor of wholehearted fidelity. Because members of the audience hear this confession at the same time Odysseus does, their viewpoint is, to that extent at least, assimilated to his. Winkler astutely reminds us that the narrator uses a sudden shift of focalization in the simile of the sailors (233–39) to equate Penelope's experience with Odysseus':[41] as land is welcome to shipwrecked men, so her husband is a welcome sight to *her*. Yet the effect may be not so much to remind us that Odysseus' view is incomplete (as Winkler asserts it does) as to allow us, by equating the experiences of husband and wife, to ignore the substantial differences between them.

The third and final exchange of stories between Odysseus and Penelope immediately follows the reunion. When Odysseus hints at the further wanderings enjoined on him by Tiresias, Penelope asks to hear of them at once, and Odysseus gives her a detailed account of the prophecy (248–84). Then, when they have made love, they entertain one another with the stories of their separate adventures. As if to equate the pleasures of lovemaking and storytelling, the same verb is used of both: τὼ δ'ἐπεὶ οὖν φιλότητος ἐταρπήτην ἐρατεινῆς, / τερπέσθην μύθοισι, πρὸς ἀλλήλους ἐνέποντε (23.300–301). Penelope speaks first of "all that she *endured*" at the hands of the suitors (302); her story is summarized in four lines. Odysseus follows with an account of "all the pains he *caused* others and all those he himself *suffered*," (306–7); the summary—in indirect discourse, like that of Penelope's tale—takes thirty-two lines and is prefaced by the narrator's report that Penelope was pleased (and not put to sleep!) by it (308–41). I find it interesting that Penelope's most important initiatives—the web, the soliciting of gifts from the suitors, and the bow contest—are here passed over, so that her role is reduced to the passive one of "enduring" the suitors' insults. Of course, to recall the solicitation and the contest would be to reopen the issue of her motivation—her apparent flirtation with infidelity. But this censorship (presented as self-censorship) reduces the already limited parallels between the adventures of wife and husband. Odysseus boasts

of inflicting as well as suffering pains; Penelope is reduced to the patient
sufferer—a figure whose story is quickly told.[42] Odysseus' tale also displays
signs of self-censorship: thus, for example, he dwells on Circe's treachery,
not on her yearlong entertainment of him (321).[43] But his story corresponds
in detail to the one he told the Phaeacians; it is not noticeably diminished
for Penelope's benefit, and it includes his affair with Calypso (333–37). It is
the story of his *nostos* (homecoming), now crowned, if not completed, by the
recovery of his home and wife. If I am right about the portrayal of Penelope
as an ideal female listener, it is at this point that she relinquishes any claim
to the roles of actant-subject and focalizer and accepts the roles of object and
appreciative listener to Odysseus' tale.

In the morning, Odysseus draws one last comparison between
Penelope's sufferings and his own (350–53) before delineating the separate
spheres of husband and wife: while he sees to his outdoor property and
seeks a reunion with his father, she must stay in her chambers with her slave
women and refuse to speak with anyone inquiring about the suitors (354–65).
Though he does not use the formula with which Telemachus and Alcinous
dismissed the claims of Penelope and Arete, and though he observes that
Penelope is herself "astute" (361), his speech has the effect of bringing to
a close the period in which Penelope's ambiguous status has allowed her to
behave in unprecedented ways. As Helene Foley has cogently argued, the
*Odyssey* displays the pattern, common to festivals and comedies in many
cultures, of "a world disrupted or inverted, then restored or renewed." In an
extended discussion of the "reverse similes" that compare Odysseus to female
figures and Penelope to males, Foley shows how these contribute to the
pattern of temporary disruption and restoration. The "hierarchical social and
sexual relations" specific to Ithaca are resumed only after "they have been
re-argued, reclarified and voluntarily reaffirmed by all parties concerned."[44]
With the reunion, however, this liminal period comes to an end, as Odysseus'
"morning-after" speech makes clear.

Yet Penelope's story is retold one more time, by the ghost of the
suitor Amphimedon in the so-called Second Nekuia of book 24 (99–204).
And this final retelling is highly paradoxical in its effects. On the one
hand, by making the dead suitor assert that Penelope acted on Odysseus'
orders in setting the bow contest (167–69), the account seems to fit the
pattern whereby the narrator, Odysseus, and Penelope herself affirm her
fidelity. (The story of the woven and unwoven shroud is also brought, in
the suitor's retelling, to a conclusion that dovetails with Odysseus' return,
147–50.) On the other hand, however, by flatly eliminating the uncertainty
so carefully cultivated throughout the earlier passage, the affirmation has
the effect of a contradiction—or, at the very least, of an oversimplification.

As Nancy Felson-Rubin has argued,[45] this oversimplification can be seen as undermining Agamemnon's effusive praise of Penelope (192–98), which is based on the suitor's false assumption that she simply obeyed Odysseus. In this case, at least, an apparent move in the direction of narrative determinacy has the paradoxical effect of creating, or reviving, an opening.

It seems clear from the preceding discussion that in the *Odyssey*, gender is a variable that affects the roles of both narrator and listener, as well as the forms of power associated with both roles. As a check on some of my conclusions, I turn to a pair of stories in which both narrators and listeners are male, although of different classes. In books 14 (192–359) and 15 (390–484), the disguised Odysseus and his loyal swineherd Eumaeus exchange life histories. That proffered by Odysseus is a "lying tale," one of the series he tells while in disguise in Ithaca. Yet its broad outlines and many of its details tally with those of his "true" history as told first to the Phaeacians and then to Penelope. It can thus be seen as yet another *mise en abyme*, a recapitulation in miniature of the epic plot. It is a failed, or at least an interrupted, *nostos*. Eumaeus' tale, though quite different from Odysseus', can itself be seen as a failed *nostos*: that of the young Eumaeus' nurse. Because the narrative context involves a testing of Eumaeus' hospitality and loyalty to Odysseus, the exchange of tales also provides an interesting contrast both to Odysseus' reception by the Phaeacians and to the dialogue of Odysseus and Penelope in book 19.

The "lying tale" told to Eumaeus at 14.192–359 invites comparison with Odysseus' narration in books 9–12—and with the epic narrative as a whole—by its explicit references to the conditions for storytelling and their attendant pleasures. As he had done in book 9 (2–11), Odysseus alludes to the food, wine, and leisure that provide the setting for a good long tale (14.193–95), and he contrasts the pleasure of the telling and listening with the sorrows of the events as he has experienced them (9.12–15, 14.196–98). Given the right conditions, it would be possible to extend the storytelling indefinitely ("for a year," 14.196–97; cf. 11.356–61, 373–76). Once again Odysseus is both narrator and actant-subject of the story. As the account of a man who has risen and then fallen in the world, it cannot be considered a claim to *kleos*; but it is calculated to appeal to Eumaeus, who, although a slave, is of noble birth. It is also the unfinished tale of a suppliant, whose fortunes may yet improve as a result of his listener's favor. In its broad outlines, the story is that of Odysseus' own adventures, recast in realistic terms and without any of the fabulous episodes recounted in books 9–12.[46] After taking part (at first reluctantly, 237–39) in the Trojan expedition, the "Cretan stranger" says he led a raid on Egypt (14.257–72) that resembles Odysseus' raid on the Cicones (9.39–61); seven years of luxury and inaction follow, like those spent with Calypso, after which the "stranger" alone survives a shipwreck brought on by the sailors' impiety (note the close verbal parallels between 14.301–4 and 12.403–6, 14.305–9 and 12.415–19). He is rescued on the shore of Thesprotia by the king's son[47] and offered conveyance, but wicked sailors again dupe him (as Odysseus had unjustly accused the Phaeacians of doing, 13.209–16) until he manages to escape their clutches on Ithaca.

There are of course important contrasts between this story and Odysseus' "true" adventures. The "stranger" is of illegitimate birth, though half noble, and has made his own fortune by raiding; at the same time, he admits an aversion for peacetime work and a wanderlust (14.222–26, 244–45) that contrast with Odysseus' longing for home. Thus his wanderings are described as taking place *after* an uneventful return from Troy. The "stranger" also admits to having surrendered when outnumbered in a battle (14.273–80)—a distinctly unheroic step. It is as though Odysseus had decided to retell his own story with a different protagonist—a rather disreputable sort who anticipates the unscrupulous Odysseus of Attic tragedy.[48] As in the case of Penelope in book 19, the epic narrator leaves us in the dark about Odysseus' motives for creating this new alter ego. The theme of enslavement is comprehensible as an appeal to the sympathy of Eumaeus, who suffered the same fate; but Eumaeus is portrayed as a dutiful and unimaginative type whose watchword might be the οἰκωφελίη (care for the household) so uncongenial to the "stranger" (14.223). Indeed, the point might be precisely to project a foil for Eumaeus, one whose antics will entertain him while providing a contrast to his stolid dependability. There is also a joke at Eumaeus' expense that can only be meant for the implied audience: Eumaeus believes the whole story except for the one bit of truth it contains, namely, that Odysseus is on the way home (14.361–65). In this respect, his response anticipates that of Penelope to the same story (19.312–15). Perhaps the most interesting thing about this "lying tale" is that its falseness, when compared with Odysseus' "true" adventures, is paradoxically commensurate with its realism and hence its plausibility to a character like Eumaeus.[49] Where gender roles are concerned, this greater realism amounts to substituting males for females in some major roles: an Egyptian king for Calypso, and a Thesprotian prince for Nausicaa. It might be thought that these changes reflect the all-male composition of Eumaeus' household and hence of Odysseus' audience for this tale; but no female characters play active roles in any of the lying tales, whose audiences include Penelope and the slave woman Melantho (19.71–82).[50]

Eumaeus' answering tale resembles Odysseus' in its thoroughgoing realism; yet it too is introduced in terms that invoke comparison with epic performance, as the swineherd describes the long evenings of leisure and the companionable wine drinking that accompany such performances (15.390–402). Like the "stranger," Eumaeus tells of his own wanderings, and he contrasts the griefs of which he tells with the pleasure of the retelling (15.400–401; cf.14.193–98, 9.5–15). In contrast to the tension and ambiguity that prevails in the exchange of tales between Helen and Menelaus, and even in the dialogue between Odysseus and Penelope in book 19, the atmosphere here is one of trust and reciprocity; not even Odysseus' disguise seems to interfere with the convivial mood. If this is a scene of "testing," it has none of the anxiety associated with the testing of Penelope. Odysseus and Eumaeus use their stories as mutual confidences that draw them together despite their differences.

In Eumaeus' tale, in contrast to Odysseus', a woman—Eumaeus' Phoenician nurse—plays a central role. In fact, the shape of the tale is such that the woman could easily be seen as the real subject of the action: her desire to return home triggers the plot and leads to the kidnapping and sale of Eumaeus. Yet although her fate resembles Eumaeus' own—the child of wealthy parents, she was likewise kidnapped and sold (15.425–29)—the parallels become less prominent than the contrasts as the woman, in pursuit of her own freedom, causes the enslavement of Eumaeus. Her gender would not seem to be a significant factor in the story except that it is emphasized by Eumaeus: in his view, the woman is corrupted by sleeping with a Phoenician sailor, as all "female women" are corrupted by sex (15.419–22).[51] Moreover, she is not allowed to profit by her theft of Eumaeus: on the journey to Sidon, Artemis kills her, and she is thrown overboard, "prey for the seals and fishes" (478–81). Though her death is not described as a punishment, it parallels the deaths of the sailors who kidnap the "stranger" in his tale, and these deaths are explicitly identified as Zeus' punishment of the kidnapping (14.300, 305–9).[52] In Eumaeus' tale, however, punishment does not overtake the sailors (who actually profit by Eumaeus' sale) but the slave woman who used him to barter for her own freedom. It should be noted that Eumaeus does not himself blame the woman; he records only his sorrow, child that he was, at being left alone (15.481). The disguised Odysseus reminds him that he was fortunate, after all, to have been bought by a "gentle" master (15.488–91).

The primary effect of the exchange of tales is to forge a bond between Eumaeus and the "stranger" on the basis of similarities in their experiences: both have suffered enslavement or the threat of it; both have endured loss of home and status. This sense of kinship in suffering is conveyed by the two men's parallel responses to each other's tales (14.361–62, 15.486–87). A similar effect is produced in the exchange between Odysseus and Penelope in book 19 (though there it is displaced somewhat because the emphasis is on the sufferings of the "absent" Odysseus, 19.253–60; cf. also 350–52). In each case, an emphasis on common suffering creates a bond and an impression of similarity between the hero and a character whose status is actually subordinate, though temporarily superior, to his.

Indeed, by assuming the role of a social inferior to both Penelope and Eumaeus, Odysseus can appeal to their sympathy on the grounds that he has suffered more than they (15.341–43, 488–92; 19.107–22, 166–71). This contributes to the strategy of inclusion I have identified in chapters 2 and 3, whereby Odysseus (and by implication the epic narrator) extends the normative audience for epic performance to include members of other groups—specifically, noble women, and in the case of Eumaeus, a man of slave status. By portraying those included in this way as loyal to Odysseus, the epic narrator suggests that the privilege is a reward for such loyalty. (By comparison, the tales told to "bad" characters, such as Melantho and the suitors, are very brief and have an overt cautionary message; cf. 17.419–44, 1975–88).[53]

A striking exception to the pattern of inclusion, and one that warrants further examination, is the figure of Eurycleia. Here is a character whose loyalty to the hero is unimpeachable, and who, as Odysseus' nurse from birth (19.353–55) might be expected to occupy a position of greater trust than Eumaeus. Odysseus does rely on her help after the suitors have been defeated,[54] but he gives her a minimum of information even then; and in book 19, he reacts with violent anger and distrust when she recognizes his scar. Seizing her by the throat, he asks, "Why do you want to destroy me?" and threatens to kill her with the other disloyal slaves (479–90). Even granted the seriousness of the danger to Odysseus should his identity be revealed to the treacherous maids, some of whom may be within earshot,[55] the violence of his reaction seems disproportionate to the threat posed by an old woman who has just expressed grief at the loss of her master (361–81). Paradoxically, after the revenge has been accomplished, Eurycleia is again rebuked, this time for showing too much delight in the suitors' destruction: as she begins to raise the *ololugmos*, a woman's ritual cry of triumph, Odysseus silences her on the grounds that it is not a pious act to vaunt over men whom the gods have punished (22.407–16). In contrast, Eumaeus is invited (with the cowherd Philoetius) to participate in the revenge on equal terms with Telemachus, and he is promised not only his freedom but the possessions and status of a noble as his reward (21.209–16). The privilege of narration granted to Eumaeus is briefly shared by Eurycleia, who carries important messages, most notably when she informs Penelope of the revenge (23.1–84). But here too, despite the truth of what she says, she is rebuffed, even scolded, by her listener (11.24, 59–68, 81–82).[56] Her own history is summarized by the narrator when she is introduced in book 1 (428–35), as befits a character of some importance. Yet here again there is a strong contrast between the treatment accorded her and the much fuller first-person account of Eumaeus' past, narrated and focalized by himself.

What can account for this failure to grant Eurycleia the privileges, enjoyed by both Penelope and Eumaeus, of narration and of inclusion in Odysseus' audience? I believe it is because of the conjunction of her servile status and her gender. On the grounds of loyalty, Eumaeus can be raised above his servile status and Penelope can be portrayed, if only for a liminal period, as her husband's equal. But as my analysis of Penelope's role has shown, gender is the more obstinate barrier—at least in this poem—because of the prominent male-focalized fear that females will betray males. The betrayal may, but need not, be sexual (as in the cases of Clytemnestra, Helen, and Penelope); while Melantho and the other "bad" female slaves show their disloyalty by sleeping with the suitors, Eurycleia is scarcely of an age to do so. In her case, the intimate knowledge (especially of the scar) that her very closeness to Odysseus has given her raises the prospect of betrayal.[57] Moreover, it is partly by displacing the threats of exposure and outright infidelity onto the female slaves—including Eurycleia—that the epic narrator succeeds in casting Penelope as an exceptional figure.[58] This strategy extends to the ugly aftermath of the revenge, where Eurycleia's unseemly joy and eagerness to call Penelope are checked by Odysseus until *the guilty maids* have cleaned away the traces of slaughter and themselves been put to death (22.428–94).[59] Penelope is equally dissociated from the enjoyment of revenge expressed by Eurycleia and from the mortal punishment of the slave women who consummated the "infidelity" she had merely contemplated.[60]

Because of Eurycleia's role in both the recognition of Odysseus and the account of his naming that it evokes (19.399–412), it has been claimed that she should also be seen as the focalizer of the account of Odysseus' scar that follows (413–66).[61] She does speak lines 363–81 and is the one to recognize the scar in the lines framing the episode (392–93, 467–75); she also speaks to Autolycus, Odysseus' grandfather, in the flashback to Odysseus' naming (401–4). If this part of the flashback is to be attributed to one of the characters in the scene, it must be to Eurycleia, since Odysseus was an infant at the time of his naming. But the entire passage is reported in the third person by the epic narrator, who does not identify it as Eurycleia's recollection. Moreover, lines 389–91 are clearly focalized by Odysseus, who is seized with fear at the belated realization that Eurycleia is likely to recognize the scar. While the story of his naming comes next (399–412), it is embedded in a far longer account (393–466) of how Odysseus got the scar in a hunt on Mount Parnassus; and this scene cannot be focalized by Eurycleia, who was not present when it took place.[62]

I agree with Peradotto and Dimock that the juxtaposed accounts of the naming and the scar should be seen as emblematic (in Peradotto's terms, an "identifying description") of Odysseus' character as one who both inflicts and suffers pain.[63] The boar hunt might even be seen as yet another *mise en abyme* in that it recapitulates in a single adventure the essential elements of Odysseus' entire "career": the journey (with the avowed aim of collecting gifts, 413), the aggression displayed and encountered, the victory at a cost, and the return home. The epic narrator also goes to unusual lengths to convey the impact of his hero's violence on his victims; in, for example, the speeches of Polyphemus at 9.447–60 and 507–21, the reaction of the suitors taken unawares in Odysseus' trap (22.9–25, 42–59), and the simile of the woman taken captive (8.523–31).[64] In an extreme example, line 444 of the hunt scene can only be focalized by the *boar* as, hidden in its lair, it hears the approaching footfalls of men and dogs. But the epic as a whole is focalized by its hero, and by a narrator who admires and even emulates him. As I see it, the perspectives of Odysseus, Autolycus,[65] and even Hermes (Autolycus' patron god, 19.395–98)[66] rival Eurycleia's as the flashback begins, and that of Odysseus dominates the hunt scene. Eurycleia has an important role to play, but it is that of Odysseus' potential helper or opponent rather than that of primary focalizer, even in this limited passage.

While Eumaeus should also be seen as a helper, he is permitted to tell and focalize a lengthy account of his own life in exchange for a version of Odysseus' story that the hero has especially tailored for him. Despite Odysseus' temporary dependence on Eumaeus for survival, moreover, there is no hint of the potential for betrayal that colors Odysseus' relationship to Eurycleia. This is especially surprising given that another male slave, Melanthius (brother of the female slave Melantho), sides with the suitors and helps them during the battle (22.135–200; cf. 17.212–58). With Eurycleia, it would seem, Odysseus cannot enjoy the easy familiarity he shares with Eumaeus. Even where slaves are concerned, then, gender seems to be a factor in the assignment of narrative and audience functions to characters in the epic.

Do the tales exchanged by Odysseus and Eumaeus—a disguised master and a slave—create any openings in the narrative fabric? I believe they do. The "lying tale" of Odysseus, in particular, raises the issue of narrative "truth" by portraying a "falsehood" as more plausible than the authorized version of Odysseus' adventures presented earlier in the epic. This effect is reinforced by the similar editing for plausibility that all the "lying tales" evince. It is true that the tale is shaped for Eumaeus, and in this perspective the false episodes of enslavement can be seen as an appeal to the listener's sympathy. But once we acknowledge the possibility of altering a tale to suit a particular audience, the "authorized version" itself becomes suspect, since it too was told to an audience on whom Odysseus depended for hospitality and conveyance home.[67] Other details contribute to the uncertainty, as when Odysseus declares to the Phaeacians that he is famous for *doloi*, "contrivances" (9.19–20)—a trait in which he resembles the grandfather who named him (19.395–97). In his exchange with Eumaeus, for example, he first swears he "hates like death" the man who lies for profit (14.156–57); then he tells an eminently profitable lie himself: the tale of an ambush at Troy, which earns him the loan of Eumaeus' cloak (457–522).

The plausibility of Odysseus' tale and its juxtaposition with Eumaeus' history create a further opening by undermining the self-evidence of the class hierarchy portrayed in the poem. As Murnaghan has argued, the fact that Odysseus assumes the role of beggar as a disguise he can remove at will suggests that he is immune to an actual loss of status. (With the magical aid of Athena, he is allowed to treat even age as a disguise.)[68] Eumaeus, however, undergoes two changes of status: noble by birth (son of a *basileus*, "prince" or "king," 15.413), he has been reduced to slavery and even proved a model slave; then, with the cowherd Philoetius, he fights at Odysseus' side in the revenge as if he were a noble, and Odysseus promises to raise both herdsmen permanently to that status (21.212–16). Eumaeus' nurse, as we have seen, is a child of wealthy parents who also suffers enslavement (15.425–29); that the same is true of Eurycleia is suggested by the high price paid for her and by the fact that her father and grandfather are named (1.429–31).[69] The poem thus acknowledges the possibility of radical changes in status for some of its minor characters. In Odysseus' "true" adventures, loss of status is never a threat; instead, he is faced with physical dangers and temptations (some of them fabulous) that could lead to loss of *kleos*. The "lying tale," however, and its plausibility to a character like Eumaeus, raises in a "realistic" context the possibility that a hero of the Trojan War could be reduced to beggary. The danger is contained by the disguise motif and by the joke about Eumaeus' incredulity: only the part of the tale that the swineherd disbelieves is "true." As Katz has noted, however, Odysseus' disguise "does not simply misrepresent reality, but also transforms it."[70] As long as he "pretends" to be dependent on Eumaeus, Odysseus is so, to the extent of being forced to angle for a cloak on a cold night.[71]

As the treatment of Eurycleia and the other female slaves shows, however, the conjunction of gender and class inferiority is insurmountable in the *Odyssey*. The epic narrator, by granting Eumaeus the roles of narrator and privileged listener in reciprocity with Odysseus, invites his audience to imagine the two, if only temporarily, as equals. He does the same thing with Penelope and Odysseus in book 19. In each case, however, one or more female slaves are invoked to cement the privileged listener's relationship to Odysseus by marking the limits of privilege. Thus Eumaeus' nurse is not permitted the *nostos* she seeks at Eumaeus' expense; thus the disloyal maids, and even the loyal Eurycleia, draw the explicit violence that the privileged Penelope is spared. In the case of Eumaeus, the result is that an equivalence is suggested between the subject position of a male slave and a male master; in the case of Penelope, the equivalence is between an aristocratic wife and a husband of the same class. These are potentially radical equations; but they are contained by being portrayed as rewards for individual fidelity to the hero. At the same time, the epic invites members of the implied audience to identify with the privileged characters and to ignore the similarities between these and the subordinate characters used as "limiting cases" (or, in the case of the disloyal maids, as scapegoats). What Eumaeus has in common with his nurse, and what Penelope has in common with her female slaves, is thus downplayed in favor of what both have in common with Odysseus—who is restored to his position of privilege with their help.

Within the plot structure of the *Odyssey*, the role of narrator and the subject position associated with it are highly privileged. By granting the narrator's role to female characters and to a male character of low status, the epic potentially subverts the gender and status hierarchies it portrays as normative. But this subversive potential is largely contained insofar as the interaction of female narrator and male listener is assimilated to the larger actantial pattern limiting females to the roles of helper or opponent of a male subject. Repeatedly the accounts of female and male narrators are paired so as to reflect, on the level of narration as well as that of content, an implicit gender rivalry—a contest for meaning and control. In most of these paired accounts, the male has the last word. Yet there remain implicit contradictions or inconsistencies between the accounts, which can be seen as destabilizing the narrative authority of male as well as female narrators. To what extent does the destabilizing effect extend to the authority of the epic narrator? It is to this question I turn in chapter 5.

## NOTES

1. J. H. Finley, *Homer's Odyssey* (Cambridge, Mass.: Harvard University Press, 1978), 3, has also observed that Agamemnon's praise of Penelope's *kleos* in book 24 "comes near making our *Odysseia* [Greek for *Odyssey*] a *Penelopeia*."

2. For the evidence on cults of Helen, see Martin L. West, "Immortal Helen" (inaugural lecture delivered at Bedford College, London, April 30, 1975), and Jack Lindsay, *Helen of Troy: Woman and Goddess* (London: Constable, 1974).

3. For a good discussion of the problematic relationship between goddesses and human women, see Nicole Loraux, "What is a Goddess?," in *A History of Women in the West*, ed. Georges Duby and Michelle Perrot, vol. 1, *From Ancient Goddesses to Christian*

*Saints*, ed. Pauline Schmitt Pantel (Cambridge, Mass.: Belknap Press of Harvard University, 1992). A sensitive treatment of this issue that focuses specifically on the figure of Helen is Norman Austin's *Helen of Troy and Her Shameless Phantom* (Ithaca: Cornell University Press, 1994), especially chap. 3.

4. On the phenomenon of *mise en abyme*, see Lucien Dällenbach, *The Mirror in the Text*, trans. Jeremy Whitely with Emma Hughes (Chicago: University of Chicago Press, 1989), and the review of the earlier French edition by Mieke Bal, "Mise en abyme et iconicité," *Littérature* 29 (1978): 116–28. On the use of *mise en abyme* in the *Odyssey*, see the short but suggestive essay of Italo Calvino, "The Odysseys Within the *Odyssey*," in *The Uses of Literature*, trans. Patrick Creagh (San Diego: Harcourt Brace Jovanovich, 1982).

5. Thalmann, *Conventions of Form and Thought*; Bruce Louden, "An Extended Narrative Pattern in the *Odyssey*," *GRBS* 34 (1993): 5–33.

6. The *Odyssey* is remarkable for the sheer number of passages that can be said to replicate its plot or portions of it; I do not claim to have identified all of these.

7. George Dimock, "The Name of Odysseus," *Hudson Review* 9 (1956): 52–70, reprinted in *Essays on the Odyssey*, ed. Charles H. Taylor, Jr. (Bloomington: Indiana University Press, 1963), 54–72; Peradotto, *Man in the Middle Voice*, 120–70.

8. The suggestion that Eurycleia focalizes the passage was first made by Irene J.F. de Jong, "Eurydeia and Odysseus' Scar," *CQ*, n.s., 35 (1985): 517–18.

9. The term *figure of the poet* is borrowed from John Winkler, "Penelope's Cunning and Homer's," 156.

10. Olson, "Stories of Helen and Menelaus."

11. See Pedrick, "Hospitality of Noble Women."

12. "Is the poet here showing how Helen does it, how she once seduced Paris, another young guest, and can ever re-seduce her husband by representing reality as these men want to hear it? This would be a magnificent *kleos* for Helen, comparable to Odysseus' victories through deceit" (Bergren, "Helen's 'Good Drug,'" 209). As I argue in the text that follows, I see Helen as seeking to camouflage her seduction by laying claim to a more specious *kleos*.

13. A hint of confirmation for Menelaus' tale may be seen in the fact that Demodocus' song of the Horse (8.517–20, "ratified" by Odysseus' weeping) describes Menelaus on the night of Troy's fall as attacking the house of Deiphobus, Helen's husband after the death of Paris, who likewise accompanies her in Menelaus' account (4.276). In each case, the charge of a second infidelity is left implicit, but the mention of Deiphobus in these two contexts suggests that the story of Helen's remarriage was known to the poet and his original audience.

14. Bergren, "Helen's 'Good Drug,'" 213. See the discussion of Bergren, "Helen's 'Good Drug,'" in chap. 1.

15. Because of the diversity of actual audiences, the seductive effects will vary for different groups of readers.

16. Circe describes the Sirens to Odysseus (12.39–54), who then describes them to his men (158–64) before the actual encounter (166–200). All three of these accounts are presented in the context of Odysseus' narrative to the Phaeacians.

17. Circe even resembles the Phaeacians in hearing an account of Odysseus' trip to the underworld before sending him home, 12.33–35.

18. In Hesiod *Theogony* 243, Amphitrite is named as one of the daughters of Nereus; in later mythology, she is the wife of Poseidon (Apollodorus *Library* 1.2.7). In the *Odyssey*, however, all references to Amphitrite seem to serve as periphrases for the sea (3.91; 5.422; 12.60, 97).

19. A Freudian reading of this passage would emphasize the specifically sexual imagery of the narrow channel, the whirlpool, the cave, and the multiple mouths of Scylla; in my view, these images of female sexuality reinforce but cannot account for the gender antagonism that prevails in this part of the poem. See the discussion by Seth Schein in his preface to *Reading the Odyssey*; Schein is careful to note that Odysseus' adventures are focalized by the character himself, that is, by a male. It is a pitfall of classical Freudian readings to treat gender antagonism as a given—a part of the "natural" order—and, in so doing, to ignore the social configurations that sustain and particularize this antagonism.

20. See especially Charles Segal, "*Kleos* and Its Ironies in the *Odyssey*," *L'Antiquité Classique* 52 (1983): 22–47; Pucci, "Song of the Sirens"; and Pucci, *Odysseus Polytropos*, 209–13.

21. Pucci, *Odysseus Polytropos*, 212.

22. In contrast, the male gods Poseidon (107) and Zeus (whose doves are decimated by the Rocks, 62–64) are described as powerless to oppose these female forces.

23. The Sirens break this pattern insofar as there are at least two of them, acting in concert with one another. (They are referred to in the dual at 12.52 and 167, in the plural elsewhere.) As Charles Segal, "Bard and Audience in Homer," 23, notes, however, they are cut off from any larger community.

24. Arete's approval of Odysseus is expressed in book 11 (336–41), shortly preceding Circe's warnings and the paired accounts of the Sirens in book 12.

25. In contrast to the epic Muse, daughter of Zeus, and to the Muses described by Hesiod, the Sirens are unconnected with any male divinity who might authorize their utterance. See Doherty, "Sirens, Muses, and Female Narrators."

26. Here again the narrative frame provides a subtle commentary on the story's content and on the uses of storytelling: while Circe had left the decision to Odysseus, he tells his companions that she had bid him hear the Sirens (cf. 12.49 and 160).

27. Compare, for example, his compulsion to reveal his identity to the Cyclops at the end of their encounter (9.473–505) to combine praise of Neoptolemus with an insistence on his own prowess and leadership (11.505–37, especially 512 and 524–25), and to lecture the suitors on their duty to beggars (17.415–76, 18.125–50).

28. See Felson-Rubin, "Penelope's Perspective," and Katz, *Penelope's Renown*, especially 25–26 and 194. Deirdre Dionysia von Dornum, "What Voice Does Homer Use for Penelope?" (paper presented at the annual meeting of the American Philological Association, Washington, D.C., Dec. 1993), has done a thorough analysis of ways in which Penelope's speech is represented as simultaneously powerful and circumscribed.

29. Katz, *Penelope's Renown*, chap. 5, especially 139–54.

30. Felson-Rubin, "Penelope's Perspective," 67–68.

31. The problematic effects of Amphimedon's account, in book 24, of Penelope's "collaboration" with Odysseus are discussed later in this chapter.

32. Katz, *Penelope's Renown*, 218.

33. Felson-Rubin, "Penelope's Perspective."

34. Katz, *Penelope's Renown*, 138.

35. Ibid., 118–20.

36. See especially Harsh, "Penelope and Odysseus in *Odyssey* XIX," and Winkler, "Penelope's Cunning and Homer's."

37. Katz, *Penelope's Renown*, 132.

38. While Penelope invites the "beggar" to begin their interview in book 19 by telling his own story, he deflects her questioning (107–22), with the result that she tells her story

first (124–61). The passage at 23.166–230 also presents the only pair of female and male narratives discussed in this chapter that opens with the male narrative.

39. The outstanding examples of this tendency are the deferred revelations of Odysseus' identity in Scheria and in Ithaca.

40. Cf. Zeitlin, "Figuring Fidelity."

41. Winkler, "Penelope's Cunning and Homer's," 158–61, discussed in chap. 1.

42. If, as Dimock ("Name of Odysseus" and *Unity of the Odyssey*), Jenny Strauss Clay (*The Wrath of Athena: Gods and Men in the Odyssey* [Princeton, N.J.: Princeton University Press, 1983], 62–64), and Peradotto (*Man in the Middle Voice*) have persuasively argued, the combination of inflicting and suffering pain is central to Odysseus' characterization, this would enhance the thematic importance of the contrast noted here between Penelope's and Odysseus' stories as summarized in book 23.

43. Cf. Wender, *Last Scenes of the Odyssey*, 16.

44. Foley, "'Reverse Similes,'" 60–61.

45. Felson-Rubin, "Penelope's Perspective," 61–62.

46. On Odysseus' "Cretan tales," see Goldhill, "Poet Hero," 36–47, with references to earlier bibliography, and Mumaghan, *Disguise and Recognition in the Odyssey*, 166–68. The "lying tales" as a group are more fully discussed in chaps. 5 and 6.

47. Fenik, *Studies in the Odyssey*, 31–34, notes the parallel between this passage and the meeting with Nausicaa and relates both to a narrative pattern used elsewhere in the Odyssey for "the arrival of a stranger on a foreign shore."

48. For a discussion of the figure of Odysseus in tragedy, see "The Stage Villain" in Stanford, *Ulysses Theme*, 102–17.

49. A similar point is made by Murnaghan, *Disguise and Recognition in the Odyssey*, 167.

50. Still more curiously, no female *gods* are invoked in these tales, with the exception of a single reference to Athena, 14.216. The male gods referred to are Ares (also at 14.216), Helios (19.275), and Zeus (14.235, 243, 268, 275, 283, 300–310, 328; 17.424, 437; 19.80, 275, 297).

51. There is even a verbal parallel between Eumaeus' comment about women and sex and the blanket condemnation of women by Agamemnon at 11.432–34 and 24.200–202: in both cases, the obloquy extends "even to the woman who does what is right".

52. The sailors' deaths in Odysseus' "lying tale" further parallel the deaths of his comrades in the "true" account of his adventures; and the comrades were themselves being punished for their sacrifice of Helios' cattle (12.374–88, 405–19).

53. In his warning to Melantho, the disguised Odysseus compares her present situation with that of a wealthy male of free status ("I too was once prosperous and had a wealthy household," 19.75–76). Though it becomes clear at lines 81–82 that all she really has to lose is her physical beauty, Odysseus' warning implies that the slave woman enjoys and abuses a "prosperity" equivalent to that of the suitors.

54. 22.391–92, 417–18, 431–32, 481–84.

55. Noted by Winkler, "Penelope's Cunning and Homer's," 148–50.

56. The effect intended here is admittedly one of ironic contrast between the truth of Eurycleia's message and the stubborn disbelief of Penelope. Yet the parallel between Odysseus' and Penelope's rebuffs of Eurycleia also contributes to the larger pattern of gender and class distinctions in the epic. Even in the naming scene (19.399–412), if Peradotto is right (*Man in the Middle Voice*, 126–28), her suggestion of a name (Polyaretus, "much prayed-for") for the infant Odysseus is rejected or perversely misinterpreted by Autolycus. Victoria Pedrick, "Eurydeia and Eurynome," notes that one way Penelope

demonstrates her virtue is by resisting the advice of the slave Eurynome to adorn herself for the suitors. Pedrick argues that by keeping a distance from her female slaves, who are potential confidantes, Penelope avoids the danger of corruption by female advisors that became a topos in later classical literature (for example, Phaedra and her nurse in Euripides' Hippolytus, and Dido and her sister Anna in Vergil's *Aeneid*).

57. A subtle verbal parallel between the foot-washing scene and Menelaus' tale of Helen in book 4 points to the danger of physical proximity: the verb ἀμφαφάω, "to feel or lay hands on," is used of Helen's palpation of the Horse (4.277) and of Eurycleia's washing of Odysseus (19.475). The further curious parallel between these scenes—Odysseus' violent restraint of another person's speech that threatens to give him away (Anticlus, 4.286–88; Eurycleia, 19.476–80)—suggests that both may have shared a common template or been linked in the poet's mind, whether consciously or unconsciously.

58. A similar point is made by Katz, *Penelope's Renown*, 132–34; but Katz downplays Odysseus' mistrust and contrasts Eurycleia's fidelity with the other maids' behavior.

59. A further displacement, affecting Odysseus this time, involves the punishment of the maids and of Melanthius, Melantho's brother. After being told by Odysseus to behead the women, Telemachus hangs them on the grounds that they do not deserve a "clean death" (22.440–45, 457–73) The atrocities inflicted on Melanthius (474–77) are likewise attributed to Telemachus, Eumaeus, and Philoetius, not to Odysseus (cf. 454 and 478–79). A similar point is made by Nagler, "Penelope's Male Hand," 247–48.

60. Note that the narrative obscures, even while acknowledging, the sexual exploitation of slave women by masters, by portraying the "unfaithful" maids as willing partners (20.6–8) and by deflecting any expectation that Odysseus or Telemachus (or even Laertes, 1.430–33) might have sexual relations with their slaves (22.426–27, 495–501). (Odysseus does accuse the suitors of "dragging the slave women about," 16.108–9 = 20.318–19, but it remains unclear whether this charge has anything to do with their sexual relations with the women, which are otherwise portrayed as consensual.) Moreover, by observing that Laertes had avoided sleeping with the young Eurycleia for fear of his wife's anger (1.433), the narrator adds another small touch to the portrayal of an exclusive and reciprocal bond between aristocratic husbands and wives. Gerda Lerner, in *The Creation of Patriarchy* (Oxford: Oxford University Press, 1986), 97–98, reaches similar conclusions to mine about the role of the slave women in the *Odyssey*, but fails to note that the women are portrayed as going gladly to meet their lovers (*Odyssey* 20.6–8).

61. See de Jong, "Eurycleia and Odysseus' Scar," and Peradotto, *Man in the Middle Voice*, 125–26.

62. De Jong, "Eurycleia and Odysseus' Scar," argues that as Odysseus' nurse, Eurycleia would have heard an account of the hunt from him when he returned, as his parents are said to have done (19.462–66). But there is no direct evidence of this in the text.

63. Peradotto, *Man in the Middle Voice*; Dimock, "Name of Odysseus" and *Unity of the Odyssey*.

64. Note especially the reflexive use of οἷ at 22.14, which suggests a hypothetical focalization by the unsuspecting suitor: "Who would expect a lone man in a crowd ... to contrive death *for oneself*?"

65. The naming, viewed as an almost prophetic anticipation of Odysseus' "career," amounts to a projection of the grandfather's identity onto the grandson. Autolycus is, to be sure, the *maternal* grandfather, and Odysseus' mother and maternal grandmother play minor roles in the flashback (19.416–17, 462–64), but the emphasis is on the ways in which Odysseus resembles Autolycus, not his mother or grandmother.

66. Hermes also serves as a helper to Odysseus several times in the course of his adventures: he is sent by Zeus to Calypso (5.28–148) and apparently of his own accord gives Odysseus the moly that protects him from Circe's magic (10.275–308).

67. See chap. 6 for a fuller discussion of the issue of differential realism in the *Odyssey*.

68. Murnaghan, *Disguise and Recognition in the Odyssey*, 9. Note that the beggar disguise is also used by Odysseus in Helen's story (4.244–48).

69. Cf. Stanford's commentary on the *Odyssey*, vol. 1: 233, and Alfred Heubeck, Stephanie West, and J.B. Hainsworth, *A Commentary on Homer's Odyssey*, Vol. 1 (Oxford: Clarendon Press, 1988), 126.

70. Katz, *Penelope's Renown*, 154.

71. At the same time, the story demonstrates how, through the power of narration, a social inferior may manipulate his superior. By telling how "Odysseus" once helped him, the "beggar" persuades Eumaeus to help him in a similar way. But Odysseus gets to have it both ways: in disguise, he is simultaneously inferior to Eumaeus and superior to him.

HELENE P. FOLEY

# Penelope as Moral Agent

In his *Poetics*, Aristotle defines tragic character in relation to tragic choice. Character, Aristotle argues, reveals a *prohairesis* or a process of undertaking moral commitment in which a person chooses to act or to abstain from action in circumstances where the choice is not obvious (*Poetics* 1450b8–10).[1] The central moral decision on which the action of the *Odyssey* turns is Penelope's. She must decide whether to stay in Odysseus' house, continue to guard it, and wait for her husband's return or to marry one of the Suitors. Yet she must make this decision in ignorance of Odysseus' identity; that is, she does not know who the beggar is and hence whether Odysseus is alive or dead. Thus, as in Aristotle's exemplary tragedy *Oedipus Tyrannos*, Penelope's choice entails the tragic dilemma of a person faced with the need to act without critical knowledge of the circumstances.

A closer look at Aristotle's assumptions about women as moral agents, however, makes clear that one cannot generalize so easily from Oedipus to Penelope. In his *Politics* and *Ethics*, Aristotle defends the view, against his teacher, Plato, that women are by nature morally inferior to men. Woman's natural function is to reproduce the species and care for the daily needs of her household; man's is to live a life in the polis that offers him opportunities for rational activity, higher learning, leisure, and the exercise of the virtues suitable for political activities. Men are good absolutely, women are good

From *The Distaff Side: Representing the Female in Homer's* Odyssey, edited by Beth Cohen: 93–115
© 1995 by Oxford University Press.

for their function; women's virtues fit them to be ruled, men's to rule
(*Eudemian Ethics* 7.1237a). A woman's capacity for moral deliberation is
without authority (*akuros*; *Politics* 1.5 1260a13), hence she benefits from
the protection and supervision of a *kurios* or guardian. Man, as a naturally
superior being, thus has a permanent constitutional rule (*politikôs*) over the
naturally inferior woman (*Politics* 1.5 125961–2). As free citizens, women
must be educated to be virtuous (*Politics* 1.5 1260b13–21). Both sexes have
*sôphrosynê* or self-control, supplemented in the male by courage (a virtue
largely useless in women) and in the female by industrious habits, free from
servility (*Rhetoric* 1.1361a).[2] Yet the virtues of women differ in kind and not
in degree from those of men (*Politics* 1.5 1260a21–24). Women have need
only of right opinion, not of a genuine practical wisdom. Aristotle thus
quotes with approval the popular view that "silence brings glory to woman"
(*Politics* 1.5 1260a32).

   We should emphasize here that Aristotle's assumption that women
are fundamentally different as moral agents from men is not idiosyncratic
to himself but derives from popular Classical perceptions. Plato and some
provocative passages from drama to the contrary, most Classical writers
assume that any nonreligious public activity performed by a woman violates
the silence, invisibility, and moral dependence appropriate to a virtuous wife.
Even in private life, the wife's virtues entail obeying and serving the interests
of her spouse. Biologically, as is clear from both the work of Aristotle and
the Hippocratic medical texts, women's unstable bodies make it impossible
to rely on their ability to make rational judgments in a consistent and reliable
fashion. Legally—and this is the most telling point—Attic women were in
most circumstances not permitted to undertake significant actions without
the supervision of a *kurios* or guardian.[3]

   Given his views, it is not surprising that female characters in drama
often—seemingly more often than male characters—violate Aristotle's
assumptions about what they should be like. According to the *Poetics*, tragic
characters should be good, traditional (or like), consistent, and appropriate.
To give just one example of deviance, it is not appropriate for female
characters to be manly or clever like Euripides' philosophical Melanippe.[4]
The case of Melanippe makes clear the depth of Aristotle's potential
difficulties with female tragic figures, for to eliminate manly or clever
heroines would be to purge much of Euripides, to say nothing of Aeschylus'
brilliant and androgynous Klytaimestra.[5]

   Yet what about Penelope? To what degree does she meet Aristotle's
standards for a serious (*spoudaios*) literary character undertaking a deliberate
moral commitment? To what degree does the world of the *Odyssey* prefigure
popular Classical Athenian assumptions about women as moral agents? In

this chapter I will examine the complex interrelation between female moral capacity and female social role that conditions and is articulated in Penelope's critical choice, as well as speculate briefly on why the poem gives that central decision to a woman.

On the surface at least, the *Odyssey*'s women *are* endowed with the same moral *capacities* as men. Both men and women are praised for *eidos*, physical appearance; *megethos*, stature; and *phrenas endon eisas*, a balanced capacity for thought and feeling within (18.249 of Penelope, 11.337 of Odysseus, etc.). The same formulas are used to describe the way that they reason about questions of strategy or moral dilemmas.[6] The *thumos* (heart) of both sexes can deliberate, be divided,[7] and then decide in a rational fashion that one alternative is better than another. Both can subdue emotion through reason or bring desire into line with rational goals. Both Penelope and Odysseus are singled out for their ability to be hard-hearted and enduring in the face of suffering. Homeric women are expected to display moral responsibility in their own sphere of the household and to enforce moral standards, such as those relating to hospitality, in the absence of their menfolk.

More important, both sexes can publicly demonstrate *aretê* (excellence or virtue) and achieve *kleos* (fame) for their actions, although they exercise their capacities for virtue in different contexts and achieve fame by different routes. Odysseus wins *kleos* for his skills in battle and counsel in the Trojan War (9.20, which includes his reputation for *dolos* (trickery); 16.241; see also 8.74), for his role as king (1.344; 4.726, 816), and ultimately for his journey and his revenge against the Suitors (implied by the *kleos* of Telemachos' journey, 1.95, 3.78, 13.415 and the *kleos* won by Orestes and others for revenge, 1.298; 3.204). Penelope wins praise for her *kleos aretês* from the shade of the dead Agamemnon in Book 24 (196–97). Men will sing songs of praise for her because she remembered Odysseus (*hos eu memnêt' Oduseos*, 195). Although Agamemnon means here to celebrate Penelope's chastity (198, *echephroni Pênelopeiêi*; 194, *agathai phrenes*), the explicit emphasis on her remembering Odysseus has, as we shall see, far larger implications in the poem.[8]

In Book 2, 116–28, the Suitor Antinoos argues that Penelope knows in her *thumos* (heart) that Athena endowed her with the knowledge of beautiful works (weaving), *phrenas esthlas* (good sense), and *kerdea* (clever counsels) such as no other Achaean woman had before—not Tyro, Alkmene, or Mykene. No other woman was capable of *homoia noênzata* (similar ideas). For this, says Antinoos, she is at this very moment winning *kleos*. As the Suitor Eurymachos later adds, the Suitors thus sensibly compete for Penelope on account of her *aretê* instead of marrying other women (2.205–7). Penelope herself thinks that she will win *kleos* or good report for her correct treatment of guests, and she chastises Telemachos for permitting the mistreatment of the beggar Odysseus (18.215–25). As she says at 19.325–26 to Odysseus, disguised as a beggar, "How shall you know if I excel other women in mind (*noos*) and thoughtful good sense (*epiphrona mêtin*)," if a beggar sits unwashed in the halls? In praising men for their good sense (19.349–52) or in chastising the Suitors for their violation of hospitality or their mode of wooing in Odysseus' house (16.409–33, 21.331–33), Penelope repeatedly shows that she shares the value system of her men (see also the chastising of the immoral maidservant, Melantho, 19.91–95). In recognition of her capacity for moral responsibility, Odysseus entrusted the care of his household, his son, and his parents to Penelope on his departure for Troy (18.266).[9] Most important, in Odysseus' mind the ideal couple shares the same mental outlook (6.180–85). *Homophrosynê* (like-mindedness) is the quality most to be desired in a marriage. A husband and wife *homophroneonte noêmasin* (like-minded in their thoughts) are a grief to foes and a delight to well-wishers.

Although women in the *Odyssey* (even Klytaimestra and Helen) are generally viewed as ethically responsible for their actions,[10] they do not have the same degree of moral autonomy and self-sufficient virtue as men. All characters in Homer are subject to social constraints and divine intervention. Yet although women's ethical capacities are apparently the same, they are notably less free to ignore moral pressures from others or to define themselves and to act apart from their families, and there are many fewer areas in which they can make an independent show of virtue.[11] Penelope's beauty and *aretê*, she twice repeats, were destroyed on Odysseus' departure for Troy (18.251–53, 19.24–26; see also 18.180–81). Similarly, Zeus takes away half the *aretê* of a man on the day of his slavery (17.320–22). If Odysseus were to return, Penelope's *kleos* would, she says, be greater and better, and she would give the stranger Theoklymenos or the disguised Odysseus many gifts (17.163–65; 19.309–11; Helen gives them in the presence of Menelaos). In short, Penelope is not fully herself without her husband. A woman must also defer to the master of her household. In Book 1 (345–59), for example, Telemachos for the first time attempts to claim authority (*kratos*) over his house and tells Penelope to leave the choice of themes for song at the banquet to himself. Although the theme of the Achaeans' return from Troy is wounding to Penelope, Telemachos finds it appropriate. Penelope should go within; speech will now be a care to men. The amazed Penelope returns in silence to her quarters and lays the wise saying of her son to her heart. Virtually the same thing happens when Telemachos reclaims Odysseus' bow from Penelope in Book 21 (343–53).

Finally, the poem continually expresses doubt that even wives of basically good character, when unsupervised by a husband or his surrogate, will make decisions in the interests of their marital family. Before Penelope makes her decision in Book 19, both Helen and Klytaimestra have served as examples of what happens when wives make decisions in the absence of their husbands; in Book 15 (20–23), when Athena appears in a dream to Telemachos, she warns Telemachos about the *thumos* in the breast of a woman. She tends to forget her previous marriage and children when she weds another (yet Penelope asserts at 19.581 that this will never be the case with herself). Overall, women are vulnerable to seduction in the absence of their husbands and endowed with deceptive intelligence that can be used to destroy them if they decide on another man.

As the recent and formidable studies of Murnaghan, Winkler, Felson-Rubin, and Katz, among others, have argued, the narrative context in which Penelope acts has made both her decision to establish the contest for her hand and her behavior leading up to that decision appear ambivalent, opaque, and/or contradictory to critics from antiquity on.[12] The books of Katz and Rubin make clear that these problems deserve a book-length discussion; it is neither possible nor desirable for me to go over the same ground in detail once more in this essay. Instead, I shall take the position, at the risk of oversimplification, that although the text does not give us full access to Penelope's thoughts and feelings, her well-articulated dilemma and her stated reasons for establishing the contest make it possible to judge and make ethical sense of her decision. The first two books of the poem examine Penelope's dilemma from the perspective of the goddess Athena disguised as Mentes, the Suitors, and Telemachos. Books 18 and 19 at last give us Penelope's own views on the issue. Finally, Penelope reluctantly makes a decision to set up the contest of the bow for her hand, ironically in the presence of Odysseus disguised as a beggar. My discussion will stress the moment at which Penelope chooses to act, to establish the contest for the bow.[13]

Because we see her situation first through the eyes of others, the text emphasizes from the start the social constraints that Penelope faces. In Book 1 (274–78), Athena, disguised as Mentes, gives advice to Telemachos. He should let the Suitors depart. If Penelope's *thumos* bids her marry, let her go back to the halls of her powerful father. Her family will prepare a feast and make ready gifts that should go with a *philê pais* (beloved daughter). Shortly afterwards, Athena offers a second piece of advice on the same issue. She urges Telemachos to find out if Odysseus is dead. If he is, Telemachos should heap up a mound for his father, perform over it appropriate funeral rites, and give his mother to a husband (1.289–92). While Odysseus lives, Athena advises Telemachos to let Penelope choose to return to her father's house and to remarry. If he is dead, she advises Telemachos to act for her.

In Book 2 (50–54), Telemachos complains to the assembled Ithacans that the Suitors beset an unwilling Penelope with their wooing and shrink from going to her father, Ikarios, so that he might dower her (give her *hedna*) and give her to whomever he wishes.[14] Not so, replies Antinoos the Suitor. Penelope, not the Achaeans, is to blame in this case, for she knows wiles beyond others and has been deceiving the Suitors for almost four years (85–110). Send her back to her father, he advises Telemachos, and command (*anôchthi*) her to marry whom her father bids and whoever is pleasing to her. Penelope knows, Antinoos says, how superior she is to other women. And the *noos* (intelligence) that the gods are putting in her breast will bring great *kleos* to her, but want of livelihood to Telemachos. Thus, Antinoos concludes, the Suitors will wait until Penelope marries the Suitor whom she wishes (2.113–14, 116–28). Telemachos replies that he will not thrust from the house the mother who bore and reared him. If he willingly (*hekôn*) sent his mother away, he would have to pay back her dowry and suffer retribution from her father, Ikarios; his mother would invoke the hateful Erinyes (spirits of revenge) on her departure; and there would be *nemesis* (moral disapproval) from men (2.130–37). Eurymachos, another Suitor, then again urges Telemachos to command (*anôgetô*) his mother to return to her father for marriage and dowry. Until then, the Suitors will compete for her on account of her *aretê* (7 2.195–97). Telemachos, defeated, asks for a ship. If he finds his father is dead, he will give his mother to a husband (198–223). In Book 15 (16–23), Athena warns Telemachos in a dream that Penelope's father and brothers bid (*kelontai*) her wed Eurymachos, who surpasses the other Suitors with his gifts and now increases them. Athena advises Telemachos to look to his possessions because Penelope may decide to marry and take Telemachos' goods with her.[15] (This dream does not correspond to what the audience hears elsewhere about Penelope in Telemachos' absence.) In Book 20 (341–44), Telemachos reiterates to the Suitors the point he made in Book 2. Insisting that Odysseus is now dead (although he now knows that he is not), he bids (*keleuô*) Penelope marry whomever she wishes and offers to provide a dowry, but is ashamed to force her to depart unwillingly from the house.[16]

The text thus identifies the factors conditioning Penelope's decision in a somewhat confusing fashion. Sometimes the choice to remarry is said to be Penelope's alone; sometimes it lies in the hands of her son or father; sometimes the decision is a joint one in which Penelope will decide in conjunction with her son or father. After his return to Ithaka, Telemachos is willing to play a more active role by urging Penelope to remarry if Odysseus is dead, but he is consistently unwilling, even though the delay continually threatens first his livelihood and then his life, to force her to leave the house and remarry; Odysseus' parting instructions to Penelope reported at 18.257–70 also place the choice to remarry in Penelope's hands.

I am avoiding the use of the later term *kurios* or guardian to describe the authority male figures have over women in this context because these passages raise considerable doubt about the exact parameters involved in male guardianship of a wife in the *Odyssey*.[17] Fathers generally arrange first marriages for their virgin daughters in Homeric epic, although even here (as in the case of Helen and her suitors) the daughter's preference may play a role; this is an option in Penelope's case. Yet Telemachos suggests that a wife or widow can invoke strong sanctions against being forced to remarry against her will. Clearly, Penelope cannot create the economic conditions of a proper marriage, like the preparation of a wedding feast or the presentation of a dowry; and male relatives can play a major role in urging her to make a choice, even a particular choice. So her decision is not fully her own. Nevertheless, despite minor inconsistencies, it appears that her preference plays an essential role in the process, a role sufficiently important that she can delay the marriage and even incur from the Suitors a mixture of public calumny and grudging praise for her crafty behavior. After Book 2, because no one claims the authority to force her to remarry, Penelope is apparently left free to choose if and when she will do so. In Book 19, she herself does (after acquiring the approval of Odysseus in disguise) make the decision to set up the bow contest for her hand. Thus the *Odyssey* gives its audience the opportunity to observe a mature female moral agent making a critical and autonomous ethical decision.

When the poem returns to the issue of Penelope's marriage in Books 18 and 19, the focus is on Penelope, and we discover that she views her dilemma more or less in the fashion that Telemachos has reported to Eumaios and Odysseus in Book 16 (73–77). Here Telemachos says that Penelope's heart is divided over whether to stay with him and respect her husband's bed and the voice of the people or to follow the best of the Achaeans who offers the most gifts of wooing.

In Book 18 (257–70) Penelope reports to the Suitors, Telemachos, and the disguised Odysseus on Odysseus' parting instructions to her as he left for Troy. Odysseus put his right hand on her wrist, in a gesture that echoes the initial appropriation of a bride by a husband in marriage. This same gesture appears on the fifth-century Melian relief in the Metropolitan Museum (plate 20), where Odysseus, disguised as a beggar, takes the wrist of the mourning Penelope. Uncertain as to whether he would survive the war, Odysseus entrusted the care of the household to her and bid her wed whomever she might wish and leave when her son is bearded. Penelope asserts that all that Odysseus predicted is being brought to pass. She thus represents the timing of her remarriage as powerfully conditioned by Odysseus' parting instructions.[18]

Before the Suitors, whom she then provokes into offering new gifts of wooing, Penelope mentions only one reason why she must soon remarry. In Book 19.124–61, Penelope describes her dilemma more fully to the disguised Odysseus. The Suitors have discovered her deception with the web; she can no longer unweave each night the shroud she was weaving for Odysseus' father, Laertes. Now she cannot escape marriage or devise a new trick; her parents press her to act, her son frets, the Suitors are devouring Telemachos' livelihood, and Telemachos is a man. Later in Book 19 (524–34), Penelope gives the beggar a precise statement of her moral quandary. She says that her heart is divided over whether to stay by her son, guard the house, revere the bed of her husband, and respect public opinion (for this important influence, see also 16.75 and 23.149–51) or to marry (literally, follow a husband). Her child, who previously would not permit her to marry, is now grown and vexed over his loss of livelihood. She then tells Odysseus about a dream in which her pet geese are slain by an eagle who goes on to say that he is Odysseus (19.535–53). Odysseus affirms the dream. Penelope doubts his interpretation; in her view the dream was a false one. But, she laments, the day is coming that will divide her from the house of Odysseus and she decides to appoint the contest for her hand with the bow. Later, when she gets the bow from the storeroom, she weeps (20.55–60). She also wishes to die and dreams of Odysseus as he looked when he left for Troy (20.61–90; see also 18.202–5). Although she clearly regrets her decision to remarry, Telemachos' maturity and the threat to both his livelihood and his life make it imperative for Penelope to act.

In Book 19, then, Penelope gradually arrives at the point where she is willing to make a (at least in her own view) socially responsible decision to move toward remarriage—in contrast to expectations that the poem generates about the behavior of wives in the absence of their husbands, who generally surrender to seduction.[19] In full recognition of the suffering it will bring her, she moves to subordinate her own desires to the needs of her son and the parting instructions of her husband. Yet critics have argued that because Penelope has received repeated signs that Odysseus' return is imminent, her decision to remarry is both ill-timed and an inadvertent betrayal of her husband, who is in fact alive and present without her knowledge.[20] Her behavior has also been categorized as intuitive, irrational, passive, contradictory, indicative of a moral collapse, and even unintelligent.[21] Nevertheless, it should be stressed again that critics' questions about the decision have, often by their own admission, arisen above all from the narrative context in which her choice is made.

In my concern with the nature of Penelope's moral choice, I wish to stress the following points. First, she is facing a dilemma that she defines clearly and rationally. Penelope's moral stance is in itself, as both the poem and Aristotle make clear, intelligible, commendable, and appropriate to her role as wife. As in Aristotle's *Oikonomika* and *Politics*, the Homeric wife's virtue apparently consists in her ability to obey with intelligence and self-control the instructions of her husband, even when he is absent. Indeed, the pseudo-Aristotelian *Oikonomika* 3.1 not only asserts that Penelope fits the wifely ideal that has just been defined in these terms but also adds that she is especially to be commended for proving herself faithful (like Alkestis) to her husband in adverse circumstances. The *Odyssey* repeatedly acknowledges Penelope's virtue and casts no *explicit* doubts on her action. Even Agamemnon in the underworld of Book 11 (444–46) thinks Penelope is an exception to the general danger of women's infidelity; Odysseus' mother (11.177–79) and Athena (13.379–81) earlier affirm her fidelity; at 20.33–35, shortly after Penelope's decision, Athena again affirms the worth of Odysseus' wife and child. Finally, the shade of Agamemnon praises Penelope in Book 24. Later Greek tradition simply makes Penelope the paradigm of the virtuous wife. The disguised Odysseus twice endorses Penelope's decision to abandon her customary retirement and approach the Suitors. In Book 18 he approves Penelope's showing herself to the Suitors (18.281–83) and winning wedding gifts while her mind intended other things (see overall 18.158–303; also 2.87–92 and 13.379–81, where Antinoos and Athena interpret her intentions in other contexts in the same terms);[22] in Book 19 he approves her choice for the contest for her hand.[23] Given Telemachos' situation and Odysseus' instructions reported by Penelope in Book 19, both to remarry and not to remarry are potentially acts of moral fidelity to Odysseus.[24] Because of her ignorance of both Odysseus' identity and his fate, the critical problem for Penelope is the timing of the decision, not the decision to remarry itself.[25] Let us turn briefly, then, to the issue of timing and circumstances.

Penelope could not in good conscience have continued to delay her remarriage much longer. After Telemachos returns from his journey and recognizes Odysseus, he demonstrates his ability to take charge of the household for the first time; pretending he thinks that Odysseus is dead, he takes a more active role in encouraging Penelope to remarry (see esp. 19.159–61, 530–34; 20.339–44); at the same time, he is under threat from the Suitors. In Book 19, where she begins to move explicitly toward the decision to remarry, Penelope consistently expresses pessimism about Odysseus' Return and rejects the signs and dreams that presage it (19.257–60, 313–16, 560–68; 20.87–90; 23.59–68).[26] Even when she has reliable evidence from Eurykleia of Odysseus' Return in Book 23, Penelope refuses to recognize her husband until she has tested his knowledge of their bed. Here she apologizes to Odysseus for her insistence on testing to the last.[27] She was always afraid, she tells him, lest some man would come and beguile her with his words, for there are many men who plan such evils (23.215–17). Earlier she remarks to the disguised Odysseus in a similar vein that she pays no attention to strangers, suppliants, and heralds (19.134–35). The swineherd Eumaios, who apparently receives a positive appraisal for being equally cautious, tells us in Book 14 that Penelope repeatedly questions beggars, but that no wanderer with reports about Odysseus could persuade his wife and son (122–28). In a poem that registers with admiration an equal wariness in Odysseus himself (see especially 13.330–38), is Penelope's skepticism—a vigilance that logically increases as the temptation to give way to hope becomes more pressing—really as contradictory as many critics would have it?[28] Or does the timing of Penelope's choice seems questionable only from the perspective of a privileged access to the truth?

In my view Odysseus' approval of Penelope's choice to establish the contest is perfectly intelligible. Logistically, it creates the opportunity (heretofore missing) for him to take on the Suitors, and it is a contest in which he knows he has a chance of success. It has been argued that the plot simply demands from Odysseus a reaction that does not account for the full complexities of the situation.[29] Yet from an ethical perspective, in a context where Odysseus has chosen to test his wife rather than revealing his identity, he observes her following his own previous instructions (reported by Penelope in his presence) and maintaining a heroic and crafty defense against seductive evidence to hope and delay. From this perspective, Penelope's choice is less dubious or irrational than tragic (by Aristotle's standards): the dilemma of a good person attempting to act correctly without full and, in this case, critical knowledge of the circumstances (Odysseus' identity and fate). As in tragedy, the consequences of both alternatives are unavoidably at least partially and potentially negative.[30] For Aristotle, tragic irony of the kind created in this scene appropriately evokes pity and fear.[31] One could even argue that *it is precisely by proposing to establish the contest for her hand with such evident regret that Penelope passes the test of the faithful wife.*

Telemachos, complaining that his house is overrun with enemies who waste his livelihood, remarks that his mother neither refuses hateful marriage nor is able to make an end (16.121–28). The poem might have rescued Penelope from a decision by having Odysseus return and dispose of the Suitors while she still delayed, or it could have staged an earlier recognition between husband and wife (what the Suitor Amphimedon imagines actually occurred in Book 24.12090). Yet in my view Penelope's fidelity to Odysseus would be far less effectively demonstrated if the poem had simply taken the painful choice out of her hands. After the recognition in Book 23, Penelope raises the puzzling exemplum of Helen in relation to herself; it is certainly possible to interpret this exemplum as a recognition by Penelope that she inadvertently flirted with adultery in setting up the contest of the bow.[32] And public opinion has apparently always been on the side of waiting, although the public is neither privy to the complex events within the palace nor able to defend Telemachos. Insofar as the text does endow Penelope with desire (e.g., her sudden urge—produced by Athena and resisted by Penelope—to show herself to the Suitors in Book 18) and ambivalence (her weeping over the geese slaughtered by the eagle Odysseus in her dream in Book 19) and offers general warnings about women's vulnerability to seduction, Penelope's acceptance of the less palatable choice in Book 19 demonstrates—however ironic the scene, given the audience's knowledge of the truth—a greater moral fidelity to her spouse.[33]

Finally, although Penelope's distress makes it clear that she views the contest with the bow as the critical step on a path toward remarriage, the narrative indicates that her choice of a contest of skill and strength leaves open, in a fashion characteristic of Penelope, several possibilities. The Suitors may demonstrate that none of them is the equal of Odysseus; although Penelope has put her fate into male hands by establishing the contest, she has at least tried to ensure that the victor will be like her former husband. The contest with the bow has the potential to serve, like the web, as a tricky device to delay the remarriage. The text has led us to expect that Penelope would choose to marry the Suitor who offered the most gifts of wooing, as her family advised; the surprise choice of the contest may thus suggest that Penelope has this in mind. If all the signs and portents prove reliable, Odysseus will return and Penelope will not have to abide by the consequences of her choice. The beggar insists that Odysseus himself will be there before the Suitors have shot the arrow through the iron (23.585–87), and Penelope acknowledges, even after her choice, how pleasurable this outcome would be to her (23.587–90). In addition, the audience knows at the time Penelope makes her decision that she will be rescued from her suffering (and hence that it will have no negative consequences).

The *Odyssey* ultimately locates significant action within a social context that threatens to destroy the household of Odysseus from many angles. Ithaka does not readily submit to the returning Odysseus' authority. Odysseus' men have been destroyed during the journey home in large part over their refusal to listen to and obey Odysseus; the Suitors persistently violate the laws of hospitality. Both groups submit too readily to their appetites. Telemachos cannot imitate Orestes in avenging his father, and he could not in Book 2 mobilize public opinion for his just cause in any effective fashion; Odysseus' subjects seem to have forgotten his paternal form of kingship, his fairness and gentleness. Even when the Suitors recall Odysseus' generous leadership, it has no effect on their actions. At 16.442–44, for example, Eurymachos recalls Odysseus' hospitality to himself as a child and promises to protect Telemachos for this reason, but he is lying. At 16.424–33 Penelope reminds Antinoos, to no effect, of how Odysseus saved his father's house (see also 4.687–95, where Penelope chastises Medon, and by extension the Suitors, for not remembering Odysseus as king). The poem predicates survival on intelligence and social cooperation within the family group. Even Odysseus cannot achieve his Return without his son, wife, and servants. In making the action turn on Penelope's decision, the poem seems to privilege and celebrate the importance and even the heroism of social responsibility in a moral agent, as well as the contingencies that make taking moral responsibility problematic.[34] In Penelope's domestic world on Ithaka, there is no legitimate room either for the wrath, withdrawal, or honor from Zeus alone temporarily espoused by Achilles in the *Iliad* or for the freely chosen immortal obscurity offered by Kalypso to Odysseus.[35] The forces driving her to remarry leave little place for self-interest or for the nearly godlike freedom to shape a human destiny offered to the two Homeric heroes. She can only attempt to serve her son's interests and to obey her husband's parting instructions. The potentially notorious *kleos* Penelope won during the period of wooing, which threatened to destroy Telemachos' livelihood, becomes the permanent *kleos* won by her devotion to her husband, a *kleos* that now enhances the household of Odysseus. (See her point that *kleos* can be achieved by being *amumôn*, blameless, at 19.333.)

A poem that urges the value of conformity to certain basic social norms like hospitality in an Ithaka represented as either indifferent to them or afraid to act on them needs to make its case in a subtle fashion. As in later Greek literature, the *Odyssey* deploys to its advantage a female figure, whom no listener could imagine escaping from social encumbrance without great damage to her family and to the reputation of all women (see *Odyssey* 24.199–202). Penelope's sophisticated moral choice thus forms a key part of the *Odyssey*'s emphasis on ethical norms such as justice and on the quieter values that promote social cohesion. In Book 19, the disguised Odysseus compares Penelope to a king whose benevolence brings fertility and order to his kingdom. I suggest that Penelope's ethical behavior in part prefigures that of the restored Ithaka in a context where the paternal king Odysseus cannot as yet display his full character as leader. As was mentioned earlier, in Book 24 Penelope is awarded *kleos* in part for remembering her husband (*hos eu memnêt' Oduseos*, 195); she elsewhere insists that even if she remarries she will, unlike other women who tend to forget the previous marriage and children (15.2023), remember Odysseus' house in her dreams (19.581). In remembering Odysseus and reminding others to conform to the standards that he once enforced—and we should recall how important a theme memory is in the poem as a whole—the beleaguered Penelope continues to live by the standards of that vanished kingdom, and through her actions we can begin to glimpse what it might be. The reestablishing of order in the household—a smaller institution in which roles and responsibilities are relatively well defined—can be symbolically extended to the fragmented public arena. The poem can also stress through Penelope the heroism of social responsibility without compromising to the same degree the greater autonomy of its hero, Odysseus. Odysseus' ethical responsibilities as king are in partial conflict with his ambitions to win fame and to protect his household as hero and avenger, roles that involve in each case a dramatic destruction of his male subjects. Penelope's choice allows the returning Odysseus to retain both the heroism he won as an individual for his journey and his revenge and his future fame as a just and benevolent king.

When major Homeric characters deliberate, reasoning generally provides the basis for a course of action to be taken in a specific case. In the majority of cases, the choice to be made is narrowly strategic: how best to survive in a situation of war or danger, and how best to win a desired goal (e.g., honor).[36] The most elaborate decision of this kind is faced by Odysseus at the beginning of Book 20. First, he debates whether to punish the unfaithful maidservants immediately or to delay the punishment to a more strategic moment; then he turns to worrying over how to punish the Suitors or to escape from the consequences if he does kill them. Sometimes, although rarely in the *Odyssey*, gods intervene to influence the choice.[37] Odysseus' choice to leave Kalypso and Achilles' choice about whether to return to battle are unusual because the hero has already been told the major outlines of his fate. Penelope's critical and elaborated choice has been incomprehensibly neglected in the general literature on Homeric decision making.[38] Penelope makes a fully conscious and autonomous decision that entails rejecting hope and desire for obedience to social responsibilities; there is no question of divine intervention in the critical moments in 19 (or 23; in 18 Athena intervenes, and Penelope resists).[39] Certainly, the question of contingency is notably operational in this instance. Indeed, if I am correct, Penelope's decision best prefigures those singled out by Aristotle as particularly effective on the tragic stage and thus gives an as-yet-unrecognized depth to Homeric philosophy.[40] Most important, by forcing Penelope to make a choice so conditioned by both critical responsibilities and uncertainties, the epic takes a leap into a complex moral territory that it normally avoids (Achilles' complex decision in *Iliad* 9 is a very different matter).[41]

In my discussion, I have also tried to emphasize the ways in which the *Odyssey* defines and makes use of subtle differences between men and women as moral agents. Even when men and women share the same values and moral capacities and deliberate about ethical issues in the same fashion, as they do here, they act under different constraints and with different priorities. Contemporary feminists have also begun to try to understand such moral differences in a modern context, and this debate served as a catalyst for this paper. The sociologist Carol Gilligan, for example, has argued for the validity of what she calls a different moral voice. For Gilligan, moral problems often arise for women "from conflicting responsibilities rather than from competing rights."[42] "The morality of rights" often adopted by men "differs from" this "morality of responsibility in its emphasis on separation rather than connection, in its consideration of the individual rather than the relationship as primary."[43] As moral agents, women tend toward self-sacrifice and are, in Gilligan's view, often "suspended in a paralysis of initiative."[44] No Homeric character deliberates in terms of competing rights in the modern sense, and decisions by Homeric male as well as female characters are always heavily determined by communal standards. Moreover, as a result of the formulaic nature of oral epic, all characters tend to deliberate about moral issues in the same terms. Although I agree with recent critics of Snell such as Williams that Homeric characters are convincing moral agents, they are not ethical individuals in a post-Kantian sense.[45] Hence, even if her controversial formulation of the relation between gender and ethics proved a reliable basis for discussion of the modern context,[46] Gilligan's distinctions, to which I cannot do justice here, are not applicable in any simple sense to the *Odyssey*.

Nevertheless, the *Odyssey* makes important distinctions about male and female moral agents that correspond to some degree with—even while they also deviate from—those established by Gilligan. Relatively speaking, for example, Penelope operates more fully than any male character in the poem within a web of relationships and responsibilities from which she neither can nor wishes to withdraw. This is not simply the result of a distinction between public and private worlds because in the household of a king no such clear boundaries can be consistently drawn. Penelope's actions can affect and be celebrated by the world beyond her household and thus have public implications, yet her choices, unlike those of a male hero, are limited to defending her present household and those within it or committing herself to follow another husband. Sex roles, then, are critical to defining gender differences in moral agency in this poem. Penelope makes a choice to sacrifice her own desires in establishing the contest with the bow, and she is placed in a paralyzing position in which she can take no action that is without negative consequences. Positive actions by women in Greek literature (whether virgins or wives like Alkestis) typically involve such sacrifice and self control. Penelope is apparently the only character in either of the Homeric epics, who faces a choice between two responsibilities to others, and it may be significant that she is never, like the male heroes, permitted an ethical soliloquy, but always debates her alternatives in dialogue with other characters. There are no discussions comparable to those about Penelope's remarriage in *Odyssey* 2 over whether a male agent has or should have the autonomy to make a critical decision. Similarly, Klytaimestra's betrayal of Agamemnon is said in *Iliad* 24 to tarnish the reputation of all women, even those who, like Penelope, act appropriately (*kai hê k'euergos eêisin*, 199–202); the *kleos* of a Homeric hero does not depend in part on the presence or actions of another person, as does Penelope's (17.163–65, 19.309–11). Penelope wins *kleos* as wife, as a person powerless to act except in relation to another, not as a powerful warrior-leader defending his reputation.

Nevertheless, the particular limits under which a female agent in Homer is ideally meant to operate make giving Penelope moral autonomy in this instance an attractive opportunity to the *Odyssey* poet.[47] On the one hand, her social role makes it dangerous for a woman to claim full moral autonomy. Furthermore, feminization, or a breakdown in gender boundaries, is a fate repeatedly feared by the typical male hero; warriors taunt their opponents by associating them with women; the bodies of male heroes, lying helpless and without armor on the battlefield, are viewed as feminized;[48] Hektor in *Iliad* 6 insists on sex-role differences between men and women as a defense against Andromache's plea that he adopt a more defensive role in the battle (490–93). On the other hand, choices made from a marginal, relatively powerless position can also serve to set a new moral direction for the dominant male agents of Homeric poetry.[49] Because Penelope shares Odysseus' values and is both constrained and willing in a situation of hopeless uncertainty to sacrifice her own needs for the benefit of others, her female difference contributes to rather than undermines the social order. Indeed, this willingness to abide by the social standards of her world ultimately separates her from Odysseus' disruptive enemies, the Suitors, and makes her the figure for a future order in which respect for such standards will be the basis for a community united under the leadership of her husband. Insofar as tragic choices of the kind identified and praised by Aristotle are symptomatic of a social world in which obligations to promote civic welfare have acquired a greater ideological interest and resonance, it is not surprising that the *Odyssey*'s most nearly tragic choice is made by a character whose social role is defined so pointedly in terms of responsibilities.

## NOTES

A portion of this essay was presented at Vassar College, in spring 1992. I wish to thank the audiences at Bard, at Vassar, and at a conference on Women in Antiquity in St. Hilda's College, Oxford, in September 1993, as well as Richard Seaford and Laura Slatkin, for their comments on an earlier draft.

1. Here I accept the view of Chamberlain, 1984, that *prohairesis* entails a process of choosing a course of action and sustaining commitment to that course of action. Perception (*aisthêsis*), reason (*dianoia* or *nous*), and desire (*orexis*) play roles in the process.

2. At *Politics* 1.5 1260a21–24 Aristotle says that the *sôphrosynê* of men and women differs, and that women need courage only for obedience.

3. For a recent discussion of the legal position of Attic women, see Just, 1991.

4. Melanippe's speech seems to have contained a knowledge of science and philosophy inappropriate for a woman (*Poetics* 15.8–9, 1454a). Apparently Aristotle disapproves of behavior in a tragic character that he would have disapproved and/or found to lack verisimilitude in a real woman.

5. I address these issues in tragedy in a forthcoming paper.

6. One exception, addressed later in this chapter, is that Penelope does not have any moral soliloquies. See Russo, 1968, 280–94 on the way that the *Odyssey*'s typical scenes of deliberation depart in certain respects from those in the *Iliad*; in particular, decisions in the *Odyssey* are only exceptionally resolved by divine intervention.

7. See, e.g., 16.73 and 19.524 of Penelope, 9.299–306 and 20.9–13 of Odysseus.

8. See further Schein, Chapter 2, this volume.

9. It is also said that Odysseus left Mentor to oversee his *oikos* (2.226), but Mentor has apparently not exercised whatever authority he may have in this circumstance. As the assembly in Book 2 makes clear, the community is in general helpless to oppose the Suitors.

10. For a discussion, see Katz, 1991, on both Klytaimestra and Helen.

11. Adkins, 1960, 37, remarks that *aretê* in Homeric women is defined by men and entails the "quiet" or cooperative virtues. Because they are not called on to defend the household, they do not need competitive virtues. "As a result, Homeric women may be effectively censured for actions which Homeric heroes have a strong claim to be allowed to perform." The women of the *Odyssey* are self-conscious about such public opinion. Nausikaa seeks to compromise between her social obligations to the shipwrecked Odysseus and her reputation; she would chastise an unwed girl who consorted with men (6.286). Public opinion is a factor in Penelope's decision concerning remarriage (16.75; 19.527), and the people criticize her when they think she has chosen to do so (23.149–51).

12. Murnaghan, 1986, 1987; Winkler, 1990; Felson-Rubin, 1987, 1993; and Katz, 1991. See further, Schein, Chapter 2, this volume. In this essay I shall, except for a few brief notes on critical issues, refer the reader to extensive discussion of these questions in Katz and Felson-Rubin, 1993. My own focus on Penelope as a moral agent leads me to adopt a different interpretation of Penelope's decision to establish the contest of the bow from that of these recent critics.

13. As was said earlier, by Aristotelian standards at least, character (*êthos*) reveals *prohairesis*, the sort of thing a person avoids in circumstances where the choice (and the resulting commitment to carry through on the choice) is not obvious; speeches in which the speaker does not commit him or herself or avoid something convey no character (*Poetics* 1450b8–10).

14. Recent discussion has made clear that the word *dowry* may be misleading in a Homeric context. What is important is that at marriage gifts were exchanged among the men aiming to marry or to give in marriage a particular woman. See with full earlier bibliography Morris, 1986; and Leduc, 1992.

15. For further discussion of this passage, see Murnaghan, Chapter 4, this volume.

16. This last speech comes after Penelope has decided on the contest, but it is clear from what Penelope says in Book 19 that Telemachos has made similar statements to her earlier.

17. For further discussion, see Finley, 1955; Lacey, 1966; Vernant, 1980; Mossé, 1981; Morris, 1986; and Katz, 1991.

18. Doherty, Chapter 5, this volume, stresses the unreliability of female narrators in the *Odyssey*, but here Penelope's story is told before the teller, and he does not question it.

19. See above all Helen, Klytaimestra, and the behavior of the unfaithful maidservants.

20. See Katz, 1991, 93–113, for a summary of previous views.

21. Those critics who view Penelope as unintelligent think that she ought to have recognized Odysseus. (I am here rejecting the views of critics like Harsh, 1950, and Winkler, 1990, who argue ingeniously that Penelope has recognized Odysseus.) Critics such as Amory, 1963, and Russo, 1982, who think that Penelope has subconsciously recognized Odysseus, view her as a positive example of feminine intuition. Those who view her as irrational object to her resistance to the signs indicating an imminent return for Odysseus. For a full summary of earlier views, see Katz, 1991; Murnaghan, 1987; and Felson-Rubin, 1993. These last three critics, in different ways, view the constraints of the narrative as responsible for Penelope's multivalence in the eyes of the reader. I agree with Katz, 92–93, that the audience's knowledge of Penelope's moral dilemma as reported by Telemachos in Book 16 helps to give coherence to the scene in Book 18. Penelope has no character beyond what the poem gives her, hence we cannot fill in the gaps in her motivation. Yet a divided self can still in a strictly limited sense be psychologically and characterologically coherent, and the narrative has established the terms by which an audience—particularly an audience whose expectations are shaped by the conventions of oral narrative—can and (despite textual ambiguities) inevitably will construct a plausible agent from Penelope (for this position, see Felson-Rubin, 1993).

22. Does the text at the same time represent Odysseus as repeatedly deceived by Penelope? In Book 18, it is clear, as critics have pointed out, that Penelope's motives for appearing before the Suitors are not quite as clear-cut as Odysseus imagines. Athena intends her to excite the Suitors and win greater honor from her husband and son. Penelope herself resists the impulse Athena instills in her. She laughs *achreion* ("pointlessly," 163) as she tries to explain the sudden urge to show herself to her wooers, although they are hateful to her. Eurynome interprets Penelope's move here as one toward remarriage, yet Penelope refuses to beautify herself as Eurynome suggests, denies her beauty, and wishes for death. She says she wants to warn Telemachos, and she actually does chastise him over the treatment of the beggar (at 16.409–33 Penelope similarly decides to appear before the Suitors and chastise them because of her fear for Telemachos). Showing herself to the Suitors is no decision to remarry, although it prepares for her later moves to do so; in Book 19, she represents herself as still struggling with the decision in the terms that Telemachos laid them out in Book 16, where he represents Penelope as continually divided between staying and remarrying. In 18, Penelope acts the part of a prospective bride, but her mind is still divided over the gesture (she is also still playing the mother to Telemachos). Hence, she can be said to be intending simultaneously things other than

those that are apparent to the Suitors, and Odysseus is not incorrect in interpreting her actions in the light of what he has heard from Athena and Telemachos. Furthermore, because Penelope represents the move toward remarriage in the light of Odysseus' original instructions and denies her beauty even as it is melting the Suitors, he has no reason to be other than delighted with her actions. He knows that the Suitors' gifts will remain his and that Penelope is attempting to be faithful to his intentions. For extensive discussion of this scene, see especially Katz, 1991; Emlyn-Jones, 1984; and Felson-Rubin, 1993, with full bibliography.

23. The ambivalence that Penelope shows in the dream with the geese (19.535–81, weeping over their slaughter) goes unregistered. Katz, 1991, 119, sees Odysseus' approval as a patriarchal maneuver that denies Penelope a set of meanings and interests separate from those of her spouse and makes the couple appear more compatible than they are. At the same time, in her view, feminist readings like Felson-Rubin's, 1987, give Penelope an autonomy that the text does not support. In my view both Penelope and Odysseus subscribe to a patriarchal ideology; the text makes a point of giving Penelope the autonomy to make a nevertheless severely circumscribed choice; in judging Penelope as a moral agent, what is important is what action she takes and the role that reason and emotion play in that choice. (See Murnaghan, Chapter 4, this volume, on the male-dominated ideology of the poem.)

24. Thornton, 1970, 109–10, 113, argues that Penelope's choice is appropriately conditioned by Odysseus' instructions, although her overall discussion does not come to terms with the full complexity of the circumstances.

25. See, e.g., Katz, 1991, 148, who argues that Telemachos' coming of age on the one hand legitimates the decision to remarry, yet in the light of the surrounding narrative the decision also becomes a form of (unintentional) betrayal (153; Murnaghan, 1987, Felson-Rubin, 1987, 1993; and others take a similar position) that is forestalled only by Odysseus' interpretation of Penelope's choice as faithfulness (147). It is true that Penelope comes close to inadvertent adultery, but in my view this does not make her morally suspect. As long as we accept her lack of trust in the portents as rational, her behavior is not incoherent.

26. The earlier portents to which Penelope reacts are as follows. In Book 17, Telemachos reports on the account of Proteus to Menelaos. The news rouses the heart in Penelope's breast (17.150). Theoklymenos says Odysseus is already there and planning evil for the Suitors (17.157–59). Penelope wishes it might come to pass (17.163). At the end of 17, Penelope hopes Odysseus might arrive and avenge the violence of the Suitors (17.539–40). Telemachos sneezes. Penelope interprets the sneeze as a sign the Suitors will meet their fate (17.545–47). The text repeatedly stresses that Penelope wishes to believe in the portents, but resists that wish, either at once or by the time we next return to her in the text. Her momentary optimism in 17 does give way to the desire (which puzzles Penelope herself to approach the Suitors in Book 18. Yet the continuing dilemma as defined by Telemachos in Book 16 has not evaporated in 18, nor has there been any direct sign of Odysseus' return. I endorse the view of Emlyn-Jones, 1984, 3, that, by and large, Penelope's skepticism rarely wavers, "only occasionally straying into the optative in the face of a particularly convincing prediction." Moreover (5), it "enables the poet to exploit dramatic irony."

27. Penelope's final decision about whether to test Odysseus or fall into his arms (23.85–87) parallels Odysseus' concerning Laertes in 24. Both decisions have raised questions in the minds of readers, but the poem seems overall to offer a positive appraisal of seemingly hard-hearted caution. See Athena on Odysseus' exceptional caution at 13.330–38. Eurykleia displays hardness of heart over Odysseus' secret about the scar (hard

as stone or iron, 19.494). At 19.209–12 Odysseus pities Penelope, but refuses to lament as she does—his lids are of horn or iron. Although Penelope is criticized for her hardness of heart in 23 (72, 97, 103), she gives a good explanation for her resistance during the recognition.

28. See Zeitlin, Chapter 7, this volume, on how Penelope's bed trick serves to test the heroine as well as Odysseus; Penelope here proves that she never gives in too easily.

29. As Murnaghan demonstrates, Athena plays a large role in setting up and directing this plot.

30. In the *Poetics*, ignorance concerning the identity of a relative (or of one's own identity) is the typical tragic error. This is part of the issue here. But in the *Nichomachean Ethics* (2.1.15–17, 1110b–1111a), when Aristotle is discussing by what standards one may treat an act as voluntary (blameworthy) or involuntary (to be pitied and forgiven), he broadens the ways in which an agent may be considered ignorant of his or her interests. One may be ignorant concerning the agent (one's own identity), the act, the thing or person affected by the act, the instrument, the effect of the action, and the manner. In 2.6.11–12 1108b, when discussing the emotions that moral agents feel, he argues that time, occasion, purpose, and manner are critical. It seems likely that Aristotle would have wanted these broader standards to apply to tragic ignorance as well.

31. One might argue—from the perspective of critics who think that the narrative denies coherence to Penelope's actions and feelings—that tragic irony is blurred in this case because clear lines between what the character and the audience know do not exist. From a strictly ethical perspective, I have tried to demonstrate that this is not the case.

32. On the complex issues raised by Penelope's use of Helen as an exemplum in this scene, see especially Katz, 1991; Murnaghan, 1987; and Felson-Rubin, 1993, with further bibliography.

33. The text clearly takes a risk, given these cultural preconceptions, on giving Penelope what amounts to sexual autonomy. At the same time, by acting, Penelope becomes a far more convincing example of the faithful wife. The fact that Penelope's desire for marriage (and/or the disguised Odysseus) is gradually reawakened in Books 18–23 at the same time that she resists it does not compromise her as a moral agent. Desire is a legitimate part of the ethical process in the views of most Greeks, including Aristotle, as long as it serves the dictates of reason. Indeed, knowing that Penelope has complex emotions of grief and desire simply makes her decision to suppress her own wishes more impressive.

34. Murnaghan, 1987, 128–29, 134, 146, rightly stresses that the plot makes Penelope far more vulnerable to contingency and less able to control her circumstances than the disguised Odysseus. In her view Penelope is "defeated ... by the incompatibility between her fidelity to her husband and her social position"; hence she forces "us to acknowledge the element of chance that turns the contest of the bow into Odysseus' triumph" (1986, 113). Because I view Penelope's final decision as an act of loyalty to Odysseus, I find her choice less disturbing. Nevertheless, I agree with both Murnaghan and Felson-Rubin, 1987, 1993, that Penelope's ignorance is central to our understanding and judgment of her situation and actions in Books 18–23.

35. See further, Schein, Chapter 2, this volume.

36. For examples, see Sharples, 1983; Gaskin, 1990. The implications of these decisions may, as in the case of Achilles' choice in *Iliad* 9, entail larger issues concerning the quality of a hero's life.

37. Athena intervenes in a decision-making scene only in this instance. See further, Russo, 1968, 292–93.

38. The debate, inaugurated by Snell, 1960, 1–22; and Voigt, 1933 (see also Fraenkel, 1975; Adkins, 1960), has concentrated largely on the nature of the Homeric moral agent and whether such agents can be understood to act as integrated beings (see most recently Sharples, 1983; Gaskin, 1990; and Williams, 1993). Most of the more detailed discussion has justifiably centered on Achilles in *Iliad* 9 (the bibliography is too extensive to cite here). Williams recognizes that the case of Penelope is more complex and hence decides not to address her decision in detail (1993, 48). Surprisingly, Nussbaum, 1986, did not turn to Penelope in a study that makes the problem of moral contingency in Greek literature a central concern.

39. As Murnaghan, Chapter 4, this volume, points out, Homeric characters rarely resist divine suggestion. Penelope's defiance of convention in this respect may serve to underline her self-control.

40. Gaskin, 1990, 14, thinks that Penelope comes close to tragic *amêchania* in 4.787–94, where she helplessly debates over the threat to Telemachos' life by the Suitors. He argues that most decisions in epic lack the complexity of the tragic dilemmas facing an Agamemnon or Orestes: "While Achilles' decision in the *Iliad* to avenge his friend is to be sure tragic, it is so in a different and much simpler sense than Agamemnon's.... Achilles has no difficulty reaching his decision; he faces no insoluble moral dilemma, with disaster threatening him on either side of the choice. All that is required of him is courage, and that is a virtue he can unproblematically supply" (14). By these standards, Penelope's decision to approach remarriage is more deeply tragic.

41. Williams, 1993, 41–42, notes that duty in the modern sense has not been thought to play a role in Homeric decision making. The term does not occur in Homeric vocabulary, but Penelope's choice perhaps comes closer than any other Homeric decision to invoking what we might call duty as a basis for her choice. Hektor, whose representation is so closely linked with that of his city, is the male character most similar to Penelope. In his decision about whether to stay outside the walls and fight Achilles or to retreat into the city, as his parents wish him to, Hektor weighs the taunts of those who will accuse him of ruining his people by his mistaken strategies if he goes into the city and his fear that Achilles would not negotiate with him against risking death with glory (*Iliad* 22.98–130). Even here, however, Hektor's own honor as warrior ultimately takes precedence over his responsibility to protect his city or at least to delay its fall.

42. 1982, 19.

43. Ibid.

44. Ibid., 82.

45. Williams, 1993, esp. 21–29, is the most recent of the critics of Snell.

46. Gilligan's work has been criticized on multiple grounds. For a representative critique with further bibliography, see Porter, 1991, 142–93. In the case of the *Odyssey*, the differences between male and female moral agents arise from differences in socially defined sex roles, not from differences in the moral capacities and proclivities of the agent. In this respect, the present study may have something to contribute to the modern debate, in which Gilligan has been accused of essentialism, or of being insufficiently attentive to the contexts (e.g., public or private) in which decisions are made. In addition, the difficulties encountered by scholars in defining Penelope's character may result in part from the inextricable embedding of female characters in their social role.

47. For a recent general discussion of sexual ideology in the *Odyssey*, see Wohl, 1993.

48. See Vermeule, 1979, esp. 101–3, 105.

49. The role played by the marginal figure Thersites in the *Iliad* also serves to reshape

our perspective on the ethics of Homeric heroes. In tragedy also, female experience can be educative to the male. See, e.g., Foley, 1992, for Penelope and Odysseus serving as a paradigm in this respect for Helen and Menelaos in Euripides' *Helen*, as well as Zeitlin, 1985, on Phaidra and Hippolytos. In its use of reverse similes, which often assimilate male and female experiences, the *Odyssey* similarly plays with dissolving gender role boundaries. See further, Foley, 1978.

FREDERICK AHL AND HANNA M. ROISMAN

# Rival Homecomings

As the *Odyssey* opens, the poet asks the Muse, the daughter of Zeus, to sing in him the man who suffered much, saw much, and experienced much in the attempt to save his own life and the lives of his comrades after the sack of Troy (*Odyssey* 1.1–10). He invites the Muse to commence with events leading up to the destruction of Odysseus's crew for their consumption of the cattle of the Sun. Once the appeal is completed, the Muse's voice takes over, we are invited to believe. The poet, who appears to know the story he is prompting the Muse to recite through him, vanishes from view and does not intervene again.[1] The Muse does not take her mandate very literally. She begins not as the poet suggests, but with Odysseus on Calypso's island—after his crew has already perished. And, as we have noted, most of Odysseus's men die well before they have an opportunity to eat the cattle of the Sun.

Activating the narrative of Odysseus's homecoming, as the Muse represents it, is a matter of crucial timing: the decision can be taken among the banqueting gods with some guarantee of success only because Poseidon, who would object, is banqueting elsewhere—among the Ethiopians (1.11–26). The Muse instantly establishes that Odysseus's return is the final return, the last homecoming of a survivor of the Trojan War (1.1115). For his part, however, Zeus is thinking ahead to the long-term consequences of the return of Agamemnon, the commander in chief. Agamemnon, murdered by his

From *The* Odyssey *Re-Formed*: 27–42 © 1996 by Cornell University.

wife's lover, Aegisthus, has just been avenged by his son, Orestes (1.26–43). Zeus, that is to say, is already preoccupied with the deeds of the next generation. Odysseus threatens to fall between the cracks of the narrative, marooned for eternity on the island of Calypso, "Concealer," lost to, and in, time. The goddess Athena, Odysseus's protector, expresses precisely this fear to Zeus and adds that Odysseus may himself be beguiled and forget his desire to return (56–57). That, at least, is how the Muse represents the matter. But, as she does, she upstages the revenge myth of the next generation by setting it in her narrative before, rather than after, Odysseus's return.

Odysseus's seven-year stay with Calypso could indicate, as such stays often do in Celtic myth, not a specific length of time but removal from time. The Irish hero Bran, for instance, returns from his travels to discover that no one knows who he is, though they have ancient stories about him.[2] The Homeric muse may herself be "rescuing" Odysseus from a similar never-never land to which other tradition (including Hesiod) assigns him, in which he fathers, among others, Nausithous and Teledamus upon Calypso and Telegonus upon Circe, and in which his return occurs at a rather later date.[3] After all, Telegonus and Nausithous would be at least ten years younger than Telemachus. If Telegonus and other sons such as Euryalus, who are mentioned in various traditions, are to arrive in Ithaca in search of their father at around the same time as Odysseus returns home from Troy, then the twenty-year absence of the hero postulated in the *Odyssey* is not nearly long enough. The Homeric Athena is acting in a Hesiodic manner: arranging and rationalizing a confused and disparate tradition, giving, indeed establishing, a kind of "historical" sequence to bring Odysseus back to Ithaca closer to the end of the Trojan War.

The return of Agamemnon, leader of the Greeks, and its consequences in the next generation, then, become the narrative warp upon which the return of Odysseus is woven. Agamemnon is subsumed into and subordinated to the narrative substructure of the *Odyssey*. The process of making one's rivals one's footnotes has begun. In fact, Agamemnon, or rather his ghost, appears at two convenient junctures later in the *Odyssey* to comment on events (11.405–61; 24.106–19, 192–202).

Athena, the Muse tells us, puts Odysseus back in Zeus's mind by means of a sound play which links Odysseus's name not only to its resonances of pain (*odynê*), but, perhaps, to Zeus's own name.[4] It thus becomes harder for Zeus to think about himself without also thinking about Odysseus. The ploy pays off. When Zeus responds to Athena, he places his own self, *egô*, "I," in between Odysseus's name and the adjective *theioio*, "divine," which qualifies (and adds divine color to) that name (1.65). Not only is there now something of Odysseus in Zeus, but something of Zeus in Odysseus. In the

Muse's narrative, then, Athena (born, as Hesiod *Theogony* 886–91 would have it, from Zeus's head after his ingestion of Metis, "Thought") insinuates Odysseus into the mind of Zeus and takes control of the situation, ensuring the dispatch of Hermes to Calypso to secure Odysseus's release, and herself going to Ithaca to dispatch Telemachus to Sparta in search not of his father, but of some narrative of his father's return, his *nostos* (1.81–95).[5] Her dispositions are important. Had she gone to Calypso's island and Hermes to Ithaca, we would move closer to other traditions, often described as sub-Homeric, where Hermes travels to Ithaca and becomes Penelope's lover and father of the goat god, Pan.[6] Athena is controlling the switch points to guide her train onto totally different, even possibly newly laid tracks. Zeus is given no chance to object.

As the poet has invited the Muse into his head to tell the story, the Muse describes Athena putting the story into the head of Zeus and authorizing her own intervention in the narrative. The connection between the act of returning and the presence of thought is nicely made by Douglas Frame in his discussion of the relationship between the Greek words *nostos* (return) and *nous* or *noos* (thought).[7] As he points out, Odysseus's companions lost their *nostos* because of their lack of *nous*. And Odysseus will not be able to return until the thought of his return is again in Zeus's mind. "It is very significant," Frame adds, "that noos is associated with a 'return from death.'"[8] There are those in Ithaca who consider Odysseus dead because he is lost to their own and others' perception. Zeus, the devourer of *mētis*, "thought," must again concern himself with the hero who is himself full of *mētis*, as his epithet *polymētis* implies.

Control of narrative and of events is now firmly in the hands of the divine and feminine: the Muse, Athena, and Calypso. Little wonder Samuel Butler thought that the poet of the *Odyssey* must be a woman. Once Athena, according to the Muse, sets events in motion, she quickly moves to become a participant in, rather than the narrator of, what she has begun. In fact, the distinction we often make between narrator and participant is systematically blurred in the opening of the *Odyssey*. *Odyssey* 1 is Athena's book, as the Muse narrates it. Thus, appropriately enough, her name is the last word of *Odyssey* 1.[9] Aside from the narrative Muse, no one other than the now-distant poet deserves the honor more.

Athena, as the Muse narrates the story, goes to Ithaca and is introduced, albeit disguised as a male mortal, into the human scene, where she meets Telemachus, gives him a fictional narrative of her assumed identity as Mentes, and then orders him, in effect, to leave this part of the epic (1.179–212, 279–97). Athena thus prompts Telemachus to search for a narrative on his own. While he is away, he picks up a few gifts, makes friends with Peisistratus, son of Nestor, king of Pylos, and is an audience for the narratives of Helen and Menelaus, whose ruptured marriage caused the war from which Odysseus has failed to return. But Telemachus achieves hardly anything that he set out to find. Athena's action in sending him away does not protect him or Penelope from potential dangers at home. Penelope, courted by 108 suitors, is left more vulnerable to their attentions. And it is easier for the suitors to plot to dispose of Telemachus discreetly (and anonymously) while he is away, instead of doing so in his home, thereby alienating Penelope.

The Muse, however, may have other considerations. Most obviously, Telemachus's absence provides a narrative pretext for incorporating two other stories of return into the substrate of her own narrative: those of Nestor and Menelaus. But there is more. If we note how persistent is the motif of a son of Odysseus searching for his father throughout the variants of the "return of Odysseus" theme in later writers, matters become more complicated. Euryalus, Odysseus's son by Euippe, daughter of the king of Thesprotia, comes to Ithaca in search of Odysseus, as does Telegonus, his son by Circe. The first is killed by Odysseus; the second kills Odysseus.[10] Granted our assumption that these versions may have been in the mythic "pool" available to Homeric audiences, the listener hearing the *Odyssey* for the first time has no reason to suppose that the quest by a son of Odysseus for his lost father would necessarily culminate in recognition and mutual acknowledgment. Nor would it yet be evident that Telemachus was Odysseus's only son.

When Athena mentions Orestes, already in Zeus's mind and famous for avenging Agamemnon and killing his mother's lover, she invites Telemachus to rival his epic contemporary with deeds of his own (1.298–300). There is an uncomfortable undertow in this allusion to that divinely approved mythic paradigm: Orestes had to avenge the murder of his father (killed on his return from Troy) when he himself returned from what amounted to exile. The parallel is further enriched when Telemachus, while away, strikes up a friendship with Peisistratus of Pylos, and the two youths travel together, much as Orestes, in most versions of his myth, traveled with his faithful companion, Pylades. When Telemachus and Peisistratus arrive at Menelaus's palace in Sparta, the king's daughter is marrying not Orestes (her promised husband in most traditions) but Achilles' son Neoptolemus, and Menelaus seems nervous that Telemachus, who does not immediately introduce himself, may be Orestes. But more on this matter later. Suffice it to say for now that as the *Odyssey* opens there is some reason to suspect that the Muse is innovating and, perhaps, attempting to codify her version against the backdrop of competing variants.

Once Athena has put Odysseus in Telemachus's mind, as in Zeus's, she metamorphoses into a bird and vanishes from the scene (1.320–23).

Telemachus joins the suitors and the musical program in progress. The minstrel Phemius is singing (what else?) the return of the Achaeans from Troy, made miserable by the very goddess who has just departed (1.325–28). But scarcely has Phemius begun when Penelope sweeps into the room and orders him to play a different song; the tale of the return is too melancholy and painful for her to bear (1.329–44), perhaps because it would not include Odysseus's return. The details of Phemius's song are not specified, and speculation as to its nature is pointless, though the ancient scholiast suggests Phemius is telling a false story about Odysseus's death, and some modern scholars accept this notion.[11] Since the Muse is already singing the song of Odysseus's return, Penelope's desire to silence songs of return is surely ironic. Its thread must be completed before the hero can get back to Ithaca, before it is a complete *nostos*, a complete song of return. In fact, as Telemachus will discover on reaching Sparta in his quest for news of Odysseus, part of Odysseus's return is already known—though not, it appears, in his home. Telemachus and Penelope seem not to know (and perhaps it is just as well) what Menelaus knows: that Odysseus is marooned in space and time (for Menelaus holds no high hopes that Odysseus will escape) in Calypso's land. Penelope's reluctance to hear songs of return does not help her keep apace of the latest tales. She seems intent on stopping a narrative of which she is about to become a part, a narrative progressing both externally with the Muse and internally with Phemius toward Odysseus's return to Ithaca.

Penelope's intervention in this delaying capacity is not altogether surprising. She has a talent for procrastination, for unweaving what she has woven. And weaving is a common metaphor for song and narrative in the *Odyssey*. Because Penelope puts the suitors off by weaving her father-in-law's death shroud, there is something about her which is not only reminiscent of the Moirai, or Fates, who spin the threads of people's lives, but of the rhapsode, the poet, who reweaves the threads of traditional tales. Penelope has been, for three years, almost as much the controller of time as Calypso, who holds Odysseus in suspended existence. Why only three years? Are these the years in which Telemachus has come of age?[12] As Odysseus has several years unaccounted for on Calypso's island, several years in Penelope's life are similarly isolated from the narrative and unaccounted for.

Shrewdly, the Muse presents Penelope's three-year strategy of the loom through the perceptions and words of one of her suitors, Antinous, who reports that she is masterfully deceitful and untruthful. She put a large loom (*megas histos*) in her hall, so that, she said, "I can weave the shroud and not let my work go for nothing" (2.98). Greeks of later years would certainly have found some ironic humor here, since the expression "to work the loom of Penelope" was proverbial for an exercise in futility. There may be a little wicked irony in Antinous's words too. Penelope is famous in myth as the waiting wife, faithful—or otherwise. Odysseus's return will end that phase of her existence and her fame rivaling that of famous women of the past, such as Tyro, Alcmena, and Mycena (whoever she was)—a fame, Antinous concedes, she has won by her actions (2.115–28). Comparison of Penelope with Tyro and Alcmena is not entirely what a faithful wife might appreciate, since both women are famous for being tricked by gods into sexual relationships: Tyro with Poseidon, whom she mistakenly thought was the river Enipeus; Alcmena with Zeus (unwittingly in some traditions) while her husband was away fighting.[13]

A passage later in the epic adds force to the mention here of Tyro, Alcmena, and Mycena. Odysseus claims to have met Tyro and Alcmena among the spirits of the dead in his catalogue of famous (in some cases notorious) women (11.235–47, 266–68). But this is as close as the Muse comes to conceding infidelity on Penelope's part. She passes over in silence all Penelope's activities in any but three or four of the nineteen years Odysseus was away. There are strong traditions elsewhere that Penelope was seduced by Antinous, sent away by Odysseus, and that she went to Mantinea in Arcadia, where she bore the god Pan to Hermes.[14] It is thus at least of passing interest that the Muse has Antinous, Penelope's seducer in other traditions, make sarcastic allusions to Penelope's fame as a waiting wife while the Muse maintains her chastity.

The *histos*, the loom, is Penelope's protection and security when all else fails her. Similarly, the security of Odysseus's *histos*, his ship's mast, is his salvation as he travels. The words "loom" and "mast," different in English, are identical in Greek. Odysseus is tied to his *histos* as he hears the Sirens' song. It saves him from drowning during a storm as he leaves Calypso's island.[15] As the ship's mast symbolizes what enables both vessel and sailor to move, so women (or goddesses) working at the loom are the picture of fixity and immobility: domestic tranquillity, or the illusion of it.[16]

Telemachus, in contrast to Penelope, has every reason to want the narrative to continue and takes his mother to task for stopping the song of returns. His rebuke takes the form of an order that she return to her room and weave, leaving narrative (*mythos*) to men, and especially to himself in his capacity as master of the house (1.358–59). Although Penelope's attempt to stop Phemius seems unsuccessful, the bard's narrative of the return is, in effect, brought to a halt. The suitors lust for Penelope, dispute with Telemachus, then dance. Phemius, it seems, does not return to his tales of homecoming at this point. He is prevented from usurping, with his own narrative, the Muse's narrative rights. It is her story, not his, and she (as narrator and controller) allows Penelope to succeed, by default, in silencing the song of Odysseus's return until book 5. At that later point the Muse herself, not Phemius, spins the yarn.

When Telemachus travels to Pylos, his questions about Odysseus mostly result in a series of miniature homecoming tales pertaining to Nestor, Menelaus, Agamemnon, and an aside or two about Idomeneus, Diomedes, and others. Further, the tale of Orestes' vengeance—the latest, and, presumably, most popular, song—threatens to upstage the others by assimilating Telemachus to its pattern. As Odysseus's son leaves Pylos, he has with him a faithful, friendly, and rather more worldly wise young companion, Peisistratus, to enjoy the improbable chariot ride over the mountains to Sparta much as Orestes, in most traditions, has Pylades as his usually more savvy companion. The insistent allusions to Orestes and to other motifs of the house of Agamemnon heighten the apprehension in a newcomer's reading of the *Odyssey*. Telemachus's lot may, in some ways, parallel Orestes'. Thus the idea, once popular among scholars, of the thematic separateness of the Telemachus narrative seems, in retrospect, both puzzling and unnecessary.[17] The Muse, in reminding us of the potentially centrifugal forces of myth, readies us for her centripetal assumption of control. The problem is that the *Odyssey* is too familiar to scholars: we do not let ourselves get caught up in the intricacies of its possible (but unfulfilled) developments. It is precisely in the element of narrative suspense generated by the active search of Telemachus for Odysseus that the dramatic tension (in which the *Odyssey* arguably surpasses all other Greek and Roman epics) lies.

Three centers of interest have been established: one static (yet, paradoxically, seething) with Penelope and the suitors in Ithaca; one with Telemachus, now moving away from Ithaca; one with Odysseus (whom we have yet to meet), of uncertain location but about to move. The roads to bring about the convergence have been built, but remain separate, as roads do. But that does not mean they are not part of a planned system. Some artist somewhere in the process made them meet.

## AT THE COURT OF MENELAUS

In *Odyssey* 4, Telemachus and his companion Peisistratus arrive in Menelaus's Sparta in their quest for information about Odysseus. We share Telemachus's curiosity, since we have not yet "seen" Odysseus in the Muse's narrative. It is tempting to summarize what Menelaus and Helen tell Telemachus, then pass to book 5 and Odysseus himself.[18] Yet if we do so, we are assuming that the Muse introduces Helen and Menelaus primarily to provide information to (and a safe haven for) Telemachus. True, their narratives yield the first apparently "new" information about Odysseus.

Yet these narratives are so evidently shaped by Helen's and Menelaus's own experiences with each other that they tell us more about them than about Odysseus. But we must not get ahead of ourselves. Let us return to the beginning of book 4.

When the Muse brings Telemachus and Peisistratus to the palace of Menelaus and Helen in Sparta, a double wedding celebration is in progress. Hermione, Menelaus's daughter by Helen, is being sent away to marry Achilles' son Neoptolemus, also known to tradition as Pyrrhus. This marriage in process provides a further reminder that we are moving into the next mythic generation. The second wedding is more curious. Megapenthes, Menelaus's otherwise unimportant son by an unnamed slave girl, is being married in Sparta to an equally mysterious woman brought from Sparta (which is odd, since Menelaus is in Sparta at the time). The bride is the unnamed daughter of Alector—a man Eustathius calls the son of Pelops and Hegesandra (herself the daughter of Amyclas and thus closely associated with Sparta's "twin" city, Amyclae).

The double marriage is a rather ironic comment on events in the royal household. Menelaus clearly did not live a celibate life before his marriage to Helen, if we presume Megapenthes is marrying at an age over, rather than under, twenty-one, as was usual for Greek males. If we assume Megapenthes is younger than twenty-one, then Menelaus did not go unconsoled during his years without Helen. That such a situation might have caused some comment in the world of the *Odyssey* we may perhaps discern later from comments about Eurycleia, with whom Laertes would have had an affair had it not been for fear of his wife.[19]

Helen is thus involved in double marriage preparations which place her presumably legitimate daughter Hermione on a par with the child of a "slave girl."[20] And her daughter's marriage was, in most mythic traditions, a troubled one. Neoptolemus, Hermione's groom, brought back Andromache, Hector's widow, from Troy as his concubine and was himself murdered, with Hermione's connivance, by Orestes, as we see in Euripides' *Andromache*. Orestes had been promised Hermione's hand, but either the marriage was denied by Menelaus (who favored Neoptolemus) or Hermione was taken away from Orestes after their marriage had taken place.[21]

If, as is generally contended, the Homeric muse does not know these "other" versions, we might well ask why she bothers to connect the arrival of Telemachus and Peisistratus with the wedding at all. She is as careful to keep the king's two young visitors away from the wedding festivities for Hermione and Megapenthes as is Menelaus himself. Yet Telemachus and Peisistratus are more central to the attentions of Helen and Menelaus than are the bridal parties. Menelaus remains with the two guests throughout their stay, neglecting the feast that is presumably going on. The only significant allusions he makes to weddings of any kind are a backhanded slap at Helen's relationship with Deïphobus (her second Trojan husband) and a description of bedding down in the vile-smelling concealment of sealskins "beside a sea beast," *para kêteï*, in Proteus's cave (4–443). *Para kêteï* may even suggest, given the marital context, some kind of play with the word *parakoitis* (bedmate) and conjures an image of sexual revulsion rather like that suggested in Patrick Fermor's description of the stench when the garments a Sarakatsani woman has worn all her life are finally removed on her death.[22]

Helen, Hermione's mother, is not at the feast either. She spends her time either in her upper chamber or with the newly arrived guests (4.120ff.). Throughout the episode, both king and queen behave as if entertaining Telemachus and Peisistratus were the only social and familial event of importance at the time. Only when Telemachus is about to leave does Megapenthes appear and help Menelaus carry gifts to Telemachus's chariot as the latter prepares to return to Ithaca (15.97–123). Since Hermione is being sent away to marry Neoptolemus, Achilles' son never appears at all.

The Muse's decision is prudent. The famous Neoptolemus, not to mention Hermione, would, if introduced, cast Telemachus into the shadows. Neoptolemus, besides, was the killer of Priam, the father of both of Helen's Trojan husbands, Paris and Deïphobus. Thus Menelaus's selection of Neoptolemus as Helen's son-in-law would perhaps have had a bitter aftertaste for Helen too. As it happens, then, Menelaus not only fails to introduce Telemachus and Peisistratus to the marriage parties; he accommodates Telemachus and Peisistratus not in his opulent palace, but on the porch. They are hardly made as comfortably welcome as Telemachus was by Nestor at Pylos. Things could have been worse, though. At least Menelaus does not accede to his servant's suggestion that he send them off to find accommodation elsewhere.[23] Yet he treats them very gingerly. He seems a little worried one of the newcomers may be Orestes, who Menelaus fears might blame him for Agamemnon's death and for neglecting his duties as an uncle. He avoids even the most oblique allusion to what, in Apollodorus, is his own broken promise that he would marry Hermione to Orestes. Telemachus's companion, similarly, might be Pylades. In later writers, Orestes is almost always represented as traveling with Pylades. Finally, quite apart from any thought of broken promises to Orestes, Menelaus may have some reason for worrying about the arrival of princely, youthful visitors as he prepares to send Hermione off to wed Neoptolemus. Helen herself had been kidnapped shortly after her marriage, an event neither she nor Menelaus has forgotten.

The failure to introduce formally and in an engaging episode the son of the hero of the *Iliad* to the son of the hero of the *Odyssey* is one of the Homeric muse's most maddening (and probably deliberate) omissions. She whets our appetite for the encounter only to let it slip by without overt comment. But what is particularly delicious, as the scene proceeds, is the potential confusion of Telemachus with the feared Orestes. The parallel between the two has been drawn insistently since the Muse took up the narrative in book 1. And even if she "does not know" about the marriage rivalry of Neoptolemus and Orestes, she does seem aware that Menelaus has some explaining to do about why he did not protect his brother Agamemnon, Orestes' father, from Aegisthus's murderous hand.

As Menelaus and his young visitors settle down to dinner, Telemachus, of course, knows who Menelaus is (4.49ff.). But when does Menelaus realize who his guests are? The Muse leaves us to detect this for ourselves. The princely status and age of Menelaus's visitors allow for several possibilities. At first, Menelaus addresses his visitors in the dual, as a pair, but as hospitality ritual (as presented in the *Odyssey*) and etiquette require, he does not ask the guest's identity until the guest has been bathed and has dined.[24] When he overhears Telemachus's whispered admiration for the Zeus-like wealth around him in the palace, he must notice that Telemachus addresses his companion as "son of Nestor" (4.71). Thus one visitor is identified.

"No mortal," Menelaus responds to Telemachus, "would compete with Zeus; ... maybe there's a man who competes with me—but maybe not" (4.78, 80). Menelaus underscores his pride in his wealth, then appends a lament that his riches have come at a price: Agamemnon (Orestes' father) was murdered while he, Menelaus, made his fortune in Egypt (4.90–93). Yet though Menelaus ostentatiously blames himself for not being present to help his brother, he does not now explain why he did not, on returning from Egypt, avenge Agamemnon. When the mention of Agamemnon's name produces no reaction from his listeners, Menelaus drops the subject. Further explanation of his failure to avenge he postpones until the following day when his visitor's identity as Telemachus is firmly established. On that occasion Menelaus says Proteus, the Old Man of the Sea, had urged him to hasten home to catch Agamemnon's murderer, Aegisthus—unless Orestes had beaten him to it (4.543–47). Even then, Menelaus gives no sense of how long he was in Egypt, though he is clearly prompting the conclusion that he returned too late for vengeance: Orestes had already acted.

Menelaus goes on to allude, obliquely, to what he calls his personal pain: presumably the rape of Helen by Paris and the subsequent Trojan War—their fathers must have told them about it, he declares to the youths (4.93–95). This time the response might, understandably, be more mixed—

though the Muse does not describe it. Peisistratus's father, Nestor, is never averse to storytelling, but Telemachus has no father around to tell him about the war. Narrowing his target, Menelaus adds a wish that he could have his lost friends back, especially Odysseus, who must be greatly missed by Penelope and Telemachus (4.97–112). This series of names *does* provoke a reaction: Telemachus weeps, though he tries to hide his tears (4.113–16). Nothing, we will note, has been said directly, as yet. But Menelaus now knows who his second guest is (4.116–19).

It is doubtful, in this instance, that the weeper is trying to win recognition from his interlocutor by means of his tears, as is certainly the case in *Odyssey* 8.487–554, where the listening Odysseus weeps and attempts to disguise his tears for the express purpose of conveying to the watchful observer that the narrative of Odysseus and Troy has a special poignancy for him. We may be tempted to assume it is the purest accident that Menelaus mentions only Odysseus, of all the Greek heroes from Troy, and that he goes on to name Odysseus's wife, Penelope, and his son, Telemachus. Some have even argued that Menelaus is stupid (as he sometimes is in Euripides). But, if we look ahead, we will see that Menelaus observes a few lines later how struck he was by the physical resemblance of Telemachus to Odysseus. We must allow for the possibility that Menelaus spoke as he did to test a hunch about his visitor's identity.

Appreciation of this scene is often spoiled by the scholarly assumption that meaning lies only in what is explicit and underscored. In the *Odyssey*, it is routine for acknowledgment of what is observed to be postponed, even withheld altogether.[25] As in real life, so in epic: when someone sees us and does not greet us, he is just as likely to be ignoring us as to have failed either to notice or to recognize us. In the *Odyssey*, recognition and communication in general are *normally* indirect, by innuendo, in disguise.

Ill-timed self-disclosure, even in triumph, can be dangerous, as Odysseus points out in his narrative of the Cyclops (9.500–542). Sometimes it is simply tactless, as it would be if Alcinous made it plain that he sees Nausicaa's eagerness to launder clothes for her brothers, who are of marriageable age, as a hint of her own readiness for marriage (6.66–67). When Menelaus does not acknowledge Telemachus's identity after the Muse tells us he knows it (4.116–19), his caution is understandable. Knowing *who* Telemachus is does not explain *why* he is present. Relatives of warriors in the Trojan War might resent the king whose wife could be considered its cause. Better to discover what is on Telemachus's mind before admitting you know who he is. So Menelaus bides his time. Withheld acknowledgment allows expressions of kindness about Odysseus and his son to appear uncalculated, and thus genuine. Penelope adopts a similar strategy later in the *Odyssey* with

Odysseus. She almost certainly figures out who he is well before she actually acknowledges him; the test of the bow she proposes (and he accepts) is not so much to see if he is Odysseus, but whether Odysseus is the man he was twenty years ago.[26]

Menelaus is prevented from exploiting his rhetorical advantage because Helen enters (4.120–22). In contrast to the reticent Menelaus, she instantly declares the visitor must be Telemachus, since no one else could so closely resemble Odysseus. Menelaus concurs, giving details which show how carefully he has noted the youth's physical appearance; he now acknowledges he has recognized Odysseus's son (4.138–54). There is no reason to assume this is pretense on his part to avoid being outshone by Helen. Later developments show he is her match, rhetorically. And his signs of recognition are precise.

When mutual recognition and acknowledgment set the company to lamenting Odysseus and Peisistratus's brother, Antilochus (4.155–215), Helen drugs everyone's wine with a potion she obtained in Egypt from the wife of Thon. It prevents grief even if one sees one's kin killed before the city gate (4.219–34). Again we find a possible allusion to another tradition. Herodotus says Helen was stopped by Thonis and detained in Egypt by Proteus while en route to Troy with Paris until Menelaus claimed her after the war.[27] The drug administered, Helen narrates a story whose overt purpose and early statements show how great a man Odysseus is (4.235–50): he came into Troy before the city fell, disguised as a beggar; he even had himself flogged to make the effect authentic, and he fooled everyone in Troy—well, almost everyone.

At 4.250 the narrative changes direction: *pantes—egô de*, "everyone, but I ... "Suddenly Odysseus is at Helen's mercy (4.250–64): she recognized him, despite his efforts to elude her; she bathed him; she swore not to (and did not) betray him, for she now longed to return home to Sparta, regretting the mad passion for Paris which had brought her to Troy in the first place, longing for her bedroom at home and her husband.

Helen's narrative, of course, foreshadows Odysseus's recognition by Eurycleia in *Odyssey* 19.335–507 and might fulfill the useful purpose of alerting Telemachus to Odysseus's skill at disguising himself as a beggar.[28] But it is self-serving, even if it is "true." And there is no means of telling whether it is true or not. Helen's story here sharply contrasts with that in Euripides *Hecuba* 239–48, where Hecuba appeals to Odysseus on the grounds that she saved his life when he came into Troy and was recognized by Helen. Helen told her (though only her) about her discovery, and Hecuba kept the secret when Odysseus begged her for his life. The Euripidean Odysseus concedes that this is what happened. The Homeric Odysseus makes no reference to the incident, but the Homeric Helen clearly states that she told no one. Her point is that though Odysseus was disguised, she, Helen, saw through it. We can credit the Homeric Helen's claimed powers of observation, for she recognized Telemachus immediately on seeing him. But she has now revealed to us that she was unable to restrain herself from declaring her recognition instantly. Could she really have kept Odysseus's identity secret if she had discovered him in Troy? Was she really ready to betray Troy and return to Greece with Menelaus? Even more to the point, why was Odysseus with her (if he really was), and what was it about him that she recognized and why? At the very least she is claiming a personal contact and companionship with Odysseus such as would have made him run the risk of detection and betrayal.

The Muse does not overlook our questions. When Helen comes out of her chamber to entertain Telemachus and Peisistratus she is compared to Artemis, the virgin goddess par excellence, who has no interest in men or marriage. The insertion of the theme of celibacy and chastity has an ironic effect (and warns us to be careful about taking even comparisons of Penelope to Artemis too literally). We might cite the similarly puzzling comparison of Dido and Aeneas to Diana and Apollo—just before they have their famous and almost certainly sexual rendezvous in the cave (*Aeneid* 4.498–504). Similes in the *Odyssey* are generally remarkable for their appropriate inappropriateness. Odysseus's tears on hearing tales of Troy are compared to those of a captive Trojan woman (8.522–30). Similarly, the comparison of Eumaeus's tears on welcoming Telemachus home to those of a man who has not seen his son for ten years has to be read against the fact that when Telemachus enters Eumaeus's hut, he is also seen, but not acknowledged, by his real father, Odysseus, who has not seen him for twice the length of time noted in the simile.

At first, Helen's drug and her narrative seem to work: Menelaus declares Helen's story marvelous. But then he appends a tale of his own, introduced by a line almost identical to that used by Helen to introduce her narrative of Odysseus (4.242 and 271), telling how Odysseus had saved the Greeks concealed in the wooden horse (4.265–89). The story is not overtly self-promoting. On the contrary, Menelaus narrates as an observer. Helen, he says, accompanied by Deïphobus, walked three times around the horse, hailing the Greek warriors by name, and imitating the voices of their wives. One warrior, Anticlus, would have cried aloud in response, and the Greeks would have been detected, had Odysseus not clamped his hand over the man's mouth and silenced him until Athena led Helen away. In his story, then, it is Odysseus who prevents Helen from betraying the Greeks: precisely the opposite point from the one she is attempting to establish.

We may wonder, at this stage, what has happened to the power of Helen's potion, since Menelaus's story is a total refutation of hers, not just an addition to heroic lore about Odysseus.[29] The chronological setting is subsequent to Helen's: the eve of the fall of Troy. Menelaus's allusions to Deïphobus, Helen's *second* Trojan husband, and to her treacherous behavior undermine Helen's claims that she came to regret leaving Menelaus for Paris and that her sympathies had reverted to her husband and home. Menelaus has not forgotten the pain.

## HELEN'S EXPULSION

Helen has blundered rhetorically by allowing her narrative to be undermined by her behavior, and by making her claims so blatantly that she invites refutation, and is refuted. Menelaus's counternarrative is successful (if not necessarily "true") and puts a chill on the evening. Although Telemachus tactfully ignores the undertones of the rhetorical duel, he observes to Menelaus, first, that Odysseus's iron heart did not save him from destruction and, second, that it is now time to sleep (4.290–95). Nor does he miss either the irrelevance or the nasty undertow of the couple's exchanges. He follows up Menelaus's narrative of Odysseus in the Trojan horse by suggesting that this tale only makes things worse, since Odysseus was obviously lost subsequently anyway (4.290–93). In other words, neither of their stories has any bearing on his quest. Perhaps to avoid further altercation, he suggests that it's time for bed, for sleep (4.294–95). This observation prompts Helen to leave the room and supervise the sleeping arrangements. She is relegated to housewifely duties. When the narrative resumes the next day, Helen is not present. Menelaus is free to launch into a protracted narrative of his own return from Troy and his own adventures in Egypt and encounter with Proteus. In this Menelean tale, Odysseus is purely incidental, and Helen is completely absent.

Yet Menelaus is careful not to be rude. Although he refutes Helen's account of her longing to return to Greece, he never outrightly calls her a liar. She, as daughter of Zeus, is his passport to Elysium. That is all he needs her for. Nor does Menelaus claim, in his own voice, that he is superior in divine blessings to Odysseus. He adopts the kind of approach which Demetrius praises as a special part of formidable speaking, *deinotês*: "The effect is more powerful because it is achieved by letting the fact speak for itself rather than having the speaker make the point for himself" (*On Style* 288). Menelaus achieves an abusive, discrediting effect without actually using abuse, *loidoria*. He lets his narrative do the necessary work for him while he himself stands back and treats Helen with formal courtesy and speaks with huge admiration for Odysseus.[30] The force of what is communicated, as Demetrius notes of *deinotês* (*On Style* 241), lies not in what is said, but in what people pass over in silence.

When conversation resumes the next day, and Menelaus tells of his own return from Troy, Helen does not seem to be present. If she is, she is silent. Menelaus is free to narrate in his terms, to make himself the narrator-hero. We might think, as does Herodotus 2.113–20, that Helen was not with him on his return. When he describes himself withdrawn from his men and walking the Egyptian beach deep in thought, he is alone (4.367). He mentions Helen only as he reports what the Old Man of the Sea, Proteus, told him. In Proteus's "revelations" (as reported by Menelaus), the most striking detail is how much more blessed Menelaus is than any other returning hero (4.491–592). Locrian Ajax is dead "among his long-oared ships." Agamemnon's troops return alive, but Agamemnon dies. Odysseus survives; his troops are lost. Menelaus, by contrast, survives with most of his forces intact. Odysseus, Menelaus's chief rival as "returned hero," is shown as alive, but miserable, stranded, and helpless, having neither crew nor ship, and essentially a captive of Calypso, "who keeps possession of [*ischei*] him" (4.557–58). There is no allusion to Calypso's hope of giving him immortality, a matter the goddess later raises with Hermes in *Odyssey* 5.135–36. Odysseus's prospects look bleak.

Proteus's version of Menelaus's future (as reported, of course, by Menelaus) is more promising. He will find bliss and eternal springtime in Elysium, not death in Argos, when his time comes. "You," Proteus says, "possess Helen [*echeis Helenên*] and are son-in-law to Zeus" (4.569). The contrast with Odysseus is sharp: Telemachus's father is possessed by a goddess, whereas he, Menelaus, is possessor of the daughter of Zeus, and through her the certainty of immortality. There was, then, more than first met the eye when Menelaus, the previous evening, had rebuked Telemachus, albeit gently, for comparing his palace to Olympian Zeus's: "No mortal would compete with Zeus; ... maybe there's a man who competes with me—but maybe not" (4.78, 80).

The wily king has crushed Helen's attempt to tell her story to her own narrative advantage by using her "superiority" to Odysseus as a means of advancing her own claims to fame and recognition. Menelaus has taken over the narrative, as he takes control of Proteus despite Proteus's constant metamorphoses, and makes it tell the story his way: how much more blessed he is than any returning hero, including Odysseus. And Helen is his key to ultimate status: a family connection with Zeus, and immortality, part of the godlike affluence of his palace. That is all she is.

The two competing tales about Odysseus in *Odyssey* 4 are weapons in a struggle for narrative rights between husband and wife, the outcome of which will determine Helen's image in subsequent tradition. Odysseus, however central to Telemachus's search, is as incidental to Menelaus as he is to Helen. He is the heroic corpse each struggles to expropriate in a battle of narratives that Menelaus seems to win.

Heroism in the *Odyssey* is to some degree determined by one's ability to seize and exploit the narrative initiative. Helen attempts and fails. Menelaus seems to succeed, momentarily, by crushing Helen yet using her, and by co-opting the inner narrative voice of Proteus to build his own boastful stature. But he has not persuaded Homer's muse to invert the *Odyssey* and make it the tale of Menelaus.[31] His riches, status, and now housebroken wife are not to be the stuff of Homer's epic. Indeed, Menelaus is robbed of the status he seeks even as he thinks he is winning it. Homer's muse is about to usher Odysseus into the center with her own authorial voice, and then to give Odysseus the second largest narrative voice after her own: four of the epic's twenty-four books. During that narrative Odysseus will attempt to advance his kind of heroism beyond Achilles' Iliadic glory. He will claim to have heard Achilles' lament that he would rather be a slave of the poorest man on earth than king of the dead. The heroic choice of the *Iliad* dissolves in the face of death. How remarkable, then, Odysseus must be to reject the chance of immortality with Calypso, since he knows what death is! But in alluding to Odysseus's rejection of unheroic immortality with Calypso (while consigning Menelaus to an even more bourgeois version of the same with Helen), the Muse reinserts Odysseus into the world of heroic homecomings and consigns Menelaus to the sidelines.

There will, presumably, be other rounds in this ongoing fight. When we are offered another glimpse of the Spartan king's rather strained marriage, Helen gains narrative revenge by offering a neat explanation of an omen which utterly baffles her husband. But by then the listener's attention is far removed from Menelaus and Helen's war of polite words.

## Notes

1. That is why it seems to us that the supposed tension and rivalry between poet and muse which has much preoccupied scholars is rather beside the point. See Pedric, "The Muse Corrects," and references cited by Pedric (especially on p. 39).

2. A. Rees and B. Rees, *The Celtic Heritage* (London: Thames and Hudson, 1961) 316.

3. Apollodorus *Epitome* 7.17. Telegonus was recognized by Hagias in his epic, *The Returns*, and by another Cyclic poet, Eugammon of Cyrene, who composed an epic about the adventures of Telegonus called the *Telegony*. According to Eugammon, Telegonus was a son of Odysseus by Calypso, not by Circe. See G. Kinkel, *Epicorum Graecorum Fragmenta* (Göttingen: Vandenhoek and Ruprecht, 1988) 56, 57ff.; Eustathius on Homer

*Odyssey* 16.118, op. 1796 adds Telademus. Hyginus (*Fabulae* [*Myths*] 125) gives him two sons, Nausithous and Telegonus, by Circe. As to Telegonus, see Apollodorus *Epitome* 7.36ff.

4. For *odynê*, see W. B. Stanford, *The "Odyssey" of Homer*, 2d ed., 2 vols. (New York: St. Martin's Press, 1965) on 1.62. For the Odysseus/Zeus wordplay, see M. Steinrück, *Leise Laute: Arbeiten über das Verhältnis von Rhytmus und Lautresponsion bei Archilochos* (Lausanne and Basel: Petra Tergum, 1991) 5. For the connection of the name Odysseus with *odyssaomai*, see the extensive discussion of Clay, *Wrath of Athena*, 59–65, 70 n. 31. Clay does not, however, connect the name Odysseus with Zeus; see p. 63.

5. For a discussion of Athena's dominance over the action of the *Odyssey*, whether through her presence or absence, wrath or support of Odysseus, see Clay, *Wrath of Athena*, 40–53, 182–83, and passim.

6. Pindar frag. 100 (Snell); Apollodorus *Epitome* 2.38; Servius on *Aeneid* 2.44.

7. D. Frame, *The Myth of Return in Early Greek Epic* (New Haven: Yale University Press, 1978) 33.

8. Frame, *Myth of Return*, 37.

9. For last words of first books, see F. Ahl, *Metaformations: Soundplay and Wordplay in Ovid and Other Classical Poets* (Ithaca, N.Y.: Cornell University Press, 1985) 167–68.

10. See Sutton, *Lost Sophocles*, 46, 88–94, and the sources cited. These references will be discussed in more detail below.

11. See Pucci, *Odysseus Polutropos*, 198–99; J. Svenbro, *La parole et le marbre: Aux origines de la poétique grecque* (Lund: Studentlitteratur, 1976) 20–21; against this, see Ford, *Homer*, 108–9.

12. The suggestion by K. Atchity and E. J. W. Barber, "Greek Princes and Aegean Princesses: The Role of Women in the Homeric Poems," in *Critical Essays on Homer*, ed. K. Atchity with R. Hogart and D. Price (Boston: G. K. Hall, 1987) 29, that the kind of garment Penelope was weaving takes three years to produce is interesting—though a competent modern Turkish or Iranian weaver could produce several large and spectacular carpets in three years.

13. About Mycena we know very little (unless, as daughter of Inachus, she is identical with Io, beloved of Zeus); but as the eponymous heroine of Mycenae, it is not unlikely that she too was involved in some relationship with a god.

14. Apollodorus 7.38; Pausanias 8.12.5ff.; Cicero *On the Nature of the Gods* 3.22.56; Tzetzes, scholia on Lycophron 772; Servius on *Aeneid* 2.44.

15. *Odyssey* 12.50–51 and 161–62 (he ties himself to the base of the mast [*histopedê*]); 12.421–25 and 438 (the mast saves him from Scylla and Charybdis); 14.310–12 (riding on the mast, he drifts for nine days till he reaches the land of the Thesprotians); 5.315–16 (the mast is broken during a storm after he leaves Calypso's island).

16. 5.62 (Calypso's idyllic tranquillity as Hermes arrives); 7.104–10 (the Phaeacian women at work); 10.221–26 and 253–54 (Circe and the illusory tranquillity of her residence); 13.107–8 (the nymphs in the bay of Phorcys).

17. A. Kirchhoff, *Die homerische "Odyssee" und ihre Entstehung* (Berlin: Wilhelm Hertz, 1859) esp. viii, also 136ff.; cf. id., *Die Composition der "Odyssee": Gesammelte Aufsätze* (Berlin: Wilhelm Hertz, 1869). The results of Kirchoff's analysis were accepted later by Wolf, Wilamowitz, and Jebb. See H. Fränkel, *Early Greek Poetry and Philosophy*, trans. M. Hadas and J. Willis (New York and London: Harcourt Brace Jovanovich, 1975) 23. E. R. Dodds, *The Greeks and the Irrational* (Berkeley: University of California Press, 1951) 10, takes the separateness of the "Telemachy" for granted. Doubts whether the Telemacheia at one time was an independent poem still creep into a number of more recent scholarly

works; see D. Page, for example, the last of the old-time Analysts, in *The Homeric "Odyssey"* (Oxford: Clarendon Press, 1955) 52–73.

18. See Ahl, "Complex Narrative Structures,"8–10.

19. 1.432–33.

20. For the marginal place of a *nothos* (illegitimate, bastard) in the Greek family, see C. B. Patterson, "Those Athenian Bastards," *ClAnt* 9 (1990) 40–73; on Megapenthes specifically, see pp. 47–48 n. 40.

21. Apollodorus *Epitome* 6.13 and 14; Euripides *Andromache* 967–81; Orestes 1653–57; scholia on Euripides *Andromache* 32; Hyginus *Fabulae* (*Myths*) 123; Eustathius on *Odyssey* 4.3; scholia on Homer *Odyssey* 4.4; Ovid *Heroides* 8.31ff.; Servius on *Aeneid* 3.297 and 330; Vergil *Aeneid* 3.330.

22. P. L. Fermor, *Roumeli: Travels in Northern Greece* (New York: Harper and Row, 1966) 46.

23. For a discussion of the scene and the social implications of Eteoneus's suggestion, see J. Roisman, "Some Social Conventions and Deviations in Homeric Society," *Acta Classica* 25 (1982) 35–41. For a list of servants' suggestions in the epic, see S. D. Olson, "Servants' Suggestions in Homer's *Odyssey*," *CJ* 87 (1992) 219–27.

24. The difficulty is that most of our picture of Homeric customs is extrapolated from the epics and not from independent evidence. It is not clear how common it was in any real-life social situation for a guest to be received and not to identify himself.

25. For further discussion, see Chapter 7.

26. The encounter between Odysseus and Penelope is one of the most intriguing scenes in the epic and has justifiably attracted endless scholarly attention. For the possibility of an early recognition and its actual postponement, whether for psychological or structural reasons, or for the sake of characterization, see, for example, P. W. Harsh, "Penelope and Odysseus in *Odyssey* XIX," *AJP* 71 (1950) 1–21; J. Russo, "Interview and Aftermath: Dream, Fantasy, and Intuition in *Odyssey* 19 and 20," *AJP* 103 (1982) 4–18; C. Emlyn-Jones, "The Reunion of Penelope and Odysseus," *G&R* 31 (1984) 1–18; and earlier treatments of the episode cited in these discussions.

27. 2.113–120. Herodotus suggests that Homer knew the story but rejected it. The potion would certainly have been more useful to her at Troy than on the journey back with Menelaus, which, in Menelaus's account in *Odyssey* 4.351–586, took them through Egypt. On Helen's drug, see Ann Bergren, "Helen's 'Good Drug': *Odyssey* IV 1–305," in *Contemporary Literary Hermeneutics and the Interpretation of Classical Texts*, ed. S. Kresic (Ottawa: Éd. de l'Université d'Ottawa, 1981) 201–14.

28. Indeed, we should recall that Eurycleia herself is found later in book 4, in dialogue with Penelope when the narrative returns to Ithaca (4.741–58).

29. Again, see Bergren, "Helen's 'Good Drug'"; id., "Language and the Female in Early Greek Thought," *Arethusa 16* (1983) 63–95, and esp. 79–80.

30. And at a time made special not only by Telemachus's visit but by the double marriage of Menelaus's two children (only one of whom is by Helen).

31. For a discussion of competition between bards, and a possible rivalry between a bard and the Muses, see Ford, *Homer*, 93–120. One can claim that to some extent any narrator in the epic becomes a pseudocompetitor with the Muse. See also Claude Calame, *The Craft of Poetic Speech in Ancient Greece*, tr. J. Orion (Ithaca, N.Y.: Cornell University Press, 1995) 27–44.

# Penelope's Perspective:
## Character from Plot

Penelope in the *Odyssey* both weaves and interprets plots; she also takes pleasure in the plots she has woven. Yet the traditional view of Penelope limits her to a single plot, MARRIAGE-AVOIDANCE, and confines her to a single role, faithful and enduring wife.[1] This single plot belongs primarily to a larger plot schema: RETURN OF HUSBAND, RECOVERY OF WIFE AS BRIDE, VENGEANCE AGAINST FALSE SUITORS.[2] As a subordinate plot, it lacks autonomy, and its heroine seems to act more to suit her husband than out of personal desire.

This univalent Penelope whom Western tradition, since Homer, has taken for granted, can be seen to originate in the *Odyssey* itself. She specifically emerges from the remarks of Agamemnon's ghost when, in book 24, he couples praise of Penelope with blame of his own wife Klytaimestra, setting the two heroines in an opposition to one another that has persisted through the centuries.[3]

But how objective and how reliable is Agamemnon as a narrator of Ithakan and Argive events? Are his praise of Penelope and his blame of Klytaimestra convincing? Do they offset those doubts about her virtue raised by the same ghost figure in the first Nekyia of book 11? I shall contend that, on the contrary, the doubts of Agamemnon of book 11, once raised (regardless of who raised them, or under what circumstances[4]), remain because the primary narrator never dispels them. Moreover, the Agamemnon

From *Reading the* Odyssey: *Selected Interpretive Essays*, edited by Seth L. Schein: 163–183 © 1996 by Princeton University Press.

of book 24 who affirms Penelope's virtue is conspicuously unreliable as a judge of female character; indeed, the primary narrator expressly undermines his evaluation of the two heroines by placing it in the context of a dead suitor's mistaken report of events in Ithaka. In explaining their slaughter, Amphimedon's shade includes this piece of misinformation:

> Then, in the craftiness of his mind, he urged his lady
> to set the bow and the gray iron in front of the Suitors,
> the contest for its ill-fated men, the beginning of our slaughter.[5]
>     (24.167–69)

The slain suitor, supposing that Penelope recognized her husband before the contest, mistakenly ascribed to Odysseus sole responsibility or blame for initiating that event.[6] Penelope thus earns praise from Agamemnon's ghost on false grounds: she is not held accountable for proposing the contest of the bow.

Other scenes, too, reveal a Penelope far more complex than the ghost of Agamemnon imagines. To recover some of that complexity, I examine passages that seem to indicate contradictory motives and inconsistent behavior and that are apt to keep the reader confused about Penelope's actual desires until that moment of clarity (for Penelope and reader) at 23.205–8, when Penelope finally embraces Odysseus as her husband.[7] Incidentally, such reasonable bewilderment has spawned numerous scholarly attempts to excise any passages that undermine the image of Penelope as unproblematically faithful.[8] I shall take a different route.

I propose to show that Homer, by withholding information from Penelope until 23.205, offers her no rational solution to her dilemma of whether to await Odysseus or not. In plot language, he assigns her roles in two incompatible types of plot: in BRIDE-CONTEST and MARRIAGE-AVOIDANCE (with each plot-type further specified for a maiden or widow and for a matron).

The multiple plots that Penelope weaves, seen from the perspective of various male characters (particularly Odysseus, the Suitors, and Agamemnon), constitute the following plot-types: BRIDE-PRIZE, ADULTERY, FRIGIDITY AND TEASE, and LOYALTY AND CUNNING. In BRIDE-PRIZE Suitors desire to marry, select a potential bride, and compete in a contest for her hand. In ADULTERY a wife betrays her husband and takes a lover. In FRIGIDITY AND TEASE, a potential bride thwarts her suitors' desires, leading them on and tormenting them, all the while not intending to marry. Finally, in LOYALTY AND CUNNING, a wife cunningly holds eager suitors at bay until her husband returns. The second and fourth plot-types unfold from the absent husband's point of view, the first and third from that of the Suitors.

From her own female-centered perspective, Penelope weaves and participates in the following, corresponding four plot-types, some virtually indiscernible from those seen by the male characters: COURTSHIP AND MARRIAGE; DALLIANCE AND INFIDELITY; DISDAIN AND BRIDE OF DEATH; and PATIENCE AND CUNNING. In COURTSHIP AND MARRIAGE, a maiden or widow enjoys male attention and/or desires to marry; she accepts courtship and sets herself up as bride-prize in a contest. In DALLIANCE AND INFIDELITY, a wife (her husband away) enjoys courtship and/or engages in a (playful?) act of infidelity. In DISDAIN AND BRIDE OF DEATH, a maiden or widow disdains unworthy suitors and prefers virginal death to any marriage. Finally, in PATIENCE AND CUNNING a wife cunningly (indeed heroically) withstands seduction and awaits her husband's return.

Though I do not use all of these terms equally, I present them here because it is important for us to know that the bride has her own story, even when it is not presented in full.[9] The second group takes into account the maiden or matron's own desires and attitudes toward her actions (to the extent that we can observe them). Note how the same sequences of action acquire a different shade of meaning and a different label depending on whether they are "focalized"[10] from a male or female center. In what follows, I pay special attention to female-focalized plots, which are often overlooked in readings of the *Odyssey*.

By keeping Penelope ignorant as to her marital status and by representing her as uncertain as to which of her several plots she is at any moment involved in, Homer gives a legitimacy and reasonableness to her multiplicity of purposes (which in turn engenders our legitimate perplexity). Much of her behavior becomes intelligible to us if we consider that she is unremittingly vexed by the question, "Am I moving toward new union or toward reunion?" Behavior shameful if her husband lives is normal if he has perished at sea.[11]

Homer has Penelope, in this state of ignorance, set up the contest. She takes this step uncertain whether Odysseus will return in time, mistrusting omens and the statements of seers or beggars. Nor does she propose the contest relying, as some have thought, on her intuition that Odysseus is home already.[12] Certainly, on the one hand, she feels she has exhausted her strategies for deferring the decision; she hopes, on the other, that her husband will arrive in time. Additional sentiments can be adduced as influencing her move: an attraction to the stranger, loneliness,[13] *ripeness for eros*, her son's coming of age.[14] None of these, however powerful, changes the fact that by setting up the contest now she risks infidelity.[15]

To these several possible motivations we may add an explanation from plot. What if Penelope, weaver of plots (as her name, from *pênê*, "woof" or "web," suggests),[16] calculated her move to fit simultaneously into several possible plots? What if, indeed, she is complicitous with her author in that she willingly takes up several strands of plot simultaneously?

We can learn much about her character by posing this question, even if we eventually discard it as overstated.[17] We then ask how Penelope weaves plots, and whether she interprets plots she has woven. Is she a character who, like Odysseus, aims to control events as they happen but, inevitably, sometimes falls short, due to obstacles unforeseen and results unintended? Does she preview and rehearse imagined sequences of events and retrospectively formulate them in a coherent narrative, like Odysseus when he "spoke to his own great-hearted spirit" (5.465–73) or "plotted out the destruction of the overmastering suitors" with Athene (13.373f.; also 20.37f.) or with Telemachos (16.235–39)?[18] In narrating her life events, does she select and reshape with the freedom of a storyteller? In short, is she a "plotting" character? Perhaps we can envision a scale for describing characters, from unwitting agents who act within whatever plot is given to them, on the one hand, to supreme plotters who seemingly control their fictional lives, on the other. Would we not place Penelope and Odysseus closer to the latter pole than the former?

Whenever she previews her destiny in dreams and fantasies, and whenever she retrospectively interprets the plots she has spun, Penelope seems empowered (by Homer) to select and arrange events. Thus, like a narrator, she makes a *muthos* in Aristotle's sense, as a *synthesis pragmatôn*, "a putting together of deeds" (Aristotle, *Poetics* 1450a4–5).

Building up Penelope's features as a creator of plots requires that we know, at each plot moment, what she knows, what beliefs and convictions she holds, what she desires and fears, what actions she thinks are possible and permissible for her to take. In other words, we may treat her as if she were a character in real life, with a world of her own.[19] We ascribe to her a psychological coherence that, admittedly, we as readers construct. We are mute on the question of Homer's absolute intentionality, since we are focusing here on the impact of the text rather than on its production.

This study aims, then, to expand the interpretation of Penelope's most frequent epithet, *periphrôn*, "thinking all around," as well as the etymological pun on her name as "weaver." From our analysis *periphrôn Pênelopeia* finally emerges as a character aware of the plots she creates and, like Odysseus, cunning in securing her own best interests in terms of survival, duty, and pleasure. Thus she acts for her own sake as well as for the limited purpose that Agamemnon's ghost assigns her, namely, to assure Odysseus' glory and safety. Agamemnon's worldview is male focalized, whereas Homer offers us a larger perspective. Examining Penelope's character from plot leads us to supplement her traditional image as a patient, faithful, enduring wife with a fuller portrait—of a complex, problematic figure who ultimately remains faithful to her absent husband but comes dangerously close, and for good reasons, to an unintentional betrayal. And in the course of her life history, she participates in a multitude of plots.

### Penelope and Plot

Penelope engages in the following actions: she offers words of encouragement and promises to each suitor; devises the trick of the web; appears before the Suitors and solicits gifts; dreams, ponders, scolds, weeps and prays; interviews the stranger and tells him her dream; sets up the contest of the bow; and eventually entraps her husband into divulging his secret knowledge of their marriage bed. Some of these activities she enacts before our eyes (mimesis); others a character recounts (diegesis).[20] I shall try to recover her motives and self-knowledge as she previews and makes her decisions and acts on them, and as she retrospectively evaluates her choices. The passages I treat are out of textual order; the first two demonstrate Penelope's sincerity in setting up the contest; the second and third are retrospections by Penelope, indicating her plot awareness; the remaining five indicate Penelope's participation in several plot-types as she makes her choices.

My analysis depends on the assumption, which the first two passages support, that Penelope is sincere in setting up the contest of the bow to determine whom she will marry, and that indeed she envisions her wedding taking place.

### Tears

> She sat down, and laid the bow on her dear knees, while
> she took her lord's bow out of its case, all the while weeping
> aloud. But when she had sated herself with tears and crying,
> she went on her way to the hall to be with the lordly suitors.
> (21.55ff.)

Penelope sheds these bitter tears in private when she has placed her husband's bow on her knees. Her mood in this passage is sombre: wanting to remain steadfast, she has run out of strategies. She weeps not only at the sight of the weapons, reminders of her absent husband, but also at the dire implications of her decision not to wait.[21]

Penelope's mournful behavior as she collects the weapons belongs, if she is a matron, not to a successful marriage-avoidance plot (LOYALTY and CLEVERNESS; PATIENCE) but to a failed one, a remarriage, which is equivalent to ADULTERY/INFIDELITY.

### HELEN APOLOGY

Penelope also reveals her sincerity in setting up the contest when, in retrospect, she tacitly acknowledges to her husband how close she had come to adultery. This is the problematic Helen passage that many consider an interpolation but that in fact illuminates the complexity of Penelope.[22]

> Do not be angry with me, Odysseus, since, beyond other men,
> you have the most understanding.... Then do not now be angry
>     with me nor blame me, because
> I did not greet you, as I do now, at first when I saw you.
> For always the spirit deep in my very heart was fearful
> that some one of the mortal men would come my way and deceive me
> with words. For there are many who scheme for wicked advantage.
> For neither would ... Helen of Argos
> have lain in love with an outlander ...
> if she had known that the warlike sons of the Achaians would
>     bring her home again to the beloved land of her fathers.
> It was a god who stirred her to do the shameful thing she
> did, and never before had she had in her heart this terrible
> wildness, out of which came suffering to us also.
> But now, since you have given me accurate proof ...
> so you persuade my heart, though it has been very stubborn.
>     (23.209–30)

Penelope's attitude toward Helen is unusually empathetic. Her remark that Helen would not have lain with a foreigner had she known that the sons of the Achaians would bring her home again, suggests that it is not the betrayal itself, but ignorance about the future that is ruinous folly (atê). Penelope implies that, had she yielded to the stranger claiming to be Odysseus or married a suitor, she too would have been subject to reproach; since she did not, she ought to be absolved from blame.[23] Thus, by exonerating Helen she hopes to exonerate herself for not immediately embracing her husband and for nearly causing a Trojan War!

Accentuating the similarity between their two situations leads Penelope to veil one conspicuous distinction, namely that Helen abandoned Menelaos out of sheer desire. Penelope's principle, that any woman might unwittingly betray her husband, hardly applies to Helen. This distortion of the comparison, for her argument's sake, reveals the degree to which Penelope understands how dangerously close she came to marrying a suitor, with her husband already nearby!

Here Penelope comes closest to reflecting on the theme of infidelity. Her worst possible scenario would have been marriage to a stranger or a suitor followed by Odysseus' return. This, she now realizes, would have earned her ill repute for all time and made her indistinguishable from Helen. Except here, she never alludes to such a possibility or hints at second thoughts about proposing the contest. Now, for the first time, she begins to minimize her near-betrayal by indirectly defending the legitimacy of a bride-contest if a woman thinks herself a widow. Her insistence on Helen's ignorance (as if Menelaos were permanently missing when Helen departed with Paris) causes me, as reader, not to object to the passage, but, relying on it, to add a dimension to my own sense of Penelope's complexity and plot-awareness as she asks her husband for double pardon.

## PENELOPE'S TALE

A second retrospection that gives us a sense of Penelope as a spinner of plots is her account to Odysseus after lovemaking. The narrator tells how Penelope, herself as narrator, reduced her plots to a single type:

> When Penelope and Odysseus had enjoyed their
> lovemaking, they took their pleasure in talking, each one telling
>     his story.
> She, shining among women, told of all she had endured
> in the palace, as she watched the Suitors, a ravening
> company, who on her account were slaughtering many oxen
> and fat sheep, and much wine was being drawn from the wine jars.
>     (23.300–305)

This is the story of holding the Suitors at bay until Odysseus' return. It is LOYALTY and CLEVERNESS, or PATIENCE, and it has no affinity with ADULTERY or INFIDELITY. Penelope's story corresponds to Odysseus' adventures seen only as obstacles to return—without reference to any pleasure the adventurer took in his travels. Each spouse/storyteller, now at last out of danger, interprets all prior events in terms of REUNION. Moreover, by depicting the Suitors as villains who attacked Odysseus' household and by focusing solely on their misdeeds, Penelope's story helps justify their slaughter. Though she blithely dismisses the other side of the story, we as readers cannot: her encouragement of them and indeed her enjoyment of their attention lessen their criminal culpability, and her omission of this aspect from what she tells Odysseus helps launder her image for posterity.

We turn now to Penelope's behavior before she embraces Odysseus in 23.205, in five passages that together disclose a multivalent Penelope.

## ENCOURAGEMENTS, PROMISES, AND AMBIVALENCE

The text is unrelenting in informing us, always diegetically, that Penelope encouraged the Suitors. Telemachos (1.245–51; cf. 16.122–28) and Amphimedon (24.126–28) state that "she would not refuse the hateful marriage, nor would she bring it about"; Amphimedon adds, "But she was planning our death and destruction with this other stratagem of her heart's devising." Thus he connects the ruse of the loom to Penelope's noncommittal behavior toward them. The suitor Antinoos (2.85–128) and the goddess Athene (13.379–81) observe that she raised the Suitors' hopes and made promises to each, but "her mind had other intentions" (*noos de hoi alla menoinai*; 2.92 and 13.381).

## THE SHROUD OF LAERTES

In the Second Nekyia the ghost of Amphimedon quotes Penelope's proposal of the ruse of the loom:

> "Young men, my suitors now that the great Odysseus has
> perished, wait, though you are eager to marry me, until
> I finish this web, so that my weaving will not be
> useless and wasted. This is a shroud for the hero Laertes."
>     (24.131–34)

Then he tells of her servant's betrayal that led the Suitors to discover Penelope "in the act of undoing her glorious weaving" so that "against her will and by force, she had to finish it" (24.145–46). Finally, "she displayed the great piece of weaving that she had woven. She had washed it, and it shone like the sun or the moon" (24.147–48).

Earlier, describing to the stranger-Odysseus her treatment of the Suitors (19.137–56), Penelope recalled how she was weaving her own wiles

(137) and how some spirit (*tis daimôn*) "put the idea of the web in my mind" (138). She quoted herself announcing the project to her suitors and urging them to wait to marry her until she finished weaving the shroud (141–47). This promise, however deceitful, contributed to the complaints the Suitors Antinoos (book 2) and Amphimedon (book 24) harbored against her.[24] It also keeps us as readers perplexed as to Penelope's real intentions.

Words of encouragement and secret promises would not in themselves prove a heightened interest in the Suitors or a turning toward men for attention, since these actions could be part of a stratagem to placate oppressive suitors (PATIENCE). Other passages contribute to our sense of an increasingly sensuous Penelope who participates actively in COURTSHIP.[25]

## SOLICITATION OF GIFTS

It is Athene who prodded Penelope to appear before the Suitors:

> But now the goddess, gray-eyed Athene, put it in the mind
> of the daughter of Ikarios, circumspect Penelope,
> to show herself to the Suitors, so that she might all the more
> open their hearts, and so that she might seem all the more
>        precious (*timiêssa*)
> in the eyes of her husband and son even than she had been before this.
> She laughed, in an idle way and spoke to her nurse and named her:
> "Eurynome, my heart desires, though before it did not,
> to show myself to the Suitors, although I still hate them."
>    (18.158–65)

Though the purpose clauses introduced by *hopôs* express the goddess's intentions in putting this idea in Penelope's mind, the expression "my heart desires" (164: *thumos moi eeldetai*) suggests to me that Athene's "intervention" does not lessen Penelope's responsibility for her decision.[26] We can assume that Athene could only influence Penelope in accord with Penelope's own character and disposition. Thus Athene's purpose, planted in Penelope's mind (*epi phresi thêke*), becomes Penelope's even though it contradicts her dominant set of feelings, hatred for the Suitors, a hatred explicit in her earlier wish for their demise (4.681ff.).

Appearance before suitors is a standard courtship motif, and Homer shows us a Penelope allowing herself to be courted. Which men does she aim to impress? Clearly, the hated suitors. Indeed, her embarrassed laugh is a sign of her own discomfort at the incongruity between her actions and this dominant, negative emotion;[27] at the same time, the laughter invites us to think of the laughter-loving goddess Aphrodite, whose influence suggests coquetry. Penelope conceals such coquetry from her nurse Eurynome, who (as an embodiment of propriety) might well disapprove of her mistress's flirtation.

Penelope's appearance has its intended impact on the Suitors (18.212–13). This, in turn, impresses Odysseus (18.281–83), who is happy "because she beguiled gifts out of them and enchanted their spirits with blandishing words, though her own mind had other intentions." That last formulaic clause reflects Odysseus' assessment of her motivations, along with the narrator's. Compare Athene's reassurances to Odysseus at 13.381, using the same formula. How accurate an assessment is it in this passage? Is the narrator totally cognizant of his own character's intentions? Does he allow Penelope to take pleasure in the Suitors as she beguiles them and possibly to overlook the cost of that pleasure, namely a plot moving rapidly toward remarriage? Is Penelope's behavior with the Suitors incautious in the same way as Odysseus' with Polyphemos?

Odysseus is not offended when he sees his wife winning male attention. He values the economic gains, which will help replenish the household. As a tactician himself, he respects her tactics. Moreover, as one of her attentive males, he is not threatened by his competition. Rather, he expects to (re-) claim Penelope, and her value for him is enhanced by the need to compete for her. For the reader, this scene emphasizes the husband's recovery of his wife as bride; i.e., it is BRIDE-CONTEST for a matron, where suitor = husband and bride = wife. Relevant here is a scene on the brooch that Penelope gave Odysseus when he departed twenty years earlier (19.225–31). The scene itself suggests an erotic conquest: the capture of a fawn by a hound who "preyed on the fawn and strangled it and the fawn struggled with his feet as he tried to escape." Odysseus is the hound pursuing Penelope, and her flirtations with others (a resistance of sorts) stimulate him rather than incurring his wrath.[28]

## DREAM AND CONTEST

The interview of Penelope with the stranger begins with Odysseus' compliment to Penelope (19.107–14) and his elaborate, persuasive lie (165ff.). It culminates with his mention of her departure gift to her husband (225–31) and with his prediction that Odysseus will presently come home (270 and 306–7). Penelope offers the stranger a bath and addresses him as "Dear friend" (350). But at the crucial point when Eurykleia recognizes Odysseus by his scar (467–77) and turns to Penelope for affirmation, Athene averts her perception (478–79).[29]

Shortly thereafter Penelope begins to share her innermost thoughts with the stranger. First, she confides her sharp anxieties over Telemachos (516–34),[30] and soon her dream of the eagle and the geese.[31]

> But come listen to a dream of mine and interpret it for me.
> I have twenty geese here about the house, and they feed on
> grains of wheat from the water trough. I love to watch them.
> But a great eagle with crooked beak came down from the mountain,
> and broke the necks of them all and killed them. So the whole twenty
> lay dead about the house, but he soared high in the bright air.
> Then *I began to weep*—that was in my dream—*and cried out
> aloud*, and around me gathered the fair-haired Achaian women
> *as I cried out sorrowing* for my geese killed by the eagle.
> But he came back again and perched on the jut of the gabled
> roof. He now had a human voice and spoke aloud to me:
> "Do not fear, O daughter of far-famed Ikarios.
> This is no dream, but a blessing real as day. You will see it
> done. The geese are the Suitors, and I, eagle, have been
> a bird of portent, but now I am your own husband, come home,
> and I shall inflict shameless destruction on all the Suitors."
> So he spoke, and then the honey-sweet sleep released me,
> and I looked about and saw the geese in my palace, feeding
> on their grains of wheat from the water trough, just as they had been.
>     (19.535–53)

To this confidence the stranger Odysseus replies:

> Lady, it is impossible to read this dream and avoid it
> by turning it another way, since Odysseus himself has told you
> its meaning, how it will end. The suitors' doom is evident
> for one and all. Not one will avoid his death and destruction.
>     (19.555–58)

Penelope's response is to deny the validity of the dream. She offers an allegory of two gates through which dreams pass: this one, she insists, passed through the gate of ivory and cannot be believed (19.560–69); it is helplessly ineffectual (*amêchanos*) and difficult to decipher (*akritomuthos*). Penelope suddenly announces her plan to hold the bride-contest (570–72).

Aside from depicting her pleasure as she watches the Suitors and her grief as she previews their death,[32] the central portion of the dream reveals a Penelope awaiting her husband's return yet reluctant to relinquish her attachment to the Suitors. The careful construction of the dream precludes our inferring that Penelope is ambivalent toward Odysseus' homecoming, or that she would continue her attachment to the Suitors if she knew Odysseus was home. For she does not mourn in her dream once eagle-Odysseus tells her, "Now I am your own husband, come home." And yet with things as she supposes them to be at this juncture, the Suitors' presence is her sole pleasure, though a mixed one. Should Odysseus not return, she desires a continuation of that pleasure, naturally disguising this from herself by expressing her grief for dead suitors in terms of grief over pet geese. At this moment, she is not the consummate "weaver of plots," for she presents herself to Odysseus in all her vulnerability.

Penelope awakens to experience a jarring discrepancy between the dream events and reality. When she finds her geese still alive, she feels the dream message doubly annulled. That is, the presence in her palace of literal geese eating from the trough undermines the dream figure's equation between geese and suitors—asserting, visually, that geese are geese and, further, that *her* geese are still alive. Moreover, if she means to sustain the dream metaphor and use "geese" to designate her suitors (a possibility that the text leaves indeterminate), then the presence in her palace of the Suitors eating like animals is incongruent with the vivid dream image of suitors slain.[33] Perhaps Penelope denies that equation by saying "geese are geese" and denies the death of the Suitors by saying "my suitors are still feeding."[34]

Penelope's predominant reaction against the gentle, dreamed suggestion that Odysseus is home and that she forego her attachment to the Suitors ("Do not fear ...") is to affirm COURTSHIP by setting up the bride-contest.

If we grant that Penelope takes pleasure in her suitors/geese, and now look back to the ruse of the web, that event (which Amphimedon's ghost saw as purely deceitful) takes on new ambiguities. The deferral tactics of Penelope the weaver serve two functions: they enable her, first, to hold off the Suitors for some years to give her husband a chance to return home in time to rescue her (i.e., prolonging the courtship for *his* sake) and second, to defer the remarriage so that *she* can take pleasure as long as possible in "watching her pet geese" (i.e., prolonging the courtship for *her own* sake). The one plot is LOYALTY and CLEVERNESS and PATIENCE, the other COURTSHIP; if, however, Penelope suspects that Odysseus is home and still enjoys COURTSHIP, the plot-type is DALLIANCE—a weak or incompleted form of INFIDELITY.

The weaving itself as a physical process is double-edged: she weaves by day (moving toward remarriage) and unweaves by night (undoing her day's progress).[35] She has told the Suitors to defer their suit until she finishes the shroud, insinuating that she will marry one of them eventually. Like her messages of encouragement to each, the project itself entices and allures and indeed entraps them. But this allurement is aimed not only at their destruction, should Odysseus return, but at prolonging their wooing as well. It perpetuates COURTSHIP *for her sake*. In short, the web for Laertes' shroud reveals and symbolizes Penelope's full ambivalence toward the Suitors and toward her situation. All the while that she weaves she is saying yes to them, but it is an outward yes, contradicted by a secret no at night. The Suitors legitimately accuse her of leading them on (TEASE); their anger has grounds. Telemachos too is aware of this coquettish side of Penelope's behavior, and it angers him as well.

Odysseus accepts a complex Penelope who laments over her geese. He consoles her in the dream but at present, in real life, he can give her only limited consolation. He cannot repeat his assurance to her that her geese are as good as dead or that Odysseus is as good as home. He must leave her in a state of ignorance as to whether or not Odysseus will return and kill all the Suitors.

Without such consolation (Odysseus has not returned, as far as she can tell), Penelope reacts to her disappointment by reaffirming COURTSHIP and MARRIAGE. She prefers this plot to no action at all. She is not ready (as her dream shows) to give up the attention of the Suitors and the possibility of marrying one of them—until she has sure knowledge that Odysseus has arrived.

Note that the idea for the contest comes to Penelope suddenly, like the brainstorm of the web. Both ideas have several facets and reflect the complexity of Penelope. The bow contest, from Penelope's focalization at the moment she proposes it, could be an event in COURTSHIP and BRIDE-PRIZE (for a widow); it could also fit into LOYALTY and CLEVERNESS. Penelope would not see it as an event in ADULTERY and INFIDELITY—the Argos plot. Like a skilled chess player, Penelope knows when she proposes the contest that she is choosing a move that will fit into more than one strategy or plot trajectory.

Compare in this connection Antinoos' comment to Telemachos that Penelope "is winning a great name (*kleos*) / for herself, but for you she is causing much loss of substance" (2.125–26). He sees Penelope's flirtations and encouragements of the Suitors as bringing her some gain. Consider, too, the sustained parallelism between her and Odysseus:[36] just as he enjoys his adventures even though they delay his homecoming, so she "loves to "watch" (*iainomai eisoroôsa*) her pet geese.

Odysseus and Penelope each have plots obstructing REUNION and plots that lead to it. Odysseus' ADVENTURES, if for the sake of learning (1.3),[37] retard his homecoming. Similarly, Penelope's COURTSHIP is not at all for the sake of, nor does it facilitate, her husband's safe return (though if she had antagonized the Suitors, they might have become destructive). Neither of these two plots moves rapidly toward closure; part of our fascination with the *Odyssey* is seeing them leisurely unfold. Either her husband's return or her marriage to a suitor will put an end to the pleasurable COURTSHIP of Penelope, unless she is wanton enough to keep it going even once she knows Odysseus is home (DALLIANCE).

### PRAYER FOR SUDDEN DEATH

This prayer echoes Penelope's earlier wish on the occasion of tempting the Suitors (18.202–5) that "chaste Artemis would give me a death so / soft, and now, so I would not go on in my heart grieving / all my life, and longing for love of a husband excellent / in every virtue, since he stood out among the Achaians." Here, for a second time, she prays for death as a better alternative than hateful remarriage:

> Artemis ... how I wish
> that with the cast of your arrow you could take the life from inside
> my heart, this moment, or that soon the stormwind would snatch me
> away, and be gone, carrying me down misty pathways,
> and set me down where the recurrent Ocean empties
> his stream; as once the stormwinds carried away the daughters
> of Pandareos. The gods killed their parents, and they were left there
> orphaned in the palace, and radiant Aphrodite
> tended them and fed them with cheese, and sweet honey, and pleasant
> wine; and Hera granted to them, beyond all women,
> beauty and good sense, and chaste Artemis gave them stature,
> and Athene instructed them in glorious handiwork.
> But when bright Aphrodite had gone up to tall Olympos
> to request for these girls the achievement of blossoming marriage,
> from Zeus who rejoices in the thunder ...
> meanwhile the seizing stormwinds carried away these maidens
> and gave them over into the care of the hateful Furies.
> So I wish that they who have their homes on Olympos
> would make me vanish, or sweet-haired Artemis strike me, so that
> I could meet the Odysseus I long for, even under the hateful
> earth, and not have to please the mind of an inferior
> husband. Yet the evil is endurable, when one ... sleeps ...
> But now the god has sent the evil dreams thronging upon me.
> For on this very night there was one who lay by me, like him

as he was when he went with the army, so that my own heart
was happy. I thought it was no dream, but a waking vision.
    (20.61–90)

In this long and complex prayer, Penelope asks for death as a new way of
avoiding remarriage. Though we know little about the myth of the daughters
of Pandareos from other sources, clearly the four goddesses (Aphrodite,
Hera, Artemis, and Athene) intended that marriage, not death, culminate the
tale.[38] Moreover, we find no hint of the maidens' reluctance to marry nor joy
at their "rescue." Unincorporated, the *muthos* was a tale not of DISDAIN, like
the myths of Io, Daphne, Cassandra, the Danaids, and others, but rather of
negative COURTSHIP and MARRIAGE—of marriage interrupted by tragic and
premature death.

   Penelope reverses the positive and negative in her use of the tale for her
own purposes, which nevertheless retains the language of violent abduction.[39]
Instead of a villainous abductor or his agent,[40] Penelope imagines a beneficent
rescuer (gods or Artemis) answering her plea. Furthermore, she fantasizes
that her rescuer will, in a second act of kindness, reunite her, in death, with
her husband. Preferring death to the upcoming remarriage, she prays not
for union but reunion. The language of marriage suits her fantasy: she will
become a bride of sorts. Thus MARRIAGE-AVOIDANCE (for a widow) becomes
BRIDE OF DEATH in Penelope's prayer. She has relinquished PATIENCE, with
husband returning in the nick of time—despite assurances by Theoklymenos
and the stranger that Odysseus will soon return.

   The language describing the readiness for marriage of the daughters of
Pandareos is sensuous and alluring, whereas Penelope casts their alternative
destiny, delivery over to the hateful Furies, in violent, harrowing terms.
Nonetheless, she prays for a similar rescue and death, with a twist: that she
will die only to reunite with Odysseus in the Underworld. As virtual BRIDE OF
DEATH she is comparable to Persephone, but, unlike Persephone, Penelope
requests this gloomy outcome. She disdains marrying a live but inferior
Suitor. Thus she expands the traditional plot-type by coupling PATIENCE
with DISDAIN, and by adding BRIDE OF DEATH.[41] And she has invented a new
pattern, a hybrid of COURTSHIP/MARRIAGE and PATIENCE—a resumption,
in death, of her present marriage, a reunion in the Underworld with her
husband. In this hybrid plot, she fuses two otherwise antithetical types of
plot.

   The sensuous language describing the virginal maidens and their
pending marriage anticipates the sensuality surrounding Penelope as she
moves toward an uncertain future. Whatever happens, this future will be
different from the state of chastity and sexual limbo in which she has lived

for twenty years. Penelope's language suits her fantasy of a reunion with Odysseus in the Underworld. For her, "blossoming marriage" may turn out to be marriage to a suitor, reunion with an Odysseus who has returned and reclaimed her, reunion in death with Odysseus, or even union with the stranger.

Penelope wants Artemis to help her avoid not only an unwanted marriage, but betrayal and infidelity as well. Her dilemma, reflected keenly in the prayer, is the need to be mindful simultaneously of Artemis as goddess of chastity and Aphrodite as goddess of sexuality: neither should she be adamantly virginal, nor should she succumb to the wrong union at the wrong time, nor hold back from Odysseus should he return. The passage anticipates her identification with Helen in book 23. As she prepares to remarry, it is easier and emotionally safer to consider Odysseus dead than about to arrive in Ithaca too late.

The interplay of Artemis and Aphrodite in the character Penelope underscores her complexity. The presence of both goddesses is often felt.[42] Whether she will turn to Artemis or to Aphrodite is a key question raised early in the text and sustained until the moment of embrace. Penelope is herself as uncertain of her divine affinities as are other characters (Telemachos, Odysseus, the Suitors). Even we cannot yet know whether Penelope will remain chaste for Odysseus or not.[43]

A network, then, of passages that can be understood as part of Penelope's plan to hold out against the criminal-Suitors, also reveals a sensuous Penelope under the influence of Aphrodite as well as Artemis. Ambiguity as to Penelope's intentions is deliberately sustained for the reader until 23.205: the release for Penelope in that passage, as her knees give way, is a release (*lusis*) for us as well; her unchanneled eroticism had felt dangerous to any of us willing to imagine that she might turn out to be a Helen or even a Klytaimestra.

Curiously, once she is safe and knows she is safe, Penelope turns playful. In a bold move she flagrantly alludes to the possibility of infidelity. This is the famous deceit of the marriage bed. The possibility to which she alludes is one that she barely managed to avoid: the intrusion of some other man into the sanctity of her marriage-bed. Only in the safety of her husband's presence, in the safety of knowing that he is back, can a playful and erotic Penelope tease him on so serious a subject as adultery.

The bold taunt admits to their discourse a theme that Folktale might have handled much more openly and crudely: the chastity test of the wife whose husband has just returned from a long journey.[44] The marriage-bed test, anticipated much earlier in Telemachos' question to Eumaios (16.33–35:

"whether Any mother endures still in the halls, or whether / some other man has married her, and the bed of Odysseus / lies forlorn of sleepers with spider webs grown upon it"), is at once a husband test and a chastity test, the latter in that by suggesting she was unfaithful—that someone moved their bed—Penelope affirms her fidelity. For Odysseus, rage at the prospect of a faithless Penelope melts into joy at full knowledge that she has waited for him and endured. Via the bed-ruse she reveals to him, on her own initiative and of her own accord, that she has chosen to be his faithful wife.[45]

## CONCLUSION: A COMPLEX PENELOPE

In book 24 Agamemnon, lacking Odysseus's subtlety, misses the mark in his assessment of two heroines, Penelope and Klytaimestra. His is a male-centered view: a woman either is or is not faithful. Any suggestion that Penelope encouraged the Suitors would have activated a misogynist condemnation, as Odysseus' characterization of Agamemnon in book 11 makes plain. As readers, we are more privileged with information than was he: the network of passages discussed above indicate a side of Penelope not entirely consonant with the side he celebrates. We are therefore faced with reconciling conflicting evidence about her state of mind. Unlike Agamemnon and Amphimedon, we know that it was she, and not Odysseus, who decided to set the contest when she did. We know she flirted and held on to COURTSHIP and MARRIAGE when Odysseus was urging her (in his interpretation of her dream) to relinquish her attachment to the Suitors. In short, we find her far more prudent about her own security and attentive to her own pleasures than others (both characters and critics) have acknowledged.

Our *periphrôn Pênelopeia* is the creator of several plots that we can label from her own female-centered perspective: COURTSHIP and MARRIAGE, DALLIANCE, DISDAIN and BRIDE OF DEATH, and PATIENCE. She dreaded INFIDELITY and wanted to avoid it at all cost. At crucial moments of decision, she showed an awareness of all these plots and, in her decisions, she fulfilled her epithet *periphrôn*, "circumspect," for she took into account her own safety and well-being along with that of her family. Her greatest challenge was recognition of her own desires, and her apologia for Helen illustrates the extent to which she realized, in retrospect, how close to a disastrous decision she had come.

## NOTES

NOTE: Please refer to the Bibliography, pp. 239–52, for full citations of works referred to by author's name only.

1. Penelope, despite rival traditions (notably, association with Pan and other love adventures; see E. Wüst, s.v. Penelope, Pauly-Wissowa, *Real-Encyclopadie*, vol. 19.1 [1937], 460–93, esp. c. 479–81), is popularly considered the paragon of the virtuous wife since Homer; cf. Wüst, ibid., col. 483.

2. Cf. my list of plot-types on p. 165; the labels for Odysseus' plots are of only marginal interest to this study.

3. For Nagy (1979, 36, n.1) this passage "reflects a formal tradition of praise poetry centering on the theme of Penelope, as distinguished by the contrasting blame poetry about Clytemnestra"; in his discussion of *psogoi* and *enkômia* (255 n.1) Nagy cites 24.201–2 as "one of the clearest instances of blame as blame poetry."

4. Agamemnon of book 11 is a creature fashioned by Odysseus to suit his purposes of winning safe and cautious convoy from the Phaiakians. It is in his interest, as teller of his own ADVENTURES, to make Agamemnon in the Underworld suspect even Penelope of potential betrayal.

5. I use Lattimore's translation. All quotations from the *Odyssey* are from W. B. Stanford, *The Odyssey of Homer*, 2nd ed., 2 vols. (London, 1958–59).

6. The observation that "dead Amphimedon's statement in the Second Nekyia ... is his own inference" dates to the scholiast (Dindorf II.725.15) and is offered by Finley (1978, 14n.6) as one of several examples of the poet showing people's wrong ideas. It is baffling that Page (1955, chap. 5) takes the ghost so seriously and relies so heavily on this "inconsistency" in the Second Nekyia to argue for contamination by "the other version" in which Penelope recognized Odysseus before the setting of the contest.

7. I see this moment, when Penelope's knees loosen, as a *lusis*, or "release," for the reader as well, perhaps even a *lusis* of the plot in the Aristotelian sense of "denouement," as opposed to *desis*, "complication" (Aristotle, *Poetics* 1455b24–1456a10). Until 23.205 even the knowing reader feels suspense as to whether Penelope and Odysseus will ever happily reunite. Note how, though we know (from 1.76–79) that Odysseus will return, we are never directly informed that Penelope will have waited for him, and the references to her possible inconstancy form a virtual leitmotif.

8. For a summary and discussion of the Analytic position vis-à-vis the so-called Continuation of the *Odyssey* (Page's term), which includes the Second Nekyia, see Page (1955, chap. 5), Kirk (1962, 245–48), Moulton (1974b, esp. 154n.7), and Wender (1978, 10–18).

To the arguments made by Erbse (1972), Moulton (1974b), Finley (1978), and others against the Analyst assertion that the first and second Nekyiai are incompatible, we can add a narratological observation. The First Nekyia, as Odysseus' "creation," need not be compatible with the second, Homer's, since Odysseus as a character-teller need not be either omniscient or truthful.

I dismiss issues concerning the genesis of the text, because my concern is rather with its impact on the reader, given its form.

9. For the comparable observation that the witch in fairy tale has her story too, see Gilbert and Gubar (1979, esp. 79). The notion of female-centered plots was suggested to me by Gilbert and Gubar and by Miller (1980, xi).

10. An illuminating discussion of the concept of focalization appears in Bal (1985, 100–114). The term comes from Genette (1980, pp. 185–210, "Perspective," and pp. 212–62, "Voice").

11. Emlyn-Jones (1984, 12) interprets her "inability to make an end" (16.126–27) as referring "not to her personal preferences or to some 'feminine' weakness but to the social situation," since "the exact situation with regard to Penelope's prerogatives in this matter

is confused." On the topic of Penelope's prerogatives, particularly the "lack of agreement on who is her *kurios*" (the person in charge of her), see Lacey (1966, 62ff.) and references in Emlyn-Jones (17, notes 51 and 52) and in Marquardt (1984, esp. 43f. and n. 12). In my opinion, Odysseus' parting words (18.259–70) define Penelope's prerogatives more than do social pressure, customs of the times, etc. (See note 27, below).

12. This position has become increasingly popular. It emerged out of the ingenious but overstated proposal by Harsh (1950) that Odysseus and Penelope communicate by code. Critiquing Harsh, Amory (1963) suggested that Penelope intuits the presence of her husband "intermittently." For Austin (1975, 232), the "spiritual harmony between the two, shown in their understanding of each other's language, makes it hardly credible that no recognition has taken place." Austin (1975) and Russo (1982) support Amory's notion of intuition. Emlyn-Jones (1984) faults all these "Intuitionists" (including Harsh) for ignoring certain passages, but mainly he is ideologically and/or temperamentally opposed to "psychologizing" (see note 13 below, where I defend and locate this form of criticism). Both Amory and Austin give full analyses of the feeling state of Penelope from the time she first encounters the stranger. Neither makes enough, in my opinion, of Penelope's self-interest, and both (together with Harsh) overestimate what she knows. Amory's Penelope emerges as an unconscious and unreflective being, very "female" in an old sense of the word but not so very "like-minded" to Odysseus. Austin perhaps overromanticizes the level of communication achieved by the pair.

My reconsideration of Penelope passages is meant to provide an alternative to the hypothesis that Penelope based her decision to set up the contest on intuition alone, and an alternative as well to the model of total communication between a husband and wife, even a couple such as Odysseus and Penelope whose relationship rests on *homophrosynê*.

13. Devereux (1957) gives a convincing psychoanalytic portrait of Penelope's lonely state, as indicated in her dream; Russo, too (1982, 6 and 9), offers a psychological interpretation of the dream of book 19. Another sensitive psychological interpreter, Van Nortwick (1979), links Penelope's divided mind in books 18 and 19 with Homer's portrayal of Nausikaa. Others cite Devereux with apparent approval.

Emlyn-Jones (1984), on the other hand, vehemently opposes postulating any "psychological 'sub-text'" for understanding characters in the *Odyssey*; he prefers a genetic explanation. In my view, the locus for a psychological interpretation is in the interpreter, who may legitimately base such inferences about Penelope's psyche on clues in the text. The problem with eschewing this whole approach is that one is left only with genetic explanations, which, even when ingenious, do not account for literary impact.

14. Among scholarly explanations that account for COURTSHIP or indeed DALLIANCE, the appeal to plot needs is prominent. Woodhouse (1930), who names his tenth chapter "Penelopeia's Collapse," states (84f.) that "a new departure on the part of Penelopeia is the only way of overcoming the deadlock" and this explains her "sudden resolve" that is "without motive, without justification, and apparently runs counter to the epithet of 'sensible' or 'wise'." Tolstoi (1934) and Hölscher (1967b [this volume, 133–40]) take the coming-of-age of Telemachos, a folktale motif, as determining the moment of Penelope's decision to hold the contest. While admiring all these ingenious contributions, I do not find that they "explain" Penelope's decision on the level that here concerns me, namely, that of the psychological plausibility and consequent intelligibility to the reader of the character Penelope.

15. See note 2, above: I mean not only adultery and infidelity, but ADULTERY and INFIDELITY as plot-types.

16. On the derivation of Penelopeia from *pênê*, "woof" or "loom," cf. E. Wüst, "Penelope," esp. c. 461. Wüst refers to Didymos in the scholion to *Od.* 4.797 and to Eustathius on *Od.* 1.343ff. as ancient sources for this etymology. Of course, name puns, to be effective, need not rely on valid etymologies, as Howard N. Porter pointed out to me long ago.

17. Consider, in Vaihinger (1968), the expediency of fictions in furthering understanding. My proposal that Penelope is Homer's accomplice in weaving strands of plot is to be taken as such an "as if" proposal, in a spirit of useful play.

18. On narration as cognition, see White (1970, 1) and Alter (1981, chap. 8, "Narration and Knowledge").

19. My approach was influenced at an early stage by several efforts by literary theorists to apply the philosophical concept (dating from Leibniz) of Possible Worlds to literary worlds, especially by Pavel (1986, chap. 3, "Salient Worlds"), Doležel (1976), Ryan (1985). Doležel uses the concept of modalities in a way that influenced my formulation of the questions we must ask about Penelope. Ryan, developing Pavel's notion of "character domain," has proposed a way to map out a world from the perspective of a character.

20. Plato (*Republic* 392d1–394c5) distinguishes three types of narration: simple diegesis (as in dithyramb), diegesis through mimesis (as in drama), and a mixture of the two (as in epic). His discussion has influenced narratologists, notably Genette (1980, pp. 162–85), where he treats the question of the relation of the narration to its own materials ("Distance"). In this study I have merely marked a passage as mimetic or diegetic without drawing implications.

21. Hölscher (1967b [this volume, 133–40]) and Finley (1978) both see the importance of Penelope's tears in establishing her sincerity.

Combellack (1973, 38) convincingly shows that Penelope's earlier tears, after the interview (19.603), and Penelope's second prayer to Artemis (20.61–90) are "completely incompatible with the Harsh-Amory woman who knows that Odysseus is asleep downstairs." Then, following Whallon (1961, 128), he asserts that Penelope believed the Suitors would certainly fail in the contest. This "solution" is, however, inharmonious with Penelope's tears when she takes out the weapons for the contest. Thornton's idea (1970), that Penelope's decision proves her "utter loyalty to Odysseus" since she is obeying his instructions, gets us back to a univalent Penelope. Van Nortwick's (1983, 24–25) Penelope has indeed decided "to bury Odysseus and her old life with him by remarrying, while Athena plots the resumption of their marital happiness." Wife and goddess are at cross purposes: Penelope weeps for the loss of Odysseus while at the same time, as a tool of Athene, she unwittingly works for his return. The coexistence of these two levels of intentionality generates irony.

Another proposal, that Penelope uses the contest as a divining test (Amory [1963], followed by Austin [1969 and 1975]), gives us a Penelope who passively allows her fate to rest "on the laps of the gods." Consider Zeus' statement in the council of book 1: would Penelope be the sort of character, like Aigisthos, to blame the gods if things did not turn out favorably? It seems unlikely. Consider as well Athene-Mentes' statement to Telemachos (1.203–5) that Odysseus will find a way home, since he is a man of many resources (*epei palumêchanos estin*). Why would we expect Penelope to be different?

22. For a summary of the arguments in favor of athetesis, see van der Valk (1949, 194–95). He claims that the lines are no interpolation "but in fact they show us very clearly the inner emotion of Penelope" (195) because "Penelope has for a long time wavered and actually failed to recognize her husband.... It is obvious she is afraid of Odysseus' reaction and wrath."

Beye too anticipates my point when he comments (1974, 97) that Penelope defends Helen on the ground that chastity is a very chancey thing," and that "within one human heart exist several desires or reactions, but some of them, while they can be acknowledged, must be suppressed." His brief study uncovers many dimensions of Penelope's character, through parallels to Helen, Klytaimestra, even Kirke.

23. It is an argument *a fortiori* (cf. Aristotle, *Rhetoric* 1358a14–17 and 1397b12–29): if Helen acted thus, and is absolved, why cannot I, who almost committed a less severe breach of faith, be forgiven? Thus Penelope distorts factual truth for her argument's sake.

24. Penelope is viewed by the Suitors as a bewitcher, almost a Kirke figure. Her web is an entrapment for them, much like Kirke's island for Odysseus' men. See the excellent discussion of Penelope as a Kirke figure in Beye (1974).

25. The ancient tradition was as ambivalent on the topic of Penelope's sensuality as modern scholars (see E. Wüst, note 1 above). Some, wanting an uncomplicated Penelope, align themselves with the character Agamemnon: they tend to excise whatever violates their image of the heroine. Others, using the *Odyssey* as social history, explain Penelope's actions as reactions to social constraints. Marquardt (1984), e.g., who collects and treats all these passages and anticipates my case for a complex Penelope (48), vitiates her own argument by underestimating Penelope's autonomy. For example, she concludes (35 and 33) that Penelope "goes through the motions of encouraging courtship" because of social constraints and obligations on her to remarry once there is no realistic hope of Odysseus' return. She sees no evidence of choice on Penelope's part, though Odysseus' parting words (quoted by Penelope at 18.259–70)—if we accept the quotation as "authentic" and not Penelope's *ad hoc* invention—make it clear that it is her decision to proceed with marriage plans or not. If we contrast Penelope's situation with that of Klytaimestra (3.267–68: "a man was there, a singer, whom Agamemnon, when he went to Troy, had given many instructions to keep watch on his wife"), we can imagine that the social fabric reflected in the *Odyssey* admitted at least these two different sorts of marital relationship.

26. For Athene as the plan and guiding hand of the poet, see Reinhardt (1960b, 45). If this is so, which plots does the goddess, in the poet's stead, further? She knows Penelope is a matron, so that eliminates all maiden plots. BRIDE-CONTEST (MATRON) (which appears to the Suitors as BRIDE-CONTEST [maiden] and is therefore a *dolos*, or "deceit") is an expedient plot for her to support; so is MARRIAGE-AVOIDANCE (MATRON). To make Penelope *timiêssa mallon ... ê paros*, "more cherished than before," is a way of goading husband and son toward competing through the bride-contest for her hand (with the son helping win her for his father—an unusual situation in bride-contests). That is, Athene increases the intensity of competition among men for a beautiful woman. The scene is archetypally powerful.

27. Levine (1983) argues that, besides representing her confusion, Penelope's laughter expresses her cunning: she "laughs at the notion of fooling the Suitors because she knows she can succeed." I link her laughter to coquetry and a new awareness of eros. Cf. the similarly arresting laughter of Earth and the Sea just before Persephone plucks the narcissus (a proleptic symbol of her loss of virginity) in *Hymn to Demeter* 14: *gala to pas' egelasse kai halmuron oidma thalassês*.

28. The brooch is a complicated symbol, since it conveys meaning both as an object and as an object decorated with images. As a departure gift from wife to husband, it binds Odysseus, reminding him of Penelope's claims. Its decorations symbolize the erotic chase, perhaps even the first capture of Penelope by Odysseus. But the chase itself is not unambiguously "male captures female." Consider Penelope's trick of the marriage bed—a

sort of verbal trap in which she ensnares her husband, an entrapment that the chase scene on the brooch may anticipate.

29. It is here that Page (1955) and others place the recognition of husband by wife in the earlier version.

30. See Marquardt's (1984) convincing analysis of the simile of the daughters of Pandareos.

31. On the irony produced by the polyphony of voices in the narration of Penelope's dream, see Delrieu, Hilt and Létoublon (1984, 192). Odysseus, the narrator, Eurykleia, and the audience know that the liar is Odysseus, and that he is already home; Penelope asserts that the dream is false but believes (perhaps) that the stranger is the Cretan Aithon.

32. Penelope mourns their death as geese in the dream as she will never mourn them later, in reality, as suitors. Dream-Penelope's grief for the Suitors is emphasized by triple repetitions (19.541–43):

> Then *I began to weep*—that was in my dream—and *cried out*
> *aloud*, and around me gathered the fair-haired Achaian women
> *as I cried out sorrowing* for my geese killed by the eagle.

33. Scholarly debate remains inconclusive as to Penelope's meaning when she says, "and I looked about and saw the geese in my place, feeding on their grains of wheat from the water trough, just as they had been." Marquardt (1984, 43n.12) reviews the literature and then sides with the Literalists as opposed to the Psychological Critics (Russo, Devereux, Van Nortwick).

For me Penelope's remark is provocatively enigmatic, as we cannot know whether or not she accepts the equation geese = suitors offered by the dream-figure Odysseus and affirmed by the stranger. It feels like a teasing gesture from the poet.

34. The dream is an explicit portent of the future. Nevertheless, to the dreamer herself the presence of the geese-suitors in waking life seems to contradict the dream message. In the dream proper the death of the geese (= suitors) is vividly felt.

On augury in the *Odyssey*, particularly in connection with this passage, see Podlecki (1967); on the possibility that Penelope used the contest as a form of divination, see Amory (1963, 109ff.), followed by Austin (1975, 235ff. and 278n.28); and on the force of conditions in prophecy, see Peradotto (1974, 822–24), who develops a typology for prophecies in the *Odyssey*.

35. This scene has contributed to the archetypal image of Penelope as virtuous wife. Scholars rarely notice that the loom deceit contains an encouragement to the Suitors.

For a different view of Penelope's weaving as part of an argument for a solar/lunar interpretation of the courtship of Odysseus and Penelope, see Austin (1975, esp. 252–53).

36. For "like-mindedness" (*homophrosynê*) as a principle of marriage, the often-cited passage from Odysseus' prayer for Nausikaa is worth quoting in full:

> May the gods give you everything that your heart longs for;
> may they grant you a husband and a house and sweet agreement
> in all things, for nothing is better than this, more steadfast
> than when two people, a man and his wife, keep a harmonious
> household; a thing that brings much distress to the people who hate them
> and pleasure to their well-wishers, and for them the best reputation.
> (6.180–85)

The reciprocity, suggested by *homophrosynê* is evident in the Penelope–Odysseus relation, in their mutual sharing of *muthoi* in the marriage bed and in Homer's allotting them parallel, multiple plots.

37. Cf. Cavafy's "Ithaca" as an interpretation of the adventures along this line.

38. Cf. Pandora's preparation by the goddesses in Hesiod, *Works and Days* 59–82 in anticipation of her marriage to Epimetheus.

39. For the persistence of the language of violent abduction, cf. lines 66, *anelonto thuellai*, and 77, *harpuiai anêreipsanto*, two parts of a ring composition framing the simile. The parallel lines in the comparant (61–62: *Artemi ... balous' ek thumon heloio* and 63: *m'anarpaxasa thuella*) also suggest violence and unwillingness.

For the language of rape, cf. *Hymn to Demeter* 19–20 (*harpaxas d'aekousan ... olophurmnenên*) and for the victim's own description of the force-feeding (an analogue of rape) and the abduction, cf. 413 (*akoraan de biêi me prosênankasse parasthas*) and 431–32 (*pherôn ... poll' aekazomenên*).

40. The figure is villainous especially (and perhaps only) when focalized by the virgin; cf. Persephone's account to her mother of the force-feeding and violent abduction by Hades (see above, note 39).

41. This is the Peleus/Thetis or Pandora/Epimetheus subtype, wherein divinities adorn the bride.

42. Cf. 18.193 and 202 just before Penelope descends to solicit gifts from the Suitors; 19.54 as she comes to her interview with the stranger "looking like Artemis or like golden Aphrodite" and 20.60–61 and 68–69 as she prays to Artemis.

43. Artemis oversees Penelope's chastity, I suggest, because Penelope is like a virgin bride.

44. These are listed under MARRIAGE TESTS (H300–499, esp. H360, 400, 430, and 460) in Stith Thompson's *Motif-Index* (1955). Woodhouse (1930) is particularly interesting in his analyses of such folktale elements, though I find his labels idiosyncratic.

45. Compare Alcestis' attempt (Euripides, *Alcestis* 280ff.) to explain to Admetos that she chose to die on his behalf despite knowing that she had other options.

STEPHEN V. TRACY

# *The Structures of the* Odyssey

W orks of art do not occur randomly. They are created.[1] Their creators dispose their material in such a way that it usually exhibits some organization or pattern, such as balance or symmetry, to take but one example. This, to put it in the simplest terms, is largely what I mean by structure.[2] In the case of poetry, the use of structuring devices doubtless both aids the poet in shaping or, in some cases surely, in controlling his material and certainly guides the audience in apprehending it. Form and meaning tend to cohere; the structure, in short, will often reinforce the meaning by throwing emphasis on what is important. At the same time, poets tend to exploit a variety of structures and sometimes seem to take delight in employing more than one at the same time. To cite an excellent example from Latin poetry—it is well-known that Vergil has organized the books of the *Aeneid* so that relatively calm books, the odd numbered ones, alternate with more emotionally charged books, the even numbered ones. The work also falls into two halves that show a fair amount of parallelism and into a tripartite structure of three groups of four books. Homer too uses, as one might expect, a variety of structures, sometimes in combination. The following essay seeks to delineate some of the more important ones; it obviously makes no claim to offer a complete structural analysis of the poem. That is an unattainable goal.

From *A New Companion to Homer*, edited by Ian Morris and Barry Powell: 360–379 © 1997 by Koninklijke Brill.

# SOME COMMON STRUCTURAL PATTERNS
## IN THE *ODYSSEY*

### *RING COMPOSITION*

Ring composition that has the shape a b c, c b a occurs frequently and appears to be a device which derives from the habits of ordinary speech.[3] One tends to respond to a series of questions by picking up with that asked last and replying in reverse order. An excellent example occurs in book 11 lines 171 to 203. There in conversation with his mother in the underworld Odysseus asks her about her death, about his father, about his son, and finally about his wife.

> What bane of terrible death overcame you?
> A long illness or did Artemis rejoicing in her arrows
> coming strike you down with her gentle darts?
> Tell me of my father and son whom I left behind.
> Is my honor still with them or does some other
> man have it since all claim that I will no longer return?
> Tell me of my wedded wife, her will and intention.
> Does she remain by her child and guard everything steadfastly
> or has some other, best of the Achaeans, already married her?[4]

In responding she takes his questions in exactly the reverse order: wife, son, father, and lastly her own death which receives thereby strong emphasis:

> Truly she abides with enduring heart
> in your home and bitter nights always
> wear her down and days too, weeping.
> No one yet has your fine honor; rather, secure
> Telemachus disposes your holdings and feasts fine
> feasts, such as befits a ruling lord to care about.
> All call on him. Your father abides out there
> in the field and does not come to town nor does he have
> beds with frames, spreads, and shiny sheets;
> in the winter that man sleeps in the house where
> the slaves do, in ash near the fire, and wears dirty clothes.
> But when summer and verdant spring come,
> indiscriminately along the flat land of the vineyard
> beds of piled leaves are thrown on the ground for him.
> There he lies in pain and great suffering grows in his heart

longing for your return. Harsh old age is on him.
So too did I perish and meet my end.
Neither did the archeress rejoicing in her arrows coming
strike me down in the house with her gentle darts
nor did some disease come on me, which especially
with hateful withering took the breath from my limbs.
No, desire for you, your counsels, and your dearness,
brilliant Odysseus, took the sweet life from me.

Odysseus has been solicitous to ask her first about herself. We may well suspect that she in reply speaks of his wife first out of kindness because she knows his eagerness to learn of Penelope. In any case, it is not any sense of modesty which forbids her to speak of herself first. Rather her response carefully builds up to and, thus, emphasizes the suffering that his absence has caused, particularly to his parents. His father grieving for Odysseus' return has retreated to the solitude of the country (195–196), while longing for him has actually killed her (202–203). The structure emphasizes the point and, as harsh as it may be, seems designed to impress on Odysseus the importance of his own return home.

Larger stretches of the narrative also reveal careful ring composition at the thematic level. A disclaimer, however, is necessary before proceeding. Although there is controversy about the book divisions as we have them, both about when and by whom they were made, there is no doubt that the poem falls into sections that the book divisions often reflect.[5] I will therefore for convenience, and because I know no other way (practically speaking) to do it, refer to the books of the *Odyssey*. The 434 lines on the bow of Odysseus contained in our book 21 are arranged in a concentric ring. The focus of this section of the poem is on the bow and the stringing of it. The passage forms a unit that begins with Penelope going to fetch the bow and ends with Odysseus still in disguise stringing it. The structure may be laid out as follows:

a. Penelope and the bow (1–79)
b. Eumaios brings the bow to the suitors and is rebuked. (80–100)
c. Telemachus (101–139)
d. Leodes and Antinoos (140–187)
  **The Recognition** (188–244)
d. Eurymachos and Antinoos (245–272)
c. Odysseus (273–358)
b. Eumaios brings the bow to the beggar amidst rebukes. (359–379)
  [Eurykleia and Philoitios lock the hall.] (380–392)
a. Odysseus with the bow (393–434)

The ring composition of this section is unmistakable. It is also marked on the verbal level at the opening and close by identical phrases used of the actions of Penelope as she sent the key home (47–48) and of Odysseus as he shot the arrow (420–421).[6] Since, as a practical matter, Eumaios is needed to carry the bow to the beggar, the book centers (188–244) on Odysseus' use of the scar to reveal himself to his two loyal servants, Eumaios and Philoitios, whose help he will shortly require. The importance of this short scene is thus emphasized. Moreover, the recognitions have a crucial function to play in the second half of the poem; through them Odysseus re-establishes himself in his various roles to the people on Ithaca. The major ones are recounted at some length, as for example the recognition with Telemachus (16.172–320), with Eurykleia (19.357–502), Penelope (23.1–240), and Laertes (24.219–360). This one necessarily must be told quite briefly, so the poet has made it central to the structure as a means of underlining its importance.

## TRIPARTITE STRUCTURES

Narrative sections often reveal a tripartite structure, which is frequently another (simpler) type of ring composition since the second of the three parts is inevitably framed by the other two.[7] The account of Odysseus' arrival at his palace (17.166–491), for example, is surrounded by passages arranged in a ring that depict Penelope. She hears predictions that Odysseus will return and wishes that it would be so (17.157–165, 525–540). Moreover, she requests news of Odysseus in each section and is rebuffed initially, in the first by Telemachus (44–51) and in the second by Odysseus himself (544–573). Penelope's fixed position in the palace has been established from the opening book. Indeed, she and the palace have become one for the audience and for Odysseus, at once a goal and a symbol of the steadfast quality of the house and their union. Her presence in the narrative at this point framing his return, just as the poet frames him visually in the door of his palace as he enters it (339–341), is very satisfying. Artistically, we have here a variation on the type of a picture contained within a picture.

The next book, by almost a mirror technique, features Penelope at the center of a tripartite structure as she appears before the suitors and beguiles gifts from them (18.158–303). Just as she tricks the suitors, so on each side of her we now see Odysseus besting the suitors and their minions (1–157, 304–428). These side panels have parallel development—in the first section of each Odysseus receives abuse from a 'follower of the suitors (Iros, Melantho), deals with one of the ringleaders (Antinoos, Eurymachos), and gets the better of them. In the second part the suitor Amphinomos behaves in a civilized manner (120–157, 412–428).'[8] The narratives of books 17 and 18 thus play off against one another to emphasize effectively husband and wife, the two protagonists who will be brought face-to-face next in the narrative, during their tête-à-tête before the fireside in book 19. There exists no better illustration of the poet's ability to manipulate the disposition of his narrative elements and to exploit simple structural devices to excellent effect.

## STRUCTURES THAT INFORM THE POEM AS A WHOLE

### SIX-PART DIVISION

Homer, like Vergil who probably copied him, was the master of combining structures. There is no doubt that the poem falls both into two halves as well as into tetrads, six groups of four books. Indeed, it is perhaps easiest to keep the poem in mind by noting that the latter arrangement is thematic. The first four books deal with Telemachus, portray him beginning to come of age and, with Athena's help, making a journey to Pylos and Sparta in search of news of his father. Real news is not to be had, but he learns from Nestor at Pylos and from Helen and Menelaos at Sparta what sort of man his father was. By learning about his father, Telemachus in reality learns about himself. That one's father is an important determiner of one's identity is true in most societies, but especially true of the ancient Greek world, for, in their naming system, a young man was named using his father's name; he was always x, son of x. His identity, then, was explicitly bound up with that of his father. Telemachus' journey in short becomes one of maturing and of learning about himself.[9] These books serve the added function of introducing us to the situation on Ithaca. We see the unruly behavior of the suitors, the desperation of Penelope, and naturally become aware of the great need for Odysseus at home.

In book 5 we meet Odysseus for the first time marooned on Calypso's island, but longing for home. Books 5 to 8 take Odysseus out of the land of his adventures to the island of the Phaeacians, his last stopping point before coming home. Having escaped the attractive, as well as dangerous demigoddess Calypso, he now encounters the innocent, but, by this very token, even more dangerous, princess Nausicaa who has marriage much on her mind. It is an extremely delicate situation which the poet develops fully by exploiting the folk-motif of the contest for the hand of the princess. In essence, Odysseus defeats the Phaeacians in an athletic contest and wins her hand, but he can not complete the final part of the story because he has a wife and child at home.

In books 9 to 12 Odysseus tells his adventures since leaving Troy to the Phaeacians, thus identifying himself to them. He takes over the role of the singer. Since singers have the power to confer what heroes want above all else, namely *kleos*, fame on the lips of men,[10]—the only kind of immortality that counts for men in Homeric poetry—the fact that Odysseus becomes the singer and sings his own song takes on powerful significance. He confers *kleos* on himself, that is to say, by singing he guarantees his own survival. In a real sense his narrative also establishes his identity for the other audiences of the poem, namely the present hearers and, in a most important way, himself. It is not inaccurate to claim that Homer here portrays via a concrete example what, thanks to relatively recent psychological theory, we can characterize as the notion that if a person can talk about his past, he has come to understand it.

After a leisurely beginning in which the poet sets the stage in the initial books, the pace quickens and tautens right through the recital of the adventures in books 9 to 12. Such a pace cannot be maintained. To begin the second half of the poem, the poet then deliberately varies things by slowing the action. Books 13 to 16 bring Odysseus and Telemachus back to the Ithacan countryside. Athena returns to the fore to aid Odysseus; this she does largely by altering his appearance to that of an old beggar. Odysseus encounters the swineherd Eumaios whom he finds to be completely loyal and in book 16 is reunited with his son. Together they begin to plot the overthrow of the suitors.

Books 17 to 20 at first continue the leisurely pace, but the tension of the situation, the inevitable doom of the suitors, soon grips the hearer. Odysseus and Telemachus go to the palace separately. In these books the theme of the abuse of a guest is emphasized, indeed in three of the four books the disguised Odysseus is actually struck by one of the suitors. The first book focuses on Odysseus as he enters his palace for the first time in twenty years, the next portrays Penelope besting the suitors by beguiling gifts from them; these carefully prepare for the emotionally charged night meeting between the two of them in the nineteenth book. The next book returns to the suitors to give us one last portrait of their blindness to the situation. The supreme irony that results from the audience's knowledge that the suitors unknowingly abuse Odysseus accounts for much of the appeal that these books undeniably exert.

The final section of the poem has four discrete subjects—the stringing of the bow (book 21), the slaughter of the suitors (book 22), the reunion with Penelope (book 23), and the necessary wrap-up, viz. the reunion with Laertes and the resolution with the families of the suitors (book 24). The final book brings the poem efficiently to an end. Some have found the ending abrupt or somewhat unsatisfying.[11] Indeed, the last book may have the feel of a hasty tidying up—this is a matter of taste—but there is no question that the reunion with Laertes and the resolution of the quarrel with the families of the suitors is an integral part of this poem's design.[12] For one thing, Odysseus' identity can not be complete without the reunion with his father. Furthermore, he can not simply kill, no matter how justified his action may be, the sons of all the leading families in Ithaca and the surrounding territory without expecting some retaliation from their families. Ancient custom demanded that they react. This problem must be dealt with, especially since the issue is specifically raised at book 23 lines 118 to 122, or else the poem will be intolerably incomplete.[13]

Who is to say, however, that Homer has not shown good judgment in bringing his story rapidly to an end? The climax of the work came at the close of book 21, the stunning moment when Odysseus strings the bow and plucks it. And, as Homer remarks, 'it sang forth beautifully like a swallow' (21.411). There is a lesser crescendo in book 23, when Penelope turns the tables on Odysseus with her deceit about their marriage bed (23.177–180). It is somehow especially fitting that she outwits him; she alone, we are made to understand clearly, is a true match for him. After these great moments a serious anticlimax could be avoided only by winding up the remaining threads rapidly.

## DIVISION INTO HALVES

The first half brings Odysseus in the narrative from Troy through his adventures to Phaeacia. The second half brings him home to Ithaca and to his rightful place in the palace. Almost exactly in the middle dividing the poem is book 11, the crucial journey to the underworld. The poet has gone to some trouble to place book 11 as close to the mid-point as possible. Indeed, I would contend that one of the primary purposes for Odysseus' narration of his past adventures to the Phaeacians in books 9 to 12 is precisely to gain this position for the account of the underworld. Why?

Conquering death constitutes logically the most difficult labor a hero can perform; thus Homer has made it central in the structure as well as in thematic importance. It is perhaps accurate to say of Odysseus that he does not conquer death by going to the underworld so much as that he symbolically dies and is reborn. In any case, he learns there what it means to be a mortal, i.e. that death is inevitable, and he also experiences the shadowy, insubstantial nature of what awaits in the underworld. It is not insensitive, then, to see the first half of the poem as a journey of self-knowledge for Odysseus in preparation for the second half in which, having gained that knowledge, he can re-establish his identity to the people on Ithaca who, one and all, have given him up for dead. And on the narratological level, of course, he does return to Ithaca almost directly from the land of the dead.

Not only is the journey to the underworld central, Homer has carefully marked Odysseus' final voyage home, with which the thirteenth book opens, as a second beginning. He has done this on a verbal level by recalling in lines 5 to 6 and again (as that journey comes to an end when the Phaeacian ship actually reaches Ithaca) in lines 90 to 92 of book 13 phrases from lines 1 to 4 of book 1.[14] Note especially how the language specifically echos the themes of wandering and suffering sounded in the initial lines of the poem.

> Tell me Muse of the man of many turns, who wandered
> very much after he sacked the holy citadel of Troy.
> Many men's cities he saw and minds he knew,
> many the pains on the sea he suffered in his own heart ...

There can be no doubt that whoever made the division of the poem at this point did so in response to these clear textual indications. There is here a new beginning that points clearly to a conception on the part of the artist of two halves. Another way, then, to look at the poem is to realize that Odysseus journeys from Troy, from the killing fields, as it were, to home where he must re-establish himself as king. The journey covers roughly the first half of the poem; the re-establishing himself as lord of his realm the second half. The *nostos*, the return home, for a warrior, perhaps for everyman, is hard, almost impossible. In some sense you can't go home again; things are never the same, but this is especially true for a soldier who has been gone for many years. By placing the underworld at the center of the journey, Homer seems to say that the only way you can accomplish it is to die and be reborn, to go through hell. One has the overwhelming sense that he knew war and its aftermath first-hand.

## OTHER OVERARCHING DESIGNS

In the work as a whole, there are certainly other overarching structures and designs. For example, there is a grand tripartite arrangement on the level of basic subject matter. The first four books deal with Telemachus and the twenty-fourth deals importantly, if not solely, with Laertes; these books surround the others, the major part of the poem, which focus on Odysseus. The hero, then, is situated structurally between his son and his father, the two parameters of his existence. This arrangement underlines the theme of fathers and sons which plays a fundamental role, as we have noted above, in the poem. The son of a hero, in the epic mind-set, should grow up to be worthy of his father. Thus Orestes, who avenged the murder of his father, is several times held up as an example to Telemachus in the first four books (1.298–302, 3.304–316, 4.546–547).

Baths cleanse; the act of bathing, then, can easily take on symbolic meaning, e.g. renewal and purification. For example, Aphrodite, as Demodokos tells the story in book 8, caught *in flagrante* with her lover Ares, returns home to Paphos on Cyprus where the Graces bathe and anoint her with oil (8.362–364). The poet also associates baths with feeding guests, often newly arrived (4.48–49, 10.364, 450, 17.87–88). And Calypso washes Odysseus before he sails away on his raft (5.264). While not heavily emphasized, the baths mark these events. In addition, each of the family members of Odysseus undergoes a bath from which or after which he is transformed. The poet explicitly avails himself of the symbolic power naturally associated with baths by adding in every instance but one a simile or a description of Athena actually transforming the individual in question.

These major baths are carefully placed, both tying the narrative together and marking important junctures in it. Telemachus' bath comes at a point when he has completed the first stage of his journey (3.464–468), Laertes' immediately after his recognition of Odysseus (24.365–367). Odysseus is bathed and transformed just after he has met Nausicaa (6.224–227) and is bathed again just before she bids him farewell (8.449–456). She has posed a real challenge to him, just as Penelope does. Not surprisingly, then, he is also bathed and transformed in preparation for the final recognition scene with his wife (23.153–155). Finally, the motif is used to suggest a parallel between husband and wife; each rejects a bath, Penelope just prior to her appearance before the suitors (18.178–179), Odysseus during his interview with Penelope (19.314, 336–348). Each apparently desires to avoid the transformation inherent in the act. But neither can quite escape it, for Athena puts Penelope to sleep and beautifies her (18.187–196), while Eurykleia recognizes her master as she washes his feet (19.392, 467–475). The bath—even the non-bath—rejuvenates or, in the case of Telemachus, marks his maturation; it also underlines crucial moments facing Odysseus and his family. Hardly anyone else, it appears significant, takes a bath in the poem.

One can see, if one isolates these major baths and what is associated closely with them in the narrative, an extended ring composition of some complexity as follows:

  a. Bath of Telemachus (book 3)
    1. Athena (371)
    2. Nestor and his sons (386–387)
    3. Bath and simile (464–469)
    4. Journey (477–497)

   b. Bath of Odysseus (book 6)
     1. Encounter with Nausicaa (127–197)
     2. Bath and clothes (224–228)
     3. Transformation by Athena and extended simile (229–235)
     [Second bath (book 8)
     2. Clothes and bath (449–456)
     1. Farewell to Nausicaa (457–468)]
   c. Penelope (book 18)
     1. Refuses bath (178–179)
     2. Athena puts her to sleep and transforms her (187–196).
     3. Story about Odysseus at the time of his departure for Troy
       (257–271)
   c. Odysseus (book 19)
     1. Refuses bath (336–348)
     2. Eurykleia washes his feet (386–392, 467–471).
     3. Story about Odysseus, his birth and his scar (393–466)
   b. Bath of Odysseus (book 23)
     2/3. Bath/transformation by Athena and extended simile
       (153–163)[15]
     1. Recognition and reunion with Penelope (166–296)
   a. Bath of Laertes (book 24)
     4. Metaphorical journey (345–355)
     3. Bath (365–367)
     1. Transformation by Athena (368–371)
     2. Dolios and his sons (387)

The baths of Odysseus in books 6 and 8 form within the larger ring an inner ring composition with each other; while the two non-baths at the center have their elements arranged parallel to each other.[16]

As the poem ends, the poet naturally returns to the beginning. We return to the palace and Penelope, the place where we started. The twenty-fourth book additionally has some specific responsions with the opening of the poem.[17] It begins with an apparent digression, the trip to the underworld (1–204), just as the poem as a whole began with another apparent digression, the Telemacheia. Moreover, in this final book an assembly in which the relatives of the suitors are in vain advised to give up their wrath against Odysseus motivates Athena to intercede with Zeus (421–471). In the opening two books Athena's intervention with Zeus leads to the thwarting of Poseidon's wrath at Odysseus and eventually to the assembly in book 2. There Telemachus pled in vain with the suitors to give up the siege of his household. Finally, the appearance of Athena disguised as Mentor at the end establishing the truce (24.546–548) recalls her appearance as Mentes at the start (1.105 ff.) to spur Telemachus to action. While there is no fully developed ring composition shaping the entire epic, these thematic responsions/echoes at the extremities of the poem do suggest a ring pattern that brings it in a satisfying way full circle.[18]

## A DOMINANT STRUCTURAL PATTERN: PARALLELISM

If there is any one dominant structural mode in the *Odyssey*, it is parallel or balanced structures of the shape a b c, a b c. Indeed, one can observe between the three tetrads of the first half of the poem and the three of the second certain specific thematic parallels:

> a. Books 1–4
>   Ithaca
>   Athena and Telemachus
>   Suitors' failure to observe proper modes of hospitality
>   Telemachus' journey to Pylos and Sparta
>   The suitors plot the death of Telemachus.
> b. Books 5–8
>   Journey to the palace of Alkinoos
>   Conflict/contest with the youngmen
>   Latent marriage contest for the princess
>   Identity of Odysseus unknown
> c. Books 9–12
>   Odysseus identifies himself and becomes the singer.
>   Tells his adventures to the Phaeacians
>   Wins the support of Queen Arete
>   Underworld/mother/heroes of Troy
> a. Books 13 to 16
>   Ithaca
>   Athena and Odysseus
>   Eumaios' exemplary hospitality
>   Telemachus' return from Sparta and Pylos
>   Odysseus and Telemachus plan the death of the suitors.
> b. Books 17–20
>   Journey to the palace of Odysseus
>   Fight with beggar and conflict with the suitors
>   Latent contest for the hand of the queen
>   Identity of Odysseus unknown

c. Books 21–24
Odysseus identifies himself to the suitors and becomes the bowman.[19]
Wins the confidence of his queen
Recounts his adventures to Penelope
Underworld/heroes of Troy/father

These correspondences do occur in the text. It should not be surprising nor a matter sparking incredulity that a storyteller, especially one working in a tradition that employs frequent type-scenes as a device of composition, could create these thematic resemblances between the larger parts of his narrative.[20] They, after all, naturally emerge from and complement the technique of recurring narrative patterns. These patterns themselves, moreover, reinforce one's sense of a story told with multiple parallels. For example, children regularly appear in the tale before their parents. This is not just the case with Telemachus and Odysseus, it is almost invariably so. Peisistratos, the son of Nestor, is introduced before his father, Nausicaa before her parents, Antinoos (and all the suitors) before his father Eupeithes (and the other parents), Melanthios and Melantho before their father Dolios, and, capping the series, Odysseus before Laertes.

Female figures who first pose a threat and then help the hero are another staple of this story. The major ones, of course, are Calypso, Nausicaa/Arete, and Circe; but, Athena in book 13, Eurykleia in book 19, and Penelope in books 19 to 21 also fit this mold. The poet also exploits this pattern in Helen's description of her encounter with Odysseus who had stolen into Troy in disguise to spy (4.244–258). Though she recognized him, she did not give him away, but helped him. Likewise, a narrative strategy that includes numerous doublets contributes strongly to this feeling of recurrent parallels. This is most easily perceived in the case of character doubles such as Calypso and Circe, Mentor and Mentes, the two mother figures Antikleia and Eurykleia, the bards Phemios and Demodokos, the loyal servants Eumaios and Philoitios, the traitorous Melanthios and Melantho, and the leading suitors Antinoos and Eurymachos, to specify some of the most obvious.[21]

Moreover, in the extensive narrative dealing with Telemachus and then with Odysseus, Homer has created many thematic parallels between father and son. They often have the same or similar experiences. One telling example—Eurykleia is said to have been nurse to each of them (Telemachus: 1.435, Odysseus: 19.482–483). Clearly the poet has done this to reinforce the audience's perception that Telemachus is truly his father's son. How much he has become his father's equal is shown to us during the contest of the bow towards the end of the poem (21.128–129) where Odysseus must nod

Telemachus off, else on the fourth attempt he would have strung Odysseus'
great hunting bow. Odysseus, of course, strings the bow with consummate
ease, but none of the others save Telemachus can even come close.

I confine myself here to noting some parallels between Telemachus in
books 1 to 4 and Odysseus in books 5 to 8. Of course, the general situation
of the two at the start of the respective sections is the same. A god (Athena,
Hermes) arrives to set events moving. Telemachus sits among the suitors
despondent; Odysseus weeps at the shore alone. After a somewhat emotional
interchange with the mistress of the house (Penelope, Calypso), the hero
departs on a journey. In each case the woman does not want him to go.[22] Once
on their way, these parallels cannot, I think, be pursued very fruitfully. The
journeys and their purposes differ strikingly. Still, certain parallels of a specific
nature are notable. Athena enhances the appearance of each so that the people
admire him as he goes to the assembly (2.12–13, 8.17–20). Telemachus weeps
and covers his face when he hears his father's name (4.114–115); Odysseus
does likewise as he listens to Demodokos' song about himself and Achilles
(8.83–86). Both hear accounts of the wooden horse on Troy's final night
(4.265–290, 8.492–520). Alkinoos' palace makes a gleaming impression on
Odysseus just as Menelaos' did on Telemachus (7.84–85 = 4.45–46). While
in the overall story of the poem the parallels between father and son suggest
their essential similarity, these parallels in the opening books surely are meant
to underline the audience's perception that Odysseus in books 5 to 8 has
experiences much like his son's in books 1 to 4. Indeed, he undergoes a series
of encounters that bear a striking resemblance to the growing pains of a young
man. Symbolically reborn at the close of book 5 (see p. 166 below), Odysseus
meets a marriageable young maiden in book 6, her parents in 7, and bests the
young men in the contest for her hand in book 8.

Let us now consider the parallel structure of a single episode, namely
Odysseus' underworld experience (11.51–627). Odysseus recounts his
meetings with six figures in the underworld and lists others briefly. The
poet separates them with the intermezzo; otherwise they are arranged in two
parallel sets of three (the first group in ascending order of length, the second
in descending).[23]

a. Elpenor (fines 51–83) 33 lines
   Odysseus speaks first.
   Elpenor speaks of his own humble death and asks for burial,
      making his appeal more poignant by reminding Odysseus
      of Penelope and Telemachus.
b. Tiresias (90–151) 62 fines
   Tiresias speaks first and asks how it is that Odysseus has come.

       Speaks of the situation at Odysseus' home
       Speaks of Odysseus' future
   c. Antikleia (152–224) 73 fines
       Antikleia speaks first.
       Odysseus attempts in vain to embrace her.
       Died because of Odysseus
   d. Catalog of Women (225–327)
   **Intermezzo** (328–384)
   a. Agamemnon (387–446) 80 fines
       Odysseus speaks first.
       Agamemnon relates his own unseemly death and
         mentions Odysseus' wife and son.
   b. Achilles (467–540) 74 lines
       Achilles speaks first and asks how it is that Odysseus has come.
       Wants to know the situation at his own home.
       Odysseus relates the past at Troy.
   c. Ajax (543–565) 23 lines
       Ajax stands off silent and so Odysseus must speak.
       Odysseus attempts in vain to converse.
       Died because of Odysseus
   d. Catalog of Men (568–627)

The first three spirits tell him about his personal future and his family; the second three are figures from his past, who teach him by their actions—they care only about what is going on in the upper world—that death, a wraithlike shadowy state, holds nothing for a hero.[24] Odysseus gains from this experience in the underworld the determination to go on in spite of the obstacles. By contrast, before it he had been increasingly discouraged and, upon being blown back from Ithaca to Aiolos' island, had even contemplated suicide (10.51). After it, even though at the end completely alone, he clings for dear life to the fig tree above Charybdis (12.431–441).

    Similarly, the adventures recounted by Odysseus in books 9 to 12, although they reveal more than one structure, have fundamentally a parallel design.[25] After the sack of the Kikonian city (a doublet of Troy), these adventures fall into two sets of four arranged around a core of ring composition (Circe/underworld/Circe) as follows:[26]

   a. Lotos eaters
       Eastern or orientalizing motif
       Temptation to forget home
       Odysseus takes his companions away by force.

   b. Polyphemos
      Monster in a cave
      Six companions are devoured.
      Odysseus thinks of using his sword, but realizes he must outwit the monster.
   c. Aiolos
      Island of the wind god
      Odysseus sleeps.
      Companions disobey Odysseus.
   d. Laestrygonians
      Cannibalistic giants
      Doublet of the Cyclops
      Odysseus and his crew alone survive.

**Circe/underworld/Circe**

   a. Sirens
      Eastern motif
      Temptation to forget home
      Odysseus' companions forcibly remove him.
   b. Scylla (and Charybdis)
      Monster in a cave
      Six companions are devoured.
      Odysseus arms to kill Scylla, but can't even see her.
   c. Helios
      Isle of the sun god
      Odysseus sleeps.
      Companions disobey Odysseus.
   d. Charybdis (and Scylla)
      Odysseus alone escapes the storm.
      Odysseus retraces the route to Charybdis.
      Doublet of a sort with Scylla

**Calypso**

In each set Odysseus is progressively stripped of the outward accoutrements of a hero, namely his men and ships, with the result that at the close of book 12 he faces Charybdis alone desperately riding a spar from his wrecked ship. Each set leads him to a demigoddess to whom he makes love and from whom ultimately he has difficulty escaping. Both goddesses have strong associations with death.[27]

As to be expected, there are other organizational principles at work here as well. Violent adventures in which lives are lost alternate with non-violent ones. Excepting the underworld, the adventures also occur in groups of three, two that are shorter and one longer; thus, we find the groupings Kikones, Lotos-eaters, Polyphemos; Aiolos, Laestrygonians, Circe; Sirens, Scylla (and Charybdis), and Helios. Since the last three adventures are told twice in the twelfth book, there are six adventures before the underworld and six afterwards. These latter schemes, however, all but ignore the encounter with Charybdis that closes the adventures. They are not then to my mind very persuasive ways to look at the structure of these adventures, for, in coming last, the episode at Charybdis attains a structural as well as thematic importance that needs to be addressed.

Form in the *Odyssey* effectively reinforces the subject matter, for these parallel structures underscore the primary theme of the poem, namely, the parallel journeys of the hero, of his son, and of his father. These journeys lead home to the palace on Ithaca and become in the telling more than geographical in nature. Telemachus' journey is one of growth and self-discovery, Odysseus' one of finding out what it means to be a mortal, and Laertes' one of reinvolvement in life. Telemachus breaks the apron strings exerted by his mother and his nurse Eurykleia by physically leaving the palace. Odysseus and Laertes both symbolically die and are reborn on their journeys.

Indeed, each one of Odysseus' journeys involves elements of death and rebirth. Most obviously the journey home from Troy via the underworld in the eleventh book carries this connotation. When, moreover, he arrives at the land of the Phaeacians at the close of the fifth book, he has escaped Calypso (the buryer) with the aid of Leukothea (the white goddess). He emerges from the sea naked. The symbolism could not be clearer. Furthermore, when Odysseus finally comes home aboard the Phaeacian ship at the opening of book 13, a deep sleep holds him, and, lest we miss the symbolism, the poet specifically describes the sleep as 'most like death' (80). He arrives on Ithaca at daybreak (93–95) and is deposited near an olive tree and cave (102–103)—all symbols of life and rebirth. Finally, even the short journey that he makes from Eumaios' but in the countryside to his own palace at lines 200 ff. of book 17 has unmistakable elements of a journey to the underworld. Evening approaches as Eumaios and Odysseus depart (191). They meet a darkling figure, Melanthios, on the road (212–253)[28] and arrive at a palace in front of whose gates they encounter a dog (291).

This motif has been so consistently present in Odysseus' journeys that when we encounter Laertes' momentary faint at the realization that Odysseus is home and his immediate recovery (24.345–349) we readily perceive it as a mini-death and rebirth. Laertes is then rejuvenated by Athena (367–369)[29] and takes the lead in facing the relatives of the suitors, in fact slaying their ringleader Eupeithes, father of Antinoos (523–525). His 'journey' has been less a physical one than an emotional one, from total discouragement and lack of involvement in the affairs of his family to total involvement, indeed leadership, as head of the household. In fact, as he kills the leader of the suitors' relatives, he momentarily displaces his son as leader.

The three heroes together, son, father, and grandfather, armed for battle (24.505–515) mark the fulfillment of these journeys and the poem. It is a striking moment, easy to visualize, tableau-like in affect. Writers have often in discussing the arrangement of the poem sought comparisons from architecture; in particular they liken such scenes to pedimental sculptures of temples.[30] This is highly appropriate. After all, we have a sense at the end of having experienced not chaos, but rather a beautifully-crafted, monumental work of art.[31]

## NOTES

1. There can be little question that the Homeric epics are the products of a living oral tradition (A. B. Lord, 1960 and 1991). The progressive creation/fixation of the texts is the subject of much discussion which it is not my place to rehearse here (see Nagy, 1992, 17–60). However the text that we have came into being, my assumption is that it exhibits a careful organization and essential unity. This is in marked contrast to the analytic approach to Homer that has dominated much of European, especially German, scholarship. On its affect on approaches to structural studies of the *Odyssey*, see Hölscher (1991) 415–422.

2. Critics interested in structure focus on 'the internal dynamics of a literary work.' See the article on structure in Preminger and Brogan (1993) 1222–1224, esp. 1222 and the bibliography there. On the importance of the disposition of the material in the *Odyssey*, Kitto (1966) 116–152. Also to be consulted are the sensible remarks of Rutherford (1985) 133–134 on structure in the Homeric epics.

3. The presence of repetition of ideas and themes (or their opposites) in this pattern constitutes ring composition. See the discussions of ring composition and bibliography in Gaisser (1969) 3–5 and in Stanley (1993) 6–9.

4. The translations throughout are my own.

5. See Heubeck et al. (1988) 33–48, for the view that the divisions pre-date Aristarchus and Stanley (1993) 249–293 for the argument that they are early, perhaps of the sixth century.

6. See further Tracy (1990) 123–124.

7. See J. L. Myres' attempt to analyze the entire poem as a series of triptychs: (1952) 1–19.

8. Tracy (1990) 105.

9. For the formulaic ways in which Telemachus is characterized, see R.P. Martin (1993).

10. G. Nagy (1979) 16–17, 317–319.

11. Eustathios on 23.296 reports that the Alexandrian scholars Aristophanes and Aristarchus regarded this verse as the end of the poem. Page (1955) 101–136, in a characteristically vigorous attack, styles the end of the poem '*The Continuation*.'

12. See, for example, Stanford (1965) 5–20 and Wender (1978).

13. Tracy (1990) 140–143.

14. On this point, see Kahane (1992) 120–121.

15. Note that the extended simile here is the same as the one in book 6 (23.157–162 = 6.230–235).

16. For another overarching ring composition based on the theme of wooing and winning the princess/queen, see Tracy (1990) 139.

17. See Bertman (1968) 115–123, esp. 121–122.

18. There is a thoroughgoing responsion between the first and last books of the *Iliad* that has often been noted. S. E. Bassett indeed has argued for a general structural similarity between the *Iliad* and *Odyssey* (1919) 557–563.

19. See Rutherford (1985) 141–144, for a sensitive discussion of the parallels between Odysseus' self-identification in books 9 and 21.

20. For an attempt to discern a single thematic pattern, repeated in rich variety, as lying behind much of the poem, see Powell (1977).

21. For a thorough discussion of doublets, including thematic and narrative doublets, see Fenik (1974) 133–232.

22. See also Bertman (1966) 18–19, 24 fig. 7.

23. Adapted from Tracy (1990) 72–73.

24. See Griffin (1980) 100–101.

25. Following a suggestion made by C. H. Whitman (1958) 288–289, most have seen a ring structure in this account—see Niles (1978) 46–60; Most (1989a); and Garrison (1989) 117–123.

26. Adapted from Tracy (1990) 55–56.

27. On Calypso, whose name signifies concealer or buryer, see just below; that Odysseus encounters Hermes on his way to Circe (10.277 ff.) assures her underworldly associations. Hermes is also (be it noted) associated with Calypso; he is sent by Zeus at the opening of book 5 to intercede with her on behalf of Odysseus. For more on Circe's and Calypso's connections with the underworld, Crane (1988) 15–60.

28. Melanthios' name derives from the word *melas* meaning 'black.'

29. The phrase used is 'larger and stouter to look upon.' In short, Athena makes him his most impressive just as she had done for his son in the encounter with Nausicaa and the Phaeacians (6.229–230, 8.19–20) and again in preparation for his reunion with Penelope (23.156–157). Penelope too is transformed in this way by Athena as she prepares to go before the suitors (18.195).

30. See, for example, Bassett (1919) 563; Myres (1952) 1; and, very recently, R. P. Martin (1993) 239. This comparison to architecture also occurs frequently in German scholarship (Hölscher [1991] 417).

31. I owe special thanks to Richard Martin and June Allison for their helpful comments on a preliminary draft of this and to Will Batstone for bibliographic advice on modern works discussing structure.

BRUCE LOUDEN

# *Kalypso and the Function of Book Five*

In this final chapter we apply the extended narrative pattern to a consideration of the structure and function of the *Odyssey*'s fifth book. The book has long been criticized for its divine council (5.3–42),[1] seen as unnecessary and derivative of the opening divine council (1.26–95). Kalypso, onstage only here, and whose role is key to any analysis of the book's structure, has also attracted a variety of interpretations.[2] While I do not fully agree with the conclusions drawn by previous criticism of the divine council or of Kalypso, as is often found, the existence of so many critical arguments is a sign that something unusual is present in the poem's structure.

I suggest that book 5 is unique in the *Odyssey* in a number of respects. Most notably, the first half (5.1–261)[3] exists outside of the narrative pattern (and thus has nothing in common with the sequence of motifs with which we have been concerned). The reader may have noted that I have not yet mentioned Kalypso, or dealt in any way with the events of the book's first half. However, though it is not part of the narrative pattern, I argue that this section has nonetheless been composed in reaction, or counterpoint, to the pattern. Second, I argue that book 5 as a whole is the most highly wrought of any in the poem, by which I mean that it is a tour de force on the part of the composer, featuring the highest density of narrative techniques such as similes, dramatic monologues, divine intervention, pivotal contrafactuals,[4]

From *The* Odyssey: *Structure, Narration, and Meaning*: 104–129 © 1999 The Johns Hopkins University Press.

and the like. I suggest that book 5 exhibits these qualities because part of its function is to insert Odysseus into the narrative pattern, a considerable feat, in many respects. We can best begin our analysis of Kalypso and of how book 5 serves this by noting the number of ways in which the Ogygian goddess differs from Kirke.

Homeric scholars usually lump Kalypso and Kirke close together.[5] Previous scholarship, while bringing to light significant similarities, has tended to suffer from a preoccupation with parallels to the exclusion of differences between the two goddesses, too often regarding them as interchangeable multiforms of the same basic character.[6] Commentators who have equated the two goddesses have observed *generic* similarities, but have, I suggest, ignored key differences in their functional relationships. Discussions of the two goddesses have further suffered from an obsession with priority. As they are so similar, go the arguments, the composer must have derived one goddess from the other.[7] The two goddesses display considerable similarities, to be sure. Both island-dwelling, chthonic goddesses entertain Odysseus for lengthy periods of time, have sex with him, swear oaths not to harm him, and offer advice, provisions, and a wind on his departure. In both episodes, Hermes intervenes for Odysseus' sake. Nagler, Crane, and others[8] have demonstrated both that these features have much in common with Near Eastern figures such as Siduri and Ishtar and that they involve motifs common to depictions of the afterlife. Scholars have perhaps been further encouraged to view the two goddesses in a similar light inasmuch as Odysseus himself twice glosses over differences between them (9.32, 10.489). However, I argue that in those instances, both in the Apologue, he has particular reasons for manipulating his immediate audience by equating the two deities.

Despite these generic similarities, the narrative pattern, as we will see, reveals Kalypso and Kirke to be virtual opposites in their relationships with Odysseus. As both goddesses are present in the poem only insofar as they interact with the protagonist, this is a fundamental distinction. In their involvement with Odysseus the two goddesses reveal strongly opposing qualities, evident in the degree of solitude in which their encounters develop, their initial attitudes toward him, their subsequent emotional engagement, their reactions as he departs, and the degree of help they offer. Kalypso is an antitype to the powerful females in the pattern, Kirke in particular. Odysseus' relations with the two goddesses can be understood as progressing through five phases, presented here in the order through which Kirke passes: (a) goddess threatens the hero, (b) Hermes intervenes on the hero's behalf, (c) goddess swears an oath protecting the hero, (d) hero and goddess make love, (e) goddess helps the hero. On Ogygia, however, these same phases unfold in almost exactly reversed order. Kalypso is at her most accommodating (e) when Odysseus first arrives. They make love (d) for the entire seven years, with the suggestion that in the early phases of the relationship Odysseus is not averse to having sex with her. Hermes intervenes on the hero's behalf (b). Odysseus, suspicious of Kalypso's motives, requires her oath (c). As he would depart, Kalypso withholds considerable information about the present and future, and her clothing almost drowns Odysseus (a).

Their relationships with Odysseus thus run in opposite directions, almost in chiastic order. Kirke, as with the narrative pattern's other powerful female figures, moves from a hostile and threatening figure to a helpful, considerate being who seems to have Odysseus' best interests at heart. Kalypso moves from a helpful, nurturing figure to a potentially threatening being who is more concerned with her own interests than with what is best for Odysseus. Kirke is most dangerous and hostile on the hero's approach but most accommodating and helpful on his departure. Kalypso is most helpful and accommodating to the hero on his approach, but more difficult and less accommodating on his departure.

A similar reversal holds for Odysseus' behavior in the two sequences. He is active and aggressive at the outset in his encounter with Kirke, as a successful hunter and a leader who rescues his men. Having achieved these tasks, however, he becomes almost entirely passive, needing a reminder that it is time to move on. Conversely, on Ogygia Odysseus is passively bewailing his fate as the narrative finally locates him, but becomes quite active once receiving Kalypso's assurance that he may leave. His vigorous industry in building the raft is the counterpart of his initial aggressive approach on Aiaia.

Furthermore, the composer uses the Kalypso section in order to depict Odysseus in a heroic context utterly unlike any encountered in the extended narrative pattern. Kalypso offers Odysseus life without conflict, life that is eternal, everlasting, and distant from humanity. Odysseus can accept or reject her offer. While he is with her, the offer still open, Odysseus is, in effect, between everything, between the states of mortal and immortal, between the heroic wanderings and the return to Ithaka. In terms of our structural analysis, while he is with Kalypso he is between the end of the Aiaian sequence (which has concluded) and the beginning of the Skherian sequence (which has yet to begin), part of neither.

Ogygia is entirely static as far as the advancement of the narrative is concerned. Kalypso, living up to her name, not only hides the hero but threatens to conceal the plot as well. The *Odyssey* twice makes use of the epic motif "the singer looks at his sources,"[9] in that two epic bards, Demodokos on Skheria and Phemios on Ithaka, both meet the hero face to face, and consequently will be able to pass on authoritative accounts about him to the subsequent tradition. Though the *Odyssey* mentions several songs sung by the two bards, none of the songs touches on Odysseus' exploits after the Trojan War. Not until Demodokos hears from the hero's own lips an account of those heroic exploits described in books 9 through 12 do they become part of the tradition, capable of being passed on. Similarly on Ithaka, Phemios comes face to face with Odysseus and personally witnesses his slaying of the suitors. Kalypso is therefore concealing Odysseus from the tradition itself by keeping him from encountering Demodokos, and eventually, Phemios. To stay with Kalypso, therefore, would mean no epic is possible, that there would be no outside knowledge of any of the Aiaian sequence, Odysseus' most heroic accomplishments. The subject matter of the *Odyssey* would be known only by deities.

Let us then consider a thematic analysis of Kalypso and Kirke's interactions with Odysseus, in terms of the five-step sequence noted above. Since Kirke, firmly woven into the fabric of the extended narrative pattern, conforms to the poem's dominant vision of Odysseus' relations with powerful females, we consider the sequence from her point of view, allowing Kalypso's differences to appear in contrast.

### KALYPSO, ALONE WITH ODYSSEUS

It should be emphasized at the outset that though the two goddesses have generically similar islands, equipped with divine attendants (5.199, 10.350–51), Odysseus' solitary circumstances when with Kalypso, as opposed to his being accompanied by his crew when with Kirke, dictate fundamentally different dynamics in his involvement with the two goddesses. Odysseus' solitary state on Ogygia is the first of many radical departures from his encounters with the narrative pattern's powerful females. There is no abusive band of young men on Ogygia counterpart to the crew, the Phaiakian athletes, or the suitors. Whatever will complicate the relationship between Kalypso and Odysseus, they will not encounter friction from any other males present. With no abusive band of young men present, book 5 further lacks all subsequent motifs of the narrative pattern in which the band takes part, particularly the violation of a divine interdiction, the punishment of which forms the climax of both the Aiaian and Skherian sequences. This is the first of many signs that in book 5 the *Odyssey* presents us with a fundamentally different type of mythic narrative than that present elsewhere in the poem.

Not only is Odysseus alone with Kalypso, with no other mortals present; Kalypso is a far more isolated figure than Kirke in other ways. Hermes, who regularly traverses vast distances, complains to Kalypso about how inaccessible her island is (5.99–102), how remote from humankind (101–2). Odysseus reiterates Kalypso's isolation, "nor does anyone, either god or mortal, associate with her" (7.246–47).[10] Kalypso's more solitary existence extends to the animal life on the respective islands. Ogygia is not said to house any fauna except birds (5.65–67). Aiaia, however, teems with animal life, whether the lions and wolves hovering about Kirke's palace (10.212–19) or the stag Odysseus catches before meeting the goddess (10.158). Though some of the Aiaian animals are transformed men, their presence is a further sign of greater traffic on Aiaia.

### DIFFERENCES IN ODYSSEUS' ARRIVALS TO AIAIA AND OGYGIA

Odysseus' respective arrivals to the two islands and goddesses could hardly be more different. Coming to Aiaia, he has a ship, and is accompanied by his crew (10.133 ff). He comes to Ogygia alone, clinging to the keel of his wrecked ship, his crew having perished (5.130–34, 7.249–53). At Aiaia, his approach to Kirke is quite complex, as is the approach to the powerful female figure in all three sequences of the narrative pattern. Initial contact is postponed as Odysseus first goes by himself to hunt for food. His hunting is thematic in some respects, as discussed below, depicting him as an active leader as he begins his stay on the goddess' island. His brief separation from the crew as he looks after their best interests anticipates the thematically parallel separation on Thrinakia, at the end of the sequence. Having feasted on the stag, the crew divides into halves, Eurylokhos' half drawing the lot to investigate the island. After Eurylokhos returns unsuccessful (Kirke having turned half of the crew into swine), Odysseus begins to approach the goddess. Before encountering her, however, Hermes encounters him: *A divine helper appears, advising him how to approach a powerful female figure*. As a result, a forewarned Odysseus now approaches Kirke.

### FIRST CONTACT WITH KALYPSO

On Ogygia, in a complete inversion of the narrative pattern, Odysseus does not approach the goddess; Kalypso comes to him, finding him alone, helpless, and near death. Unlike Kirke, who initially attempts to drug him, perhaps intending to kill him, Kalypso clearly harbors no hostility whatsoever toward Odysseus, instead taking pains to nurse him back to health (5.130, 135). On Ogygia the narrative has none of the lengthy, complicated, even deadly approach to the powerful female that is prominent in all three sequences. Unlike the trio of Kirke, Arete, and Penelope, Kalypso is not *a figure who is initially suspicious, distant, or even hostile toward him*. Though we lack a full account of their first meeting,[11] it is clear enough that Kalypso immediately welcomes Odysseus into her midst. Consequently, all but one of the other motifs in the narrative pattern relating to the powerful females are either missing or inverted in Kalypso's case: *She imposes a test on him, whereupon Odysseus, having successfully passed the test, wins her sympathy and help, obtaining access to the next phase of his homecoming. Their understanding is made manifest in her hospitable offer of a bath. Furthermore, Odysseus is now offered sexual union and/or marriage with the female.*

As far as we can tell, Kalypso imposes no test on Odysseus. She offers him help from the outset, and has considerable sympathy for his predicament. They do enter into a sexual relationship, but even this appears quite different from the relationship with Kirke, as discussed below. What Odysseus does not obtain from Kalypso, until the very end of the seven-year stay, and then only by intervention of Zeus, is *access to the next phase of his homecoming.*

### HERMES INTERVENES AT OPPOSITE POINTS

Though Hermes comes to each island out of concern for Odysseus, his role and mission differ considerably. On Aiaia he plays that role, recognizable in all three sequences of the narrative pattern, of the god in a youthful form who warns Odysseus about how to approach the powerful female, noting future difficulties involving the abusive band of young men. On Ogygia every facet of his mission is different. He does not take the youthful form required of this divine helper in all three sequences (10.278–79, 7.19–20, 13.222–23). *He does not even encounter Odysseus,* who is elsewhere on the island for the full duration of his visit. Since his errand to Ogygia brings him there only after Odysseus has been in Kalypso's company for seven years, he therefore has none of the advice which the divine helper gives to the hero in the narrative pattern's three sequences. Rather, he serves here to help Odysseus *leave,* not approach, a powerful female. Hermes' function on Ogygia is thus more like that of the cherubim in Eden supervising the hero's expulsion from Paradise (Genesis 3.24), than of the other divine helpers depicted in the *Odyssey.* In the narrative pattern, the youthful divine helper does not usually meet with the powerful female, but the hero himself.[12] On Ogygia, however, Hermes' meeting is solely with Kalypso. Hermes' motivation also differs in the two episodes. On Ogygia, he expressly conveys the command of Zeus to Kalypso, while on Aiaia, he is given no specific motivation for intervention (Crane 40). In both episodes Hermes intervenes at that point at which each goddess offers the greatest threat to Odysseus, Kirke at the beginning of the encounter, *but* Kalypso at the end.

Both goddesses, at Odysseus' request, swear oaths not to harm him (10.342–46, 5.184–89). Again, however, in function the oaths are more different than alike. Book 5 gives us Kalypso's full oath, whereas with Kirke, Odysseus merely reports that "she at once swore me the oath, as I asked her" (10.345), not retelling the oath's particulars. On Aiaia, the oath, sworn while Odysseus is still in the initial difficult stages of negotiating his agreement with Kirke, serves to protect him when he has sex with her. It marks the beginning of an agreement of trust reached between the hero and goddess. On Ogygia, the oath, in effect, signals the conclusion of their time together, and comes only after a lengthy sexual relationship.

### KALYPSO AS MORE INTIMATE THAN KIRKE

Though commentators appear to equate the sexual relationships Odysseus has with each goddess, the text suggests significant differences, springing again from the more solitary environment found at Ogygia. Kalypso has a far more intimate relationship with Odysseus than does Kirke, an intimacy permitted both by the isolation that typifies her island and the greater length of their time together. Because Odysseus is accompanied by his crew when he is with Kirke, his stay on Aiaia is permeated by that most epic of type-scenes, the feast.[13] At Kirke's behest Odysseus and crew eat and drink until they regain their spirits (10.456–70). A whole year passes in feasting at Kirke's palace. Ogygia, lacking the requisite number of participants for a feast, lacks the type-scene. Instead, the episode offers a scene closer to a romantic date, with Kalypso and Odysseus the sole participants (5.194–227).

Because of Odysseus' lack of attendants and her own solitary circumstances, Kalypso's relationship with the hero is far more intimate and more overtly sexual than Kirke's. The narrative repeatedly stresses that Kalypso and Odysseus are having sex regularly (5.119–20: εὐνάζεσθαι / ἀμφαδίην; 5.129: βροτὸν ἄνδρα παρεῖναι; 5.154–55: with frequentative ἰαύεσκεν). These retrospective accounts, all of which emphasize an ongoing relationship by virtue of frequentatives or continual aspect of present-tense verbs (εὐνάζεσθαι, παρεῖναι) are capped by a final episode of lovemaking, which occurs in the present, the night before Odysseus begins to fashion the raft which will take him away from Kalypso (5.226–27). Kalypso is the sexual aggressor in the relationship, evident in both her own account and the narrator's (5.154–55).

On Aiaia, as Odysseus is accompanied by his own crew, a less intimate atmosphere prevails, and sex is rarely mentioned. The text only once mentions Odysseus sleeping with Kirke: "and then I mounted the surpassingly beautiful bed of Kirke" (10.347). Commentators tacitly generalize on the basis of this single mention that Odysseus has sex with Kirke regularly during the whole year.[14] It must be kept in mind that Odysseus has sex with Kirke because Hermes, a god, commands him to do so (10.297). Neither Hermes' injunction nor the text suggests repeated occurrences. How does the year pass? Kirke bids them to restore their spirits (10.456–65), the next lines describing the passing of the year precisely in accord with the goddess' instructions: "Then for all the days until a year had come to pass / we sat feasting on unlimited meat and sweet wine" (10.467–68). On the day that marks the end of the year, they again feast all day (10.476–78), Odysseus approaching the goddess at sunset. A variant of "and then I mounted the surpassingly beautiful bed of Kirke," the sole mention of their having sex a year before, recurs at 10.480, but it is immediately followed by "I supplicated her by her knees." This time the formula does not suggest sex, but the urgency with which Odysseus consults the goddess on how to leave.

On Odysseus' return from the underworld, the same sequence of motifs occurs, again without sex. Again the goddess bids the crew to eat and drink to refresh themselves after their ordeal (12.23–24). When the sun sets, Kirke sits Odysseus down apart from the crew (12.33–34) and then tells him of the upcoming obstacles. No sex is involved. Though the text does not offer conclusive evidence one way or the other, the evidence suggests that Odysseus only has sex on the one occasion when Hermes instructs him to do so. On that occasion, as Hermes instructs, Odysseus is the sexual aggressor, opposite his status with Kalypso. The *Odyssey*'s larger reception, has, I suggest, distorted the nature of his relationship with Kirke, perhaps as a result of early allegorization of the episode into a hero's encounter with temptation.

Kalypso is portrayed as having a much deeper emotional relationship with Odysseus than does Kirke. Odysseus stays on Ogygia for seven years, which allows for considerable intimacy to develop between the goddess and the hero, unencumbered by his crew. Kalypso has a deep emotional investment in Odysseus as she rescues him, nourishes him back to health (5.130–35), shares intimate meals with him, and loves him; "and I gave him my love and cherished him," (5–135; cf. 12.450). Because Kalypso loves Odysseus without initially remaining aloof, or subjecting him to any tests, as do all other females in the narrative pattern, she is quite opposite to them. As a further index of Kalypso's close emotional tie to Odysseus, the poem emphasizes that she not only is aware of Penelope (5.209–10), but sees her as a rival:[15]

I declare that I am not inferior to her,
not in form and not in beauty.
   (5.211–12)

While it is dangerous for a mortal to declare rivalry with an immortal, and perhaps that is partly why Odysseus himself does not mention Penelope at this point, it is quite unusual for a goddess to put herself in the converse position, of having to justify her own beauty by mentioning a woman's. The unique moment well underscores how close Kalypso is to Odysseus, and lives up to her characterization as foregrounded at the opening of the poem, that she desires Odysseus as her husband (1.15).

Kirke, however, has little discernible emotional attachment to Odysseus. For the year he spends with her, Odysseus eats not alone with Kirke, but attended by his crew. The narrative firmly emphasizes this in his refusal to eat with Kirke before she restores the crew to their human form (10.375–87). Furthermore, considerable tension develops between Odysseus and his crew while on Aiaia: *conflict arises between Odysseus and the band of young men.* Such tension complicates the stay with Kirke, placing the emphasis on Odysseus as captain over his crew rather than on any intimate or romantic relationship between Kirke and Odysseus. Such complications are noticeably absent on Ogygia, which increases the focus on the emotional relationship between Kalypso and Odysseus. Kirke neither mentions Penelope nor shows any interest in possible female rivals, un-concerned with how attractive she herself may appear to Odysseus.[16]

## THE GODDESSES' DIFFERENT REACTIONS
## WHEN ODYSSEUS DEPARTS

Both goddesses offer Odysseus help on his departure, but again differ significantly in the degree of aid they offer and in their reactions to his desire to depart.[17] The narrative repeatedly emphasizes that Kalypso is keeping Odysseus against his will (1.14, 1.55, 4.557–58 = 5.14–15, 5.154–55; note the emphatic frequentatives in 5.154–58, 7.259–60, 23.334–37). On Aiaia, however, there is only one passing suggestion that Kirke keeps Odysseus and crew there against their will: "no longer remain in my palace against your will" (10.489).[18] Nonetheless, events in book 10 do not depict the men as remaining against their will,[19] but as living up to Kirke's suggestion that they feast until they reclaim their spirits (10.460–65).

The goddesses have opposite reactions to his departure. Kalypso lets him leave only under Zeus' threat, though she tries to dissuade him and still desires him as husband. As Odysseus prepares to leave, Kalypso becomes a greater potential threat than before. He suspects her motives when she claims that he is free to go, and manipulates her into an oath guaranteeing she has no ulterior motive. When the storm later strikes Odysseus at sea, Kalypso's clothing threatens to drown him (5.321).[20] Kalypso thus becomes increasingly dangerous as Odysseus attempts to leave, while Kirke offers more help, is far more forthcoming as to the future, makes no attempt at keeping Odysseus, and provokes no suspicion as to her motives. In full contrast to Kalypso, when Odysseus asks Kirke how to leave, she says, in effect, "Fine, here's how you do it." In a further inversion to events on Ogygia, Odysseus is not in any way suspicious of the help Kirke offers him on his departure.

Both goddesses, if they wish, are capable of offering Odysseus considerable help through their prophetic powers, their advice about future obstacles he will encounter on the next phase of his homecoming. For Nagler, this is perhaps the central function of the two figures as suggested in their shared epithet, δεινὴ θεὸς αὐδήεσσα, "dread goddess who talks with mortals" (of Kirke: 10.136, 11.8, 12.150; of Kalypso: 12.449).[21] As with every other aspect of the two goddesses, however, a generic similarity masks a functional difference. The distribution of the epithet, three to one in Kirke's favor, may suggest that it applies more centrally to her. Both are beguiling singers (5.61, 10.221, 227), but in the case of Kalypso, only Hermes is actually depicted as hearing her sing, whereas Kirke's singing is one of the qualities attracting the crew to what would have been their doom. Kirke's singing thus takes on darker overtones in its narrative context than does Kalypso's.

The central thrust of δεινὴ θεὸς αὐδήεσσα, however, lies in the goddesses' shared ability, as immortals, to foresee the future, and so to advise Odysseus. In this sense the phrase again applies more accurately to Kirke and is suppressed or stifled in Kalypso's case. Kirke twice *offers* lengthy, detailed accounts of what Odysseus must do and where he must go to obtain access to the next phase of his homecoming (10.488–540, 12.37–110, and 12.116–41). She names every stop he will encounter, noting place names and names of particular mortals and immortals he will meet. She openly proclaims that such is her function: "but I will point out the way and I will indicate each detail" (12.25–26). As such, δεινὴ θεὸς αὐδήεσσα is most operative at 11.8, when Odysseus would act upon the instructions just given in her first monitory speech, and at 12.150, when he will do so after the conclusion of her second.[22] By so advising, Kirke fully lives up to the powerful female's climactic function in the extended narrative pattern, providing Odysseus *access to the next phase of his homecoming.*

By contrast, Kalypso, true to the meaning of her name, conceals much of what she knows about the future as it pertains to Odysseus. She declares to Hermes that she will not help Odysseus depart: "I, at any rate, will not preside over his departure" (5.140). This remark would be utterly out of character in any of the narrative pattern's powerful females.[23] To Odysseus she hints at dangers awaiting him should he leave (5.206–8), but does not spell them out. She says he will reach his home unscathed, "only if the gods consent" (5.168). But in so doing she suppresses a number of points. Hermes had told her how Zeus has declared Odysseus will not die away from home, but is fated to return (5.113–15). She herself has told Hermes that she will advise Odysseus so he will return unscathed, and that she will conceal nothing (5.143–44). But when she is said to be devising his escort home (5.233), she merely provides him with tools with which to build his raft, and shows him where the best trees grow. As she sees him off (5.263–68), she offers him a bath, clothing, various provisions, and a wind. Though Kalypso does give Odysseus some particular advice on how to navigate, we are not given her advice firsthand, only through Odysseus' brief allusions. Again, however, Kalypso conceals as much as she reveals. Only after he is well at sea do we learn that she gave him advice as to celestial navigation (5.273–77). She does not, however, tell him the name of his destination, Skheria, though it is well known to both Poseidon (5.288–89) and Leukothea (5.345) and, presumably, to Kalypso as well. Kirke, who carefully named every danger and destination he would face, is far more forthcoming about the future, offering Odysseus inestimable help not once but twice.

Kirke is also more forthcoming about the roles of the gods. She immediately tells Odysseus, on recognizing him, that Hermes has earlier told her the hero would come (10.330–32). Kalypso, the "concealer," says nothing about either Hermes' visit, though it occurs while Odysseus is on the island, not in the past, or his message from Zeus.[24] Though described as δεινὴ θεὸς αὐδήεσσα, Kalypso clearly does not live up to the expected stereotype of the goddess who tells the hero everything he will encounter, as does Kirke (and Leukothea: 5.339–50).

The formula, δεινὴ θεὸς αὐδήεσσα, may more accurately apply to Kalypso in her tendency to utter charming, winning words. Athene emphasizes this aspect of Kalypso in the opening divine council:

> but always with wheedling and winning words she
> charms him, so he will forget Ithaka.
>     (1.56–57)

Athene's characterization accurately holds for all of Kalypso's speeches to Odysseus in book 5. The description serves as a summary depiction of the extent to which Kalypso departs from the role of the poem's powerful females, who neither try to restrain Odysseus from departing nor converse with him in such an indirect, oblique manner.

Other of the goddesses' epithets further underscore how greatly they differ and the opposite orders in which they behave in their treatment of Odysseus. Kirke's epithets emphasize that she poses the greatest threat on Odysseus' first approach. Before the possibility of confrontation ends by reaching an agreement, and Odysseus *wins her sympathy and help*, (10.345–47), the narrative describes her in uniquely threatening terms, "with evil thoughts in mind" (10.317). As she is both a goddess and a host, the poem depicts her in terms more appropriate to a monster, or that type of evildoer whom the hero, in Greek myth, is destined to kill for violating hospitality.[25] While maneuvering Kirke into swearing an oath by Styx, Odysseus refers to her as "planning treachery" (10.339). Her drugs are described as "evil" (10.213) and "woeful" (10.236). Odysseus describes her intelligence or motives as "malign wiles" (10.289). None of these quite negative terms is used of Kirke *after* she and Odysseus reach their agreement. We noted in chapter 1, that Arete, in some respects, best exemplifies the changes the powerful females undergo, becoming kindly disposed to Odysseus, in Athene's words, φίλα φρονέῃσ᾽ ἐνὶ θυμῷ (7.75).

The epithet, δολόεσσα, "wily," used of both Kirke (9.32) and Kalypso (7.245),[26] applies to the goddesses in opposite order. Kirke is δολόεσσα on Odysseus' approach but loses this quality after swearing an oath by Styx. Significantly, δολόεσσα is only used of Kalypso by Odysseus himself, not the principal narrator, and only after Odysseus leaves her. The term applies accurately to her behavior in the later stages of their relationship, when he tries to leave, and when he is at sea between Ogygia and Skheria.

These distinctions in their respective behaviors with Odysseus may suggest deeper differences in the goddesses' powers and identities. The *Odyssey* provides a number of other means, in addition to the narrative pattern, by which such differences are evident. Both the principal narrator and Kalypso herself suggest she has much in common with Eos, a sexually aggressive goddess, whose tendency to abduct mortal lovers is often alluded to in Homeric epic.[27] Eos' other principal function in Homeric epic is to mark time, to begin each day, to mark the narrative itself into sections.[28] Kalypso shares both traits.

The narrator suggests parallels between Kalypso and Eos by opening book 5, the only section in which Kalypso is onstage, with a dawn formula unique in the *Odyssey*: "Eos stirred from the bed of handsome Tithonos" (5.1–2). Austin (67–68) argues that the narrator departs from the usual formula to call greater attention to a specific day, in this case, the day on which Odysseus will first appear in the poem, the day on which Kalypso will be made to let her captive mortal lover go. It is no coincidence that the only daybreak formula to emphasize Eos' tendency to have a mortal lover occurs only here in the *Odyssey*. This opening reference to the sexually aggressive Eos establishes one of the principal themes of book 5. Of the several other formulas which could be used,[29] the narrator has selected the one phrase paralleling Kalypso's own circumstances, an amorous goddess with her mortal lover.

Kalypso herself continues the parallel in her complaint to Hermes over having to surrender Odysseus. Noting other mortal/immortal couplings to which the gods have objected, she compares herself to Eos, with another mortal lover, Orion:

> So once rosy-fingered Eos took Orion for herself,
> until the gods, living at ease, resented her.
>      (5.121–22)

Homeric epic offers numerous instances of mortal/immortal couplings. That the principal narrator opens book 5 by depicting Eos with a mortal lover, and that Kalypso selects Eos as paradigmatic for her circumstances shortly afterward, reiterates and solidifies the thematic parallels between Kalypso and Eos.

There is a sinister side to the amorous propensities Kalypso shares with Eos, rarely discussed by commentators. In a third mention in the *Odyssey*, Eos is described as abducting yet another mortal lover:

> But Golden-throned Eos snatched Kleitos away
> because of his beauty.
>      (15.250–51)

Kalypso does not abduct Odysseus; he has washed up on her shores. However, a similar violence, parallel to Eos' behavior, colors the episode. Odysseus is not only Kalypso's prisoner, as the poem repeatedly emphasizes, she forces him to have sex with her against his will:

> By night he would lie beside her, forced to,
> in the hollow caves, against his will for she willed it.
>      (5.154–55)

Kalypso is a rapist by this description. However, after Kalypso has sworn the oath, and, making one last but unsuccessful attempt to persuade him to stay, they make love a last time (5.227), Odysseus apparently participating willingly.[30]

In her response to Hermes, Kalypso also singles out Demeter as having had an interrupted affair with a mortal lover. Again she selects a goddess as paradigmatic for her circumstances:

> So once fair-tressed Demeter having yielded
> to her desire came together with Iasion in intercourse
> in a thrice-plowed fallow field.
>     (5.125–27)

Inasmuch as Demeter's amorous pursuits are not central to her character, Kalypso probably has in mind parallels with her more dominant traits, the ultimate nurturing, maternal figure, alluded to here in the "thrice-plowed fallow field." As she further specifies the nature of her relationship with Odysseus, her subsequent remarks reveal that she sees herself in a Demeter-like role in *nurturing* him back to health after finding him near death:

> Him I saved ...
> him I cherished and nourished, and I always said
> I'd make him immortal and ageless for all days.
>     (5.130–3)

The same motifs, a goddess nourishing and attempting to make a mortal immortal, recur in the *Homeric Hymn to Demeter*, where Demeter nurses Demophon, the same vocabulary and formulas being employed.[31] Metaneira interrupts Demeter's attempt at making the mortal immortal, the ultimate stage of being nourished by such a figure; in the *Odyssey* Hermes intrudes. Among the many goddesses who have had relations with mortals,[32] in Eos and Demeter Kalypso selects goddesses with whom she exhibits close parallels.

Kalypso also depicts herself in opposition to another deity. It is Artemis who killed Orion, ending Eos' affair with him (5.123–24), Artemis who punishes unchaste behavior.[33] In Kalypso's brief paradigm, and elsewhere in Greek myth, Artemis is perhaps the one goddess in strongest opposition to her own intimate behavior with mortals.

Neither the principal narrator nor Kirke draws parallels between herself and other goddesses, but in several respects she has much in common with Artemis, Kalypso's opposite. The emphasis on hunting and animals on

Aiaia, neither of which is mentioned on Ogygia, firmly aligns Kirke with the Mistress of Beasts, Artemis' epithet at *Il.* 21.470. Several earlier scholars have argued that Kirke is based on the *Potnia Thêrôn* figure.[34] Odysseus approaches Kirke only after successfully hunting a stag (10.144–84), an animal repeatedly linked and sacred to the *Potnia Thêrôn* (cf. *Od.* 6.102–4).[35] A Homeric Hymn refers to Artemis as the hunter of stags (27.2). Odysseus' successful credentials as a hunter implicitly permit him to approach Kirke, a goddess with an Artemis-like retinue of beasts. The only deer hunted in the *Odyssey* thus makes a fitting introduction to the entire Aiaian sequence.

While the goddesses share many generic epithets,[36] two which are not shared underscore key differences in how Kalypso and Kirke function in the larger plot. Only Kalypso is explicitly "unaging," (5.218), which emphasizes both her seductive offer of immortality to Odysseus, and again aligns her with both Eos, as a marker of time and a deity who offers immortality to chosen lovers, and Demeter, who can nurture select mortals to the same status. Only Kirke is "having many drugs," which underscores her ability to change men into animals and aligns her with Medea, never named in Homeric epic but perhaps hinted at in the *Odyssey*'s multiple allusions to the Argonautic myth.[37]

## WHY ODYSSEUS BRIEFLY EQUATES THE TWO GODDESSES

There are two passages which are inconsistent with the distinctions argued above, ones which blur the differences between the two goddesses. At the beginning of the Apologue Odysseus describes both goddesses as "desiring me as husband," λιλαιομένη πόσιν εἶναι (9.30 of Kalypso, 9.32 of Kirke). The poem consistently depicts Kalypso in just this way, but nowhere portrays Kirke as having the intimate emotional interest in the hero that the formula suggests.[38] In the account of his wanderings that Odysseus narrates to Penelope, he more accurately again describes Kalypso with the same phrase (23.334), but not Kirke. The principal narrator also uses the formula authoritatively of Kalypso at the beginning of the poem (1.15), when first mentioning her and establishing her key characteristics, but never uses it of Kirke.

Is this (9.32) a narrative inconsistency, a formula which accurately applies to Kalypso but is one time carelessly applied to Kirke? Perhaps, though an equally valid interpretation is that Odysseus, the crafty speaker, is, as often, exploiting his immediate audience. Doherty has shown that significant features of the Apologue result from Odysseus' tailoring much of it specifically for Arete, queen of the Phaiakians,[39] singled out both by Nausikaa (6.303–15) and the disguised Athene (7.53–77) as that Phaiakian whose favor is most essential to Odysseus' homecoming Odysseus thus uses his account of his wanderings to win Arete's favor. This tactic is most evident in the lengthy catalog of heroines (11.225–332) which is immediately followed by Arete's declaration that he is her guest (11.338), and by her command that the other nobles should offer him additional gifts (11.339–41). Another detail suggesting Odysseus manipulates his narrative to appeal to Arete as a female audience is the prominence given his interview with his mother, lengthier than his dialogue with Teiresias, the purported motivation for the descent to Hades.

Odysseus, in referring to both Kalypso and Kirke as λιλαιομένη πόσιν εἶναι, can also be seen as making a calculated appeal to his female audience. Odysseus increases his own stature by suggesting that not only one but two goddesses desired him as husband.[40] Emphasizing that he turned both goddesses down can be calculated to increase Arete's own possible intrigue with him, while also reiterating that he has no interest in Nausikaa, whom Alkinoos earlier implicitly offered to him in marriage (7.311–14). Attractive to females though he may be, Odysseus simply wants to return home to his own wife, to whom he has slyly made reference in the dialogue with his mother (11.224).

A similar explanation may lie behind another inconsistency noted above, Kirke's injunction, "no longer against your will remain in my palace" (10.489). Though the poem never depicts Kirke acting in such a manner, it serves Odysseus's purposes to claim that she does. He thereby provokes greater sympathy in his audience by suggesting that he was a captive, and, as before, helps to emphasize his own desirability to the opposite sex before his present female audience, Arete. As such, both inaccuracies (9.32, 10.489) work as convincing details in his subtle manipulation of Arete, for which his brilliantly exploitative speech to Nausikaa (6.149–85), with its careful emphasis on flattery, chastity, piety, and marriage, can be seen as an anticipatory echo.

## ADDITIONAL DIFFERENCES

The *Odyssey* offers further evidence of consistent, thematic differences between the two goddesses in how it structures mention of them in those sections of the narrative in which they are offstage. The poem thoroughly prepares us in advance for Kalypso, emphatically foregrounding her in the beginning of the poem (1.14, 1.51), and continuing to refer to her (4.557) in ways that accurately anticipate her role in the plot. The gods themselves discuss her in two divine councils (1.49 ff, 5.13 ff). Kirke, however, is not mentioned until 8.448, a brief reference that reveals nothing about her role in the poem. Except for Odysseus' brief and, as noted above, inaccurate reference to her at the beginning of the Apologue (9.31), she is not otherwise mentioned until Odysseus lands on Aiaia (10.135).

The stay with Kalypso, or rather its conclusion, occurs in the present time of the narrative and is narrated by the principal narrator, whereas Odysseus' encounter with Kirke occurs in the past and is narrated by the hero. On the other hand, the poem does not describe the first meeting of Odysseus and Kalypso,[41] except in truncated, retrospective accounts (5.130–36, 7.244–66, 12.448–50), whereas we are given the full beginning and ending of his relationship with Kirke.[42] This lacuna, Odysseus' approach to and first seven years on Ogygia, the nature of his relationship with Kalypso, is the largest in our information about Odysseus between Troy and Ithaka.[43] Of Odysseus' many interactions with females on his voyage home, with Kirke, Kalypso, Nausikaa, and Arete, it is only his relationship with Kalypso which is not presented from beginning to end. Furthermore, Kalypso is the only female to receive significant mention far in advance of her actual appearance.

In a final difference, both goddesses represent or articulate important, but distinct, tests for Odysseus. Though both have been seen as embodying temptation, the goddesses pose more crucial tests, tests typical of myths set in the golden age. It is through Kirke's lips that Teiresias' earlier warning against violating Helios' cattle becomes specifically a divine interdiction. Odysseus will uphold the interdiction, thus earning the gods' favor. Though he remains against his will with Kalypso for seven years, his success in obeying divine will at Thrinakia is partly responsible for the considerable aid later given him by Athene and Zeus. Once back on Ithaka, Athene appears to him often and even openly, somewhat reminiscent of the Golden Age relations that used to hold between the Phaiakians and the gods (7.201–5).

As Crane suggests (154), Kalypso can be seen as a reward Odysseus earns for successfully passing the test on Thrinakia, upholding the divine interdiction. According to one vein of Greek myth, one visible in the *Odyssey*'s account of Menelaos' afterlife (4.561–69) and the non-Homeric afterlife of Akhilleus, the hero is rewarded with a paradisiacal existence on an island at the end of the earth, with a female companion along the lines of Helen, Medea, or, in this case, Kalypso. Homeric epic, however, generally ignores a "positive" afterlife in favor of an emphasis on the hero's mortality, an epic trait reaching back at least as far as Gilgamesh. Consistent with the usual Homeric emphasis, then, Odysseus, a much fuller character than Menelaos or Akhilleus, passes this disguised test as well. Outside of Homer, Kalypso might not have been a test, but a deserved reward. In the Genesis creation myth, Adam, if obedient, could have stayed in Eden, and, perhaps, eaten of the tree of life. Adam is driven out of paradise as punishment, whereas Odysseus deliberately chooses to leave. Inside Homeric epic, Kalypso and Ogygia are demonstrably not suitable for Odysseus, and therefore she is a test.

Thus we see considerable thematic differences between Kalypso and Kirke. From a number of perspectives Kalypso is the more distinctive figure, an antitype to the other females Odysseus encounters on his voyage home. But because the audience encounters Kalypso first, sequentially, and because she shares considerable *generic* similarities with Kirke, we have greater difficulty in perceiving how different she is, and perhaps tend to see her as more like Kirke than she really is. The poem seems fashioned with an eye to deceiving us as to how different the Ogygian goddess is. As she departs so consistently from the other powerful females, she is a variation manipulated by the composer against a dominant pattern. In this sense she is "later." That Homer offers us the exception first is not only contrary to his usual practice, by which typically he offers a smaller version incorporating the same themes later stated at greater length, but one of the most unique features of the *Odyssey's* complex architectonics.

## THE FUNCTION OF THE SECOND HALF OF BOOK FIVE

We have established that events on Ogygia are not part of the extended narrative pattern which appears to underlie almost every other episode in the poem. What we have not addressed is why this may be so. I earlier suggested that book 5 in its entirety is the most highly wrought book of the poem. For the book's first episode, Odysseus on Ogygia, I argue that such is the case in the composer's elaborate inversion of the narrative pattern's usual motifs and sequence of events. When the poem's larger structure is considered there is thus a tension that exists between the first episode's very different subject matter and the more dominant matter of the narrative pattern.

Let me here document what might be thought of as the narrative density of book 5's second episode. In a relatively short span of narrative (5.282–493) the composer utilizes a number of special narrative techniques unparalleled in the *Odyssey* in a similar number of verses:

| | |
|---|---|
| 282: | divine intervention: Poseidon's first appearance in the poem |
| 286–90: | Poseidon's soliloquy |
| 299–312: | Odysseus' first soliloquy |
| 328: | first simile, parallel to that at 368 |
| 333: | divine intervention: Leukothea's only appearance in the poem |

| 339–50: | Leukothea's speech to Odysseus |
|---------|--------------------------------|
| 356–64 | Odysseus' second soliloquy |
| 366: | divine intervention: Poseidon again |
| 368–70: | second simile |
| 377–79: | Poseidon, addressed to Odysseus |
| 389: | πλάζετο, line initial, strongly enjambed, the poem's central, definitive instance of the verb, thematically governing its other occurrences |
| 394–98: | third simile; cf. 23.394–97 |
| 408–23: | Odysseus' third soliloquy |
| 426–27: | pivotal contrafactual;[44] Athene intervenes |
| 432–35: | fourth simile |
| 436–37: | second pivotal contrafactual: ὑπὲρ μόρον; Athene intervenes |
| 445–50: | Odysseus' prayer to the river god |
| 465–73: | Odysseus' fourth soliloquy (within 174 lines)[45] |
| 488–91: | fifth simile |
| 491: | divine intervention: Athene sheds sleep on him |

The episode's richness and density of composition have been well noted. Hainsworth makes the following observation: "The extensive elaboration, principally achieved by the introduction of divinities and the use of direct speech, makes it one of the most memorable [episodes] in the *Odyssey*."[46] Fenik has analyzed some patterns in the use of repeated elements (1974: 143–44). I think it is no accident that this section, with its considerable narrative complexity and density, is that part of the poem which both serves as transition into the Skherian sequence and inserts Odysseus into the extended narrative pattern. The seam begins, I suggest, with Poseidon's entrance (5.282), his first appearance in the poem, off the coast of Skheria. Poseidon will serve to conclude the same sequence, again off the coast of Skheria, when, after consultation with Zeus, he destroys the Phaiakian ship (13.162–64).

In that this section of the narrative initiates the Skherian sequence, and introduces Odysseus in the narrative pattern as a whole, the composer expends considerable time and care in the construction of this seam, evident in a number of ways. The seam is particularly marked by the emphatic use of several significant techniques noted in previous chapters. I call particular attention to the poem's key instance of πλάζω (5.389), occurring immediately after Poseidon's second appearance, and his parting threat to Odysseus (5.377–79). As argued in chapter 4, this verb offers a summary depiction of Poseidon directing his wrath against the hero, as described by Zeus in the first divine council (1.75), and suggested in the poem's second line. This particular instance of the verb serves Watkins' *memorative function*, "recalling to the mind of the epic audience what it knows already" about the nature of Odysseus' relationship with Poseidon.

## PIVOTAL CONTRAFACTUALS AND THE SEAM IN BOOK FIVE

Occurring in the backwash of πλάζετο, as it were, are two significant pivotal contrafactuals (5.426–27, 436–37). Though this Homeric narrative technique has been well studied, its tendency to appear at structurally significant plot points remains underappreciated.[47] Typically Homeric epic employs this structure to confer a climax by building a section of narrative up to a point of impending disaster, then averting disaster through having a deity intervene to save an endangered hero. We noted in chapter 4 the crucial role played by a partly parallel passage at the end of the Apologue's first episode:

> And now I would have come home unscathed to the land of my
>      fathers,
>   but as I turned the hook of Maleia, the waves and current
> and the North Wind beat me off course, and drove me on past
>      Kythera.
>   (9.79–81)

It is this passage which first signals the profound difficulties Odysseus will encounter in his homecoming. We now take a closer look at the agency responsible in this passage. The passage comes in the aftermath of a storm which Odysseus supposed to be provoked by Zeus, though Jörgensen's law, and the larger archaic Greek epic tradition, may give us cause to suspect the accuracy of Odysseus' attribution. Elsewhere in the tradition Athene is said to have provoked a storm making the Akhaians' homecoming difficult. In any case, in this passage (9.69–71) Odysseus specifies the agency responsible for driving him off course as κῦμα ῥόος τε, "the waves and current."

Regardless of how we construct the cause and effect relationship between events at Ismaros, they appear to have provoked a god-sent storm as punishment. Intriguingly, in a poem in which Poseidon is the protagonist's chief divine adversary, we have, in κῦμα ῥόος τε, agency squarely set in Poseidon's domain, which resembles the workings of Poseidon himself. Elsewhere Homeric epic sometimes uses κῦμα, in fact, to broadly suggest the larger workings of the sea,[48] as is clearly the case here. The force of the sea, incited by storm, drives (παρέπλαγξεν) Odysseus off course, just as he rounds the Cape of Maleia, complicating an otherwise easy homecoming. Though a common Homeric technique, in this instance the passage emphatically inverts a predominant tendency. Most often Homeric epic employs pivotal contrafactuals to depict a deity intervening to avert harm, to save a favorite hero.[49] In this instance the Poseidon-like agency intrudes to ruin and cause harm to the poem's principal hero.[50] The passage well conveys, with considerable pith, the sea's potential power and savagery. However ambiguous or deliberately vague the workings of that important first storm, which forces the entire Apologue on its indirect course, they suggest the workings of Poseidon, though he would not yet seem to have reason to act against Odysseus in this manner.

What does any of this have to do with Odysseus' approach to Skheria? Just as the pivotal contrafactual at 9.79–81 serves to initiate the problems Odysseus faces in the Aiaian sequence, the composer here employs the same technique, two more pivotal contrafactuals, linked in several ways with the passage at 9.79–81, to help mark the beginning of the Skherian sequence. Shortly after Poseidon leaves, having destroyed Odysseus' raft with his storm, the hero, vulnerable on the open sea, as depicted by the poem's central instance of πλάζετο (5.389), twice faces near disaster attempting to make landfall on Skheria:

> Now as he was pondering this in his heart and spirit,
> meanwhile <u>a great wave</u> carried him against the rough face,
> and there his skin would have been taken off, his bones crushed
>     together,
> had not, the gray-eyed goddess Athene sent him an inkling.
>     (5.424–27)

Note that the agency responsible for Odysseus' troubles at sea is again, as at 9.79–81. κῦμα. On this occasion there is less ambiguity: it is surely the aftereffect of Poseidon himself. The position of κῦμα in the contrafactual is here reversed, however, in accordance with the narrative technique's usual deployment. Here κῦμα is not the intervening agency, as at 9.79–81, but the already present disaster threatening the hero which itself precipitates Athene's divine intervention. The passage thus presents a miniature of the poem's two opposite deities in their typical relationship, as in the opening divine council, with Athene serving to mend the harm Poseidon causes Odysseus.

Just a few lines later, the same dynamic recurs. Having temporarily saved himself by grabbing hold of a rock, Odysseus is now threatened again by the same wave's backwash:

> Now <u>the great wave</u> covered him over,
> and Odysseus would have perished, wretched, beyond his destiny,
> had not the gray-eyed goddess Athene given him forethought.
>    (5.435–37)

Again κῦμα is the agency behind the hero's near disaster; but now Poseidon's harassment threatens to disrupt the course of destiny itself (ὑπὲρ μόρον), not to mention the continuation of the poem itself. This is just the kind of climax which pivotal contrafactuals are designed to threaten, so again Athene counteracts the destructive threat posed by the sea.

At the end of the Skherian sequence, Poseidon, in effect, places a barrier around the Phaiakians, cutting them off from the rest of the world. No longer to ferry people home, Alkinoos and his people are effectively isolated by virtue of their remote location.[51] At the beginning of the same sequence, knowing that Odysseus will be safe, destined so (5.288–89) after having reached Skheria, Poseidon serves to construct something of a barrier between Odysseus and the island, making it as difficult as possible for Odysseus to obtain landfall. The two pivotal contrafactuals function as the final markers of the narrative seam that is the beginning of the Skherian sequence.[52] The two complementary gods, serving polar opposite roles in the poem, play complementary opposite roles in the two pivotal contrafactuals, κῦμα threatening to cause destruction, Athene intervening to avert it.[53]

In a further demonstration of the structural importance of these two pivotal contrafactuals, when Odysseus selectively retells the events of book 5 to Arete (7.241–86) he repeats a version of the second pivotal contrafactual as forming the climax of his hazardous approach to Skheria:

> but there, had I tried to set foot on the land, the rough wave
> would have dashed me against tall rocks in a place that was cheerless,
> had I not backed away, and swam again, until I came
> to a river.
>    (7.278–81)

Though Odysseus is unaware of Athene's role as intervenor, again κῦμα assigned agency for the destructive potential, for the fourth time in a pivotal contractual. It is infrequent in Homeric epic for a pivotal contrafactual to repeat an account earlier given in another pivotal contrafactual. The only other instance is a similarly significant structural juncture, the *Iliad*'s account of Apollo intervening to prevent Patroklos from sacking Troy (*Il.* 16.698–701 and 18.454–56).[54] In his retelling of the same climactic incident off the coast of Skheria, the *Odyssey* perhaps suggests that Odysseus himself is aware of the significance of this boundary crossing. In any case, the repetition should serve to make us aware of the passage's role in the poem's overall architectonics.

To conclude, the second half of book 5 is a particularly complex section of Homeric narrative because of the special task it has been given, both to initiate the Skherian sequence and to insert Odysseus into the extended narrative pattern as a whole. As a consequence, Odysseus' approach to Skheria is by far the most elaborate and dramatic of all the island approaches depicted in the poem. This approach is quite unique in its length, in the difficulties Odysseus faces, and in the complexity of action on the divine plane (one deity trying to make it more difficult, two others offering varying degrees of aid). Having broken through, so to speak, Odysseus, after an immediate sleep, now initiates the narrative pattern's first step, *Odysseus, as earlier prophesied, arrives at an island, disoriented and ignorant of his location.* Only then do the narrative dynamics with which we have been concerned throughout this study get fully under way. The process we have been describing, Odysseus' struggle to break through to Skheria, is surely just what Zeus has in mind in his description in book 5's divine council:

> but he, having suffered many pains on a joined raft
> might reach fertile Skheria on the twentieth day.
> (5.33–34)

Finally, we should note the significant and distinct manner by which book 5 serves to further the *Odyssey*'s agenda of focusing on key ethical concerns. Odysseus, in the book's second episode, is thrust squarely into what we have argued are the poem's central tests, self-control as evident in the ability both to observe a divine interdiction and uphold the gods' behests in the face of adversity. However, as much of the book exists outside of the extended narrative pattern, it here presents very different contexts in which to illustrate these important motifs. We have observed that book 5, as the poem's only episode to include Odysseus and Poseidon onstage together, offers a definitive portrait of their relationship. Odysseus is sorely tested by the god, when vulnerable on the high seas. Throughout the encounter, however, both during and after, Odysseus maintains respectful relations with the gods, even with Poseidon. The book subtly emphasizes his success by presenting us with some neat inversions of the diction elsewhere used to depict divine hostility.

In the middle of the encounter, after Poseidon's blasts have disabled his raft, and briefly hurled him from it, Odysseus receives aid from Leukothea. The goddess helps him both by informing him that it is Poseidon who has caused the turmoil, and by offering him her veil (κρήδεμνον)[55] as a talisman that will keep him safe. Her parting instruction, however, calls for Odysseus, having safely reached land, to throw the veil back into the sea, having turned his face aside as he does so (5.348–50) Though she phrases her admonition as a positive command, the utterance can be interpreted as a divine interdiction, in that the encounter seems quite parallel to a widespread motif seen in the myths of Eurydike, Lot's wife, and Moses, among others.[56] It is a specific form of divine interdiction in which the deity commands a mortal not to look back upon divine workings. The divine interdiction against Pandora's opening the urn is closely related, and compare Apuleius' similar use of Venus' command to Psyche not to open the container which she retrieves from Persephone.

Though Odysseus, at this point, is rightly suspicious of all the gods' motives (5.356–64), this occurring immediately after the clothing that Kalypso had given him has threatened to drown him (5.321), he carefully observes her command. The episode offers parallels with his earlier, delicate negotiations with Kalypso. Leukothea also advises him to surrender his raft and swim for the coast (5.343–44). It is this that makes the hero suspect deception (5.356–57), as he had before with Kalypso (5.173–79), in his very first speech in the poem. As with Kalypso, he makes a considered response to the delicate dilemma presented by the necessity of obeying divine will. He will leave the raft, but only when its timbers (which he himself had cut and joined) no longer hold together. Having inserted his own modicum of control within the divine imperative, Odysseus is able to observe the goddess's behests when, after the raft does fail to hold together; and he does reach the shore by swimming, he will hurl the veil behind him into the sea (5.459–62).

However, before he can accomplish this, book 5 offers another significant index of Odysseus' relations with the gods in his interaction with the unnamed river god. Asking for pity, and declaring himself a fugitive from Poseidon, Odysseus proclaims himself a suppliant, having arrived at the river's "current" (5.449: σόν τε ῥόον). The river god immediately halts his current, ὁ δ᾽ αὐτίκα ἑὸν ῥόον, ἔσχε δὲ κῦμα(5.451). Though ῥόον and κῦμα are, perhaps, prosaic enough words, we have noted that they figure prominently in the *Odyssey*'s vocabulary to express Poseidon's hostility against Odysseus. In the pivotal contrafactual which drove Odysseus and crew off of the map in the Apologue, κῦμα ῥόον τε (9.80) are the responsible agency. In all three pivotal contrafactuals describing the force of Poseidon's destructive storms in book 5, κῦμα (5.425, 435, 7.278) is the specific agency singled out by both the principal narrator and Odysseus himself to depict the god acting on his wrath against Odysseus. The river god, then, in a neat inversion of these terms, expresses his relation to Odysseus by removing the destructive potential from the same entities.

Book 5 thus concludes with Odysseus, having displayed considerable self-control and piety, rewarded by a deity for doing so. It is worth emphasizing that the poem shows us this side of Odysseus first, before engaging him with any of the abusive bands of young men, all on their varying courses of reckless, impious action. At the same time, then, that book 5 inserts Odysseus into the narrative pattern, it firmly depicts in him the very qualities which will enable him to survive precisely where the three bands of young men will fail, due to their own recklessness.

## Notes

1. E.g., Page 70ff. Cf. Hainsworth's comments 251–52. I will not be concerned with book 5's divine council, except in passing. It is unfortunate, in my view, that so many discussions of the fifth book have focused on the opening council to the comparative neglect of the other episodes.

2. See Hainsworth 253, especially, and 260–61 for a brief survey of various opinions.

3. Hainsworth (250) notes that book 5 essentially contains two episodes: Odysseus' departure from Ogygia (1–261), and his shipwreck at Skheria (262–493).

4. Pivotal contrafactuals are past contrary-to-fact conditions in which the order of the clauses is reversed, e.g., "And now X would have occurred had not Y intervened." See Louden 1993b.

5. E.g., Wilamovitz, Scully, Cook 1992: 249–50, Nagler 1996.

6. Exceptions include Woodhouse 46–53, Stanford 1961: 47–49, Segal 1968: 421–24, Austin 149–53, Marquardt 243–46, and Olson 57, 178, 181.

7. See Crane 31, for a summary of relevant research. The issue of priority is itself rooted in nineteenth-century analyst notions of Homeric composition.

8. Nagler 1996, Crane passim.

9. On the motif in *Beowulf*, see Creed.

10. Though at 12.390 we are told of another possible visit to Ogygia by Hermes.

11. In a further indication of the unique status of the Ogygian section, unlike all three sequences of the narrative pattern, events on Ogygia are not narrated from start to finish. We enter in present time only at the end of the section, lacking a full account of the beginning and earlier stages of the relationship between Kalypso and Odysseus. I return to this topic below.

12. The only exception to this is the strange retrospective mention by Kirke of Hermes' much earlier visit to her (10.330–32). He apparently appeared as himself, however, not in the youthful form that the pattern features.

13. On the *Odyssey's* use of the feasting type-scene see Foley 1990: 265–76, Reece 1993 passim. On the type-scene as common outside of Homeric epic see especially *Beowulf*.

14. See, most recently, Olson 181: "The result is an affair powerful and satisfying enough to detain Odysseus on Aiaia for a year and make him forget everything else." This is reading a considerable amount into the text.

15. Segal 1968: 424; cf. Doherty 1995: 124 n. 84.

16. In not desiring Odysseus as her husband, Kirke parallels Arete, one multiform of the powerful female figure. Both other multiforms, Nausikaa and Penelope, however, do have a marital interest in Odysseus.

17. Cf. Stanford 1961: 47–49, Segal 1968: 421, 424.

18. The injunction parallels her earlier behest 10.457, 10.489. See Olson 57: "Unlike Kalypso, Kirke offered no overt resistance to being abandoned by her mortal lover."

19. See Clay 1994: 45 on Odysseus being under no compulsion to stay with Kirke.

20. Kahane argues (135) that, as her name is terminal in the two formulas describing her waterlogged clothing (5.312, 5.372) the positioning serves as part of a pattern that reinforces the threat she represents.

21. Nagler 1996: 148: "The traditional phrase theos audeessa invokes the life-saving ability of this goddess to report verities of the mantic world and thus induce or at least indicate the hero's return to life and light."

22. Cf. Odysseus' subsequent characterization of Kirke's warnings as θεσφαθ᾽ (12.155).

23. Cf. Alkinoös' remark, his plural including Arete, who is by his side, τὸν ξεῖνον πέμπωμεν ἐὴν ἐς πατρίδα γαῖαν (13.52).

24. Marquardt 244. However, at 12.389–90, Odysseus notes that Kalypso said Hermes told her about the divine council between Zeus and Helios (12.374–88), an apparent contradiction of Hermes' and her remarks about his not having been to Ogygia before. On which see Heubeck 140.

25. Such a dynamic lies behind Odysseus' punishment of the suitors; cf. most of Theseus' six exploits on the road to Athens, the Argonauts' encounter with Amykos, king of the Bebrykians, who forces ξεῖνοι to box with him (Argonautica, 2.1–97), and the like.

26. For discussions on the accuracy of δολόεσσα see Nagler 1996:147 and Dirlmeier 21–22, 24, who suggests Kalypso inherits the quality from ὀλοόφρων Atlas.

27. Boedeker 67: "The tradition of the mortal lover of the Dawn-goddess is an old one; in Greek epic it is surely the most obvious aspect of Eos' mythology." The Odyssey mentions three of her lovers/victims, Tithonos (5.1), Orion (5.121), and Kleitos (15.250).

28. Hainsworth 254. Cf. Slatkin 29–30: "Eos brings the day into being: in a sense she creates time.... As she brings the day into existence, and, in effect, controls time, time controls the lives of men, by aging them; yet the goddess herself is unaging, ever-renewed.... From the human point of view, she is not simply immortal; she is the agent of the process by which the meaning of mortality is fulfilled." Kahane 131: "Eos is a personification of heroic time."

29. See Kirk 1984: 119 for a complete list of the many dawn formulas available, and their occurrences. See Austin 67–68 for a brief discussion of selectivity behind their deployment.

30. On Aiaia, Kirke and Odysseus make love immediately after the oath is sworn, whereas on Ogygia, Kalypso makes her last attempt at persuasion after the oath.

31. Demeter nurtures Demophon, ἔτρεφεν (235), intending to make him immortal and ageless, καὶ κέν μιν ποίησεν ἀγήρων τ᾽ ἀθάνατόν τε (242) ἀθάνατόν κέν τοι καὶ ἀγήραον ἤματα πάντα (260). On the last expression, see Clay 1991–92.

32. Aphrodite and Anchises, Aphrodite and Adonis, Thetis and Peleus, and so on. See Sowa's comparison (39) of the Hymn to Demeter with the Hymn to Aphrodite: "Both tell of a fertility goddess who wants to make a man immortal, is balked in the attempt, and brings him increase instead."

33. Clay 1989: 179 n. 91 notes Artemis' unique interest in punishing certain negative behavior: "The only divinity who punishes unchaste behavior seems to be Artemis."

34. A. Lang 275–84, Patroni 321 ff, Christou 179 ff:

35. Arans and Shea 383.

36. Both are ἀθάνατος / ἀθανάτη, αὐδήεσσα, δεινή, δῖα, δολόεσσα, ἐϋπλόκαμος, θεά / θεός, νύμφη, and πότνια Dee 16, 106–10, provides a useful summary.

37. Stanford 1962: 424 suggests 10.108, 135, 11.235, 12.3–4, 59, and 70–72 as possibly alluding to the Argonautic saga. In that her knowledge of drugs is what enables her to change men into beasts, the epithet, however indirectly, also points to her affinities with Artemis.

38. Woodhouse is one of the few commentators to note the inaccuracy of the description: "The moment he expressed a desire to be gone, Kirke was entirely willing.... There is thus evidently no ground whatever for the bare-faced assertion of Odysseus—'and in like manner Kirke restrained me in her halls, guileful one of Aia, eager that I should her husband be.' No such proposal was ever made by her" (50). Cf. Hogan 199: "His aim is to obtain homeward passage, and he may be stretching the facts just a bit in order to impress Alcinoos."

39. Doherty 1995: 22, 67, 78, 92–93, 99, 191n, 103–4, 112. See also the discussion above in chapter 1.

40. Cf. Woodhouse 50: "Odysseus for his own glorification willfully misrepresents her [Kirke], by ascribing to her a desire that belonged to Kalypso alone."

41. Cf. Woodhouse 51.

42. A description of the middle of their relationship is missing, but only because it was, apparently, uneventfully static.

43. See Felson-Rubin (46) on the depiction of their relationship as given only retrospectively.

44. On which see Louden 1993b, Lang 1989, Morrison 1991 and 1992, and de Jong. Morrison and de Jong do not, however , discuss instances in the *Odyssey*.

45. Of Odysseus's six soliloquies in the poem, four occur in this short span (elsewhere at 13.198 and 20.17).

46. Hainsworth 279. Cf. 251 (also of book 5's second episode): "It is necessary to recognize the methods by which the epic poet seeks to compose a grand and impressive scene. He seeks quality through quantity, and doubles and trebles the hero's woes."

47. On this see especially the discussions in Louden 1993b of *Il.* 11.504–7 (185) and *Od.* 9.79–81 (186, 196–97).

48. See Cunliffe's second grouping of passages sub κῦμα.

49. See Louden 1993b: 184 n.8 for totals and a list of the relevant passages. Milton, who patterns his own use of the same narrative technique in *Paradise Lost* on Homer's example, closely follows Homeric practice in this regard, having a deity intervene through pivotal contrafactuals to avert disaster in all but one instance. On which see Louden 1996b.

50. The only other instance out of sixty-one pivotal contrafactuals in the Homeric corpus in which a deity intrudes to cause harm is *Il.* 18.454–56, in which Thetis describes how Apollo caused Patroklos' death.

51. The Argonautic Clashing Rocks are essentially the same motif (*Od.* 12.65–72), never again to allow ships to sail through.

52. They are the two closest pivotal contrafactuals in the entire Homeric corpus. See again Louden 1993b: 183 n. 5 for a complete list.

53. The Beowulf poet uses the same construction, pivotal contrafactuals, to highlight his hero's underwater battles with monsters (1054–58, 1550–54, 1655–58). On which see Louden 1996c.

54. Louden 1993b: 194–95. The passage constitutes a significant structural turning point because it leads directly to Patroklos' death, subsequently prompting Akhilleus to reenter battle.

55. Nagler 1974: chap. 2 explores the resonances of this word in Homeric epic, though I do not agree with his assertion that in this passage "the poet makes temptation suggestively present in Ino's relinquishing of her veil" (47).

56. Hainsworth notes that "the injunction usually applies to dealing with chthonic or malevolent powers" (283) and cites parallels in Thompson 331–33.

MARK BUCHAN

# In the Beginning Was Proteus

Odysseus' encounters with the Phaeacians and Cyclopes are traumatic for both species, and Odysseus is the agent who produces that trauma. A consequence is that both species begin to desire for the first time. Both stories also interrogate the related problems of beginnings and endings—that is, the general problems involved with symbolic systems of classification and their ultimate inadequacy. These themes recur, in a more abstract way, in a too rarely discussed episode of the *Odyssey*: the encounter between Menelaus and Proteus. In the case of the Phaeacians and Cyclopes, the intervention of Odysseus is a turning point in their civilizations; it signifies their emergence as properly human societies that are forced to confront their own finitude. In the story of Proteus—the god who has "first" embedded in his own proper name and yet who seems to be a being without limit, a series of endless *tropoi* or masks—the intervention of Menelaus will also radically change his conception of the universe. There is also the shared theme of deception. Odysseus deceived both the Phaeacians and Cyclopes, even as they both were species who believed themselves to be impervious to deception. In the case of Proteus, too, an infallible truth-teller seems to get deceived. But how?

The story of Proteus' deception in *Odyssey* 4 puts great emphasis on counting.[1] Proteus regularly counts his seals, and he is tricked when his system of counting betrays him: he is quite unable to account for the

From *The Limits of Heroism: Homer and the Ethics of Reading*: 50–71 © 2004 by the University of Michigan.

disguised presence of Menelaus and his three companions. I will soon argue
that the trick depends on a specific mode of counting, in particular how
Proteus counts from four to five. But before interpreting the manner in
which Eidothea tricks this obsessive counter, this "unerrring" old man of the
sea, it is worth trying to provide some context for the problems of counting.
Within the Homeric poems, what does the sequence 3-4-5 suggest?

Leonard Muellner has provided an answer from an analysis
of the *Iliad*. In that poem, he argues, the passage from three to four
symbolically defines the difference between man and god. To try and fail
to do something three times remains a normal, human pattern of failure;
to make a fourth attempt is to move into a shady realm between god and
man. Consider the transgressive assault by Patroclus on Troy. Patroclus
has attacked the wall of Troy three times and is embarking on his fourth
attempt when Apollo forces him back (16.705 ff.). Later, his fourth attack
produces his doom.

> Patroklos sprang upon the Trojans with evil intent,
> three times then he sprang upon them, <u>equal to rushing Ares</u>,
> shrieking terribly, and three times he slew nine men.
> But when he was rushing forward that fourth time <u>equal to the *daimon*</u>
> then the end of life rose up before you, Patroklos.
>     (16.783–87)[2]

Muellner notes that this fourth attempt is taboo and that Patroclus' "final
transgression is across the line that Apollo guards between mortals and
Ares."[3] The attack is therefore a fundamental challenge to the order that
guarantees the separation of men from gods, and Muellner goes on to argue
that this transgression is linked to the meaning of *menis*, the anger that is the
theme of the *Iliad*. For divine *menis* is appealed to in the course of the poem
when this order is threatened, when taboos are violated.

But though this passage from the third to the taboo fourth assault
is certainly significant, it is worth lingering over this moment of failed
transition. For in punishing the fourth assault, what remains truly taboo (and
untouched) is the possibility of a fifth attack. If Patroclus becomes equal to
the god on the fourth attempt, he is clearly not yet a god; he temporarily
takes a god's place, but this is not yet permanent identity with a god. The
narrative establishes an order through a prohibition: no humans are allowed
beyond three assaults, and if any should go as far as a fourth, they will be
punished. But its prohibition also creates a question even as it stimulates a
desire: what would happen if Apollo were not to intervene, if a human could
reach five?

If the sequence 3-4-5 is crucial to the key episodes of the *Iliad*, it is equally significant for the narrative structure of the *Odyssey*. For though we might expect the opening books to bring our attention to the twenty-year absence of Odysseus, we find out instead about the courtship of Penelope. Antinous tells Telemachus that Penelope has been frustrating the desires of the suitors for three years already, and it is soon to be the fourth (*Od.* 2.89–90). When we compare these words to Muellner's analysis of the taboo fourth assault of Patroclus, we can see how Antinous' words have a darker sense to which he remains quite blind. The narrative hints that three years is at the limit of what is permissible and that the fourth year will be a crucial one, either bringing disaster (if they cannot survive it) or ultimate happiness.

This number sequence has already played a role in the book, which opens with a speech of Aegyptius, who asks why an assembly has been called after so many years. We are provided with a brief biography of Aegyptius. He has four sons; two remain at home, one is a suitor, and the fourth went to Troy with Odysseus. An element of tragedy is introduced as we are told that his fourth son has already died, eaten in the cave of the Cyclops. The narrative emphasizes that it is the lost, fourth son that continues to haunt the thoughts of Aegyptius.

> Even so, he could not forget the lost one. He grieved and mourned
>   for him,
> and it was in tears for him, now, that he stood forth and addressed
>   them.
> (*Od.* 2.23–24)

It is the fourth son, the one that is missing and out of reach, who motivates his actions. Further, Aegyptius' feelings toward this son are characterized by a nagging uncertainty. For though he is not present, as his other sons are, Aegyptius does not know whether this absence is permanent—that is, whether he has died. His fourth son is, for Aegyptius, uneasily between life and death. The possibility that he might be alive fuels his fantasy of a paternal happiness with all of his sons alive alongside him: this fourth son is the gateway to a world without loss. There is thus once more a parallel with Patroclus, whose desire for a fourth, transgressive assault is also a desire to attain something that is out of reach, and for that very reason, his desire pushes him on further in an effort to attain it. In the *Iliad*, Apollo guards the limit beyond the fourth assault and punishes his desire with his death. In the opening of *Odyssey* 2, the narrator informs us of the ultimate futility of Aegyptius' desire by telling us of his son's death at the hands of the Cyclops. His desire for the complete safety of his children becomes an impossible desire, and Odysseus' journey to the cave of the Cyclops makes it so.

The reference to Aegyptius' son's death in the Cyclops' cave brings further relevant associations. Critics have long been keen to point out parallels between the transgressive behavior of the suitors and the actions of the Cyclops. Both pervert the laws of *xenia*; both indulge in socially prohibited forms of eating.[4] Both the Cyclops and the suitors seem to believe in the possibility of a limitless indulgence of their desires, an indulgence that fails to respect the fundamental *Iliadic* limit. The Cyclops eats transgressively because he can imagine no one who could regulate his behavior and thus impose a limit on it—he believes the Cyclopes to be better than Zeus. In book 2, Eurymachus not only threatens that the suitors will eat all of Odysseus' possessions; he imagines a permanent deferral of the only thing that could stop them—the marriage of Penelope.

> ... and his possessions will wretchedly be eaten away, there will not
> be compensation, ever, while she makes the Achaians put off
> marriage with her, while we, awaiting all this, all our days
> quarrel for the sake of her excellence ...
>     (*Od.* 2.203–6)

Both the Cyclops and the suitors live in a fantasy world where there are no limits to their ongoing enjoyment. In this context, Odysseus' careful choice of four men to help him blind the Cyclops, while he himself counts as the fifth, might assume greater significance.[5] The narrative, by emphasizing that the taboo fourth time has just arrived for the suitors and the Cyclops, suggests that the end of their indulgences is at hand.

The numerological question of the significance of the sequence 3-4-5 within the poem thus spills into the question of what it means to desire in a human as against a nonhuman way. It has long been recognized that the problem of the economy of desire, of what can and cannot be desired in the controlled economy of the *oikos*, is a central theme of the odyssey. In trying to understand the deception of Proteus, it will prove helpful to keep in mind this problematic economy produced by the creation of limits and their transgression.

Let us briefly recount the Proteus story. Driven off course to Egypt, Menelaus is uncertain about how to continue his *nostos*, until Eidothea suggests that her father, Proteus, will give him directions.[6] The catch is that Menelaus must first capture this polytropic figure. As luck would have it, Eidothea herself has a suggestion as to how he should go about it.

At the time when the sun has gone up to bestride the middle of
    heaven,
then the ever-truthful Old Man of the Sea will come out of the water
under the blast of the West Wind, circled in a shudder of darkening
water, and when he comes out he will sleep, under hollow caverns,
and around him seals, those darlings of the sea's lovely lady,
sleep in a huddle, after they have emerged from the gray sea,
giving off the sour smell that comes from the deep salt water.
There I will take you myself when dawn shows and arrange you
orderly in your ambush; you must choose from your companions
those three who are your best beside your strong-benched vessels.
Now I will tell you all the devious ways of this old man.
First of all he will go among his seals and count them,
but after he has reviewed them all and noted their number,
he will lie down in their midst, like a herdsman among his
    sheepflocks.
Next, as soon as you see that he is asleep, that will be
the time for all of you to use your strength and your vigor,
and hold him there while he strives and struggles hard to escape you.
    (*Od.* 4.400–416)

The tale is thematically charged. It involves not just any deception but one that disrupts the relationship between a single leader and his herd of seals—a motif that will recur in the *Apologoi*, when Odysseus' relationship to his companions, whose numbers come up inexorably through each death-filled encounter, is under the spotlight. Equally intriguing is the parallel between Proteus and the protean Odysseus. For Proteus, like Odysseus, is polytropic; when attacked, he has the ability to alter his appearance in order to scare off his attacker (by turning into an array of wild animals: a lion, a bear, etc.). Yet polytropic Odysseus seems to be the deceiver par excellence, while Proteus is a victim of deceit in *Odyssey* 4. If the similarity of these episodes of trickery invites a comparison between the polytropic characters, we are left with a troubling question: what is it that differentiates Odysseus from Proteus, deceiver from deceived?

Let us look more closely at the trick. Menelaus and his men seem to elude the grasp of Proteus because Eidothea hides them with sealskins, a scheme in turn made possible by the ambrosia she gives them to help mitigate the terrible stench of the animals (*Od.* 4.445 ff.). Proteus would then be fooled because he counts Menelaus and his companions as seals, not humans. However, this conventional interpretation fails to account for the emphasis the story puts not only on numbers but on the manner in which numbers are assigned; for Proteus always counts his seals, and Eidothea is careful to specify that Menelaus choose three companions. This suggests that even if Proteus fails to recognize Menelaus and his men because of their disguises, we still have a more basic difficulty. If Proteus is careful to count his seals as they come out of the water, why does he not notice that there are four extra, the disguised Menelaus and his men? He must be a peculiarly bad counter, which would seem to be a strange attribute of a god who is supposedly infallible. Or is it so strange?

Rather than take Proteus' infallibility for granted, we should perhaps pay more attention to the manner of his arithmetic and to Eidothea's ability to manipulate it. First, we should note that Proteus counts in a very specific way, highlighted by Eidothea.

> First of all he will go among his seals and count them,
> but after he has reviewed them all and noted their number,
> he will lie down in their midst, like a herdsman among his
>     sheepflocks.[7]
> (*Od.* 4.411–13)

Proteus counts in fives (πεμπάσσεται).[8] When he calculates the presence/absence of his group of seals, he does so not by cumulatively calculating their number (nor, despite his persistent counting, do we ever find out how many seals he has) but, rather, by ensuring that they make up a multiple of five. Our brief discussion of the transgression of Patroclus suggests that the form of his counting may have a wider significance: to reach five within the Homeric poems means to reach the realm of the gods, and thus Proteus counts in a perfectly divine manner. But the form of counting also points toward an obvious way to trick Proteus: if five seals are added to his flock (or, indeed, if five are taken away), his form of counting would not help him detect this. If Proteus is infallible, it is because he always thinks he accounts for all his seals. But this is because of the narrowness of his perspective rather than any particular wisdom. He is a scientist and infallible knower who never questions the prejudices that govern his counting inquiries. Yet this is not the whole of the trick Eidothea uses. Indeed, if she did simply take five seals away, Proteus would be none the wiser. Instead, she engineers something that will be much more traumatic for him: she specifies that Menelaus must choose only three other companions to join him.

Let us look at the lines that highlight Proteus' counting of the mixture of seals and disguised seals after Eidothea's addition.

> At noon the Old Man came out of the sea and found his well-fed
> seals, and went about to them all, and counted their number,

and we were among the first he counted; he had no idea
of any treachery. Then he too lay down among us.
  (*Od.* 4.450–53)

What is important in these lines is the explicit pun on the Greek verbs for
"lying" and "counting," a pun noted by commentators.[9] It is impossible
to tell the aorist middle form of λέγω, meaning "count," from the aorist
of λέχομαι, meaning "lie down." But what is the significance of the pun?
Proteus continues his normal process of counting his seals in groups of five,
but this time something important has changed; he now finds out that there
are four extra seals. He is now at the liminal point reached by Patroclus in
his *aristeia* (his conventional display of martial power)—and emphasized by
Muellner—poised between the human and the divine. Proteus, however,
reaches this in-between realm from the reverse direction. Patroclus moved
from the realm of mortals (three attacks) toward immortality (five attacks)
and was killed because of his taboo fourth assault; he never reached the
immortal realm of five. By contrast, Proteus "lives," as it were, in the
immortal realm of five, where his ability to count correctly is a sign of both
his infallibility and, consequently, his divinity. He is only forced to enter
the liminal realm of four because of Eidothea's trick.

    At this point in the story, as Proteus counts four extra seals, Menelaus,
as narrator, intervenes to insist that Proteus suspects nothing. But because
Proteus believes himself to be an infallible god, for whom his own deception is
inconceivable, he needs to find another explanation for the apparently missing
fifth seal. Here, we can make use of the pun on λέχομαι. All translators agree in
translating his action after the trick as "he himself lies down." But we can also
activate the possibility of understanding λέχομαι as the aorist middle of λέγω:
Proteus, forced to confront the missing seal that punctures his perfect world of
fives, counts himself (λέκτο καὶ αὐτός). Herein lies the subtlety of Eidothea's
trick: she understands in advance that Proteus, faced with the problem of a
missing seal, will simply count himself. When confronted with a gap in his
universe, Proteus takes himself as (fetish) object to fill up that gap.[10]

    This episode is thus much more than a joke on Proteus' poor
arithmetic. For what is at stake is how human Homeric subjects are
constituted. The story displays a pattern that we have seen occurring in
Odysseus' encounters with the Cyclopes and Phaeacians; we witness the
moment when an unerring, certain, godlike figure—in this case, Proteus—
begins to doubt himself for the first time. The episode starts with Menelaus
seeking out help from the all-knowing Proteus; but after the trick, Proteus
is the helpless one, captured against his will and utterly ignorant of which
of the gods have plotted against him.

We might chart out some consequences of this moment of doubt by looking at the way the episode complicates the relationship between the human subject and the world of objects. First, Proteus treats himself as an object, as something to be counted. Proteus himself is thus uneasily caught between his status as counting subject and that of object of his own counting—a status that formerly belonged to the seals alone: He is thus split, and this split will have important consequences for his relationship to the world structured by his counting—in this episode, signified by the herd of seals. Before the trick, we can presume that the unerring old man of the sea had never given a second thought to either the number of his seals (presuming his counting system to be infallible) or his relations with the seals as a group. But his new status as doubter invites us (and Proteus) to reconsider this relationship. What is the relationship of this doubting Proteus to his construction of the world around him, exemplified by his seals, if he can now locate himself, as object, in the world around him? Here, we can see the outlines of an ideological problem at the heart of much of the Homeric poems. What must occur for a group to be constructed symbolically as a group (say, the Greeks at Troy or the companions of Odysseus), and what happens if the master of that group doubts his mastery?

To clarify Proteus' position and this ideological problematic, we can turn to a theoretical problem within structural linguistics. Though a contemporary problem, it can provide an important tool for helping us to understand the complexities of deception within the *Odyssey*. Since Saussure, the problem of language's construction of meaning has depended on the relation between signifier and signified. How can we ever be sure that any signifier refers to any signified? For if we acknowledge (as we must) that the process of meaning is inexhaustible, that there will always be the possibility of the arrival of another signifier that will retroactively change all that went before, are we not confronted with an endless deferral of sense? A certain structuralism evades the problem by focusing attention on an arbitrarily frozen moment. By concentrating on an idealized moment in time, a closed system of signifiers is created. A signifier can then be linked to a signified precisely insofar as all the other (now finite) signifiers do not refer to it. Yet this solution, flirted with by Saussure, does nothing to evade the crucial problem. Without such a totalizing system, there can be no guarantee that any signifier refers to its signified, yet such a system is by definition impossible; for there can always be another signifier, changing all that went before.[11] In Lacanian terms, the question is one of the limits of the symbolic order. For if the symbolic has no limit, then we would seem to be forced to admit the impossibility of sense. Yet any external limit to the symbolic is equally unsatisfactory, as it denies the obvious: the possibility of another external limit, ad infinitum.

Lacan answers the problem by admitting the impossibility of any external limit to the symbolic; but he nevertheless suggests that an internal limit can be posited. If it is impossible to conceive of an external limit, it is possible (paradoxically) to conceive this very impossibility. Herein lies the internal limit to the symbolic, which provides us with the Lacanian concept of "suturing."

> Suture, in brief, supplies the logic of a paradoxical function whereby a supplementary element is *added* to the series of signifiers in order to mark the lack of a signifier that could close the set. The endless slide of signifiers (hence a deferral of sense) is brought to a halt and allowed to function "as if" it were a closed set through the inclusion of an element that acknowledges the impossibility of closure.[12]

This paradoxical function creates the conditions of possibility for what Lacan calls a master signifier. A master signifier (which gives "illegitimate" retroactive sense to the chain of signifiers) is an external element that forcibly grafts signifier onto signified.[13] Yet any master signifier is logically parasitic on this prior lack of such a signifier. This ensures that the master signifier must be an external impostor (its mastery can only work in the mode of "as if "—there is no true "master," only someone playing the role of a master); this in turn preserves the possibility of one more signifier. This logical possibility is precisely what guarantees a constitutive gap between signifier and signified, and it is in the gap between signifier and signified that Lacan locates the subject. This gap creates the breathing space for the subject by providing it with a certain freedom from the signifier. The subject is, for Lacan, that for which no signifier can account. In our Homeric story, too, it is the emergence of something that cannot be accounted for—Proteus' loss of a seal—that will introduce the god to the world of subjectivity. How? The loss of a seal opens up an empty place in the universe for Proteus, into which he is now able to project an alienated version of himself through language—that is, with signifiers. Before such a place existed, there was no possibility of Proteus existing as a subject, because his system of counting went on automatically without any subjective involvement on his part. Without this gap, there was no space available for Proteus to refer to himself. Proteus was nothing more than his infallible system of counting and thus was not a subject at all.

A clarification of Lacan's notion of human alienation in the symbolic can be of help here.

> A metaphor [for the desiring subject] often used by Lacan is that of something *qui manque à sa place*, which is out of place, not where it should be or usually is; in other words, something which is missing. Now for something to be missing, it must first have been present and localized; it must first have had a place. And something only has a place within an ordered system—space–time coordinates or a Dewey decimal book classification, for example—in other words, some sort of symbolic structure.[14]

For Lacan, the subject cannot simply be equated with a symbolic structure (e.g., language), because the symbolic structure is emphatically alien to the subject: the subject exceeds the language that tries to classify it. The symbolic structure, made up of a series of signifiers, thus can try to represent the subject, but it can never completely succeed, because all it can do—in its effort to pin the subject down—is refer to other signifiers. Any notion of something "missing" is necessarily dependent on a symbolic structure, and this is a sign of a fundamental impotence that haunts the structure; when inside the symbolic, there is no way to directly reach the world outside of it. One can only refer to it by means of further signifiers that is, within the terms of the structure itself. Nevertheless, the subject is inconceivable without such a symbolic structure; only an ordered system allows one to determine what is missing, and this gap in the structure creates a place for the subject. This helps explain Lacan's definition of the subject as that which one signifier represents for another signifier. We can relate this to Proteus; any future counting done by Proteus will occur against the background of this empty place opened up by the loss of one of his seals. His future counting will be part of an attempt to account for this empty place opened up by the loss of the seal. This empty place provides Proteus with the breathing room for self-exploration; it is also a place from which the coherence of the counting system itself can always be questioned.

Before the trick, Proteus, as a god, seems not to have been pinned down by space–time coordinates. His perfect polytropy defied spatial limitation, and his immortality defied temporal limitation. Thus, the effect of the trick played on him is to introduce him to limits—a symbolic system. Before the trick, he lived in a world that was impervious to change, and this itself seems to be suggested by the way Eidothea can predict his behavior. She *knows* he will come out of the sea at midday and count his seals, because he *always* comes out of the sea at midday and counts his seals. Proteus lives in a static universe, where the same thing happens over and over again, and this coincides with his perfect counting system; in his world free of spatiotemporal limits, he proves to himself again and again that he has the same number of seals.

It is perhaps now possible to see why the tale of Proteus opens up a crucial ideological question. What is at stake is the manner in which groups are constituted—in this case, what is at issue is the relationship of the seals to their leader, Proteus. The significant difference lies between a group that is constituted by its allegiance to a real, empirical leader and a group that is constituted by nothing other than the members' self-difference—that is, a group whose center is nothing, a void, the surplus element marking the lack of a signifier. The argument here has important ramifications, for what is at stake is the possibility of the critique of the violence imposed by the arbitrariness of numeration. I have so far concentrated on the counter, Proteus, and what is at stake for him in his counting dilemma; I now shift focus and consider the creatures counted. For humans, any constitution of a group as a group suggests some sort of acceptance (whether conscious or unconscious) of one's inclusion in the group, of being counted, and thus of the legitimacy of the system that counts you. Questioning this legitimacy is a classic first step toward enlightenment. We need go no further for illustration than the ideological dilemma faced by Achilles in the *Iliad*. He not only confronts Agamemnon; in Book 9, he questions the legitimacy of the shared ideological logic that links heroes together, the "heroic code." He thus rejects the group identity that he now believes to have been pushed on him against his will.

In the story of Proteus, counting itself assigns an identity to the seals and makes them a part of a group. Because those counted in this tale are animals, it might seem unnecessary (even absurd) to pose the question of the legitimacy *for them* of the system of Proteus' counting. After all, as animals, they are in no position rationally to question it. But as I have suggested, the narrative already puts under question the well-known structuralist divide between humans and gods by focusing on the moment when a divine being becomes subject to human doubt. Could it not also put into question the divide between humans and animals? If a god can become human by the introduction of doubt, the failure to make use of this doubt can reduce a human to the status of an animal in a herd. By an unthinking acceptance of group status, human subjects would seem to forfeit the quality that defines them as subjects. The parallel between Odysseus and Proteus is therefore deeper. Not only are they polytropic, but the ultimate sign of their cunning is their ability to gather together their subordinates—seals in the first case, human companions in the second. On this reading, the tale of Proteus would be an effort to demystify the relationships between people by redescribing them as a relationship between a god and seals. In Lacanian terms, the relationship of signs to conscious thought is the mystical world of ideology and mistaken meaning. The apparent harmony of the relationship between Proteus and his seals would thus be indicative of the way ideology legitimizes hierarchy and would give us a parallel to the apparent harmony at work between Odysseus and his men. But when we read the tale as illustrating the relationship between signifiers and the subject, we have a glimpse into the underlying structure of this imaginary ideological relationship. Proteus is an idiotic, senseless counter, and the seals are victims of this idiocy. So too Odysseus' men are ultimately attached to the idiocy of Odysseus' authority.[15]

So let us turn to the relationship of Proteus to his seals, exploring it within the terms of reference of structural linguistics already outlined. In the tale, the real, empirical seals function as referents; the concept "seal" functions as the signified; and the numbers allocated to the concept "seal" function as signifiers. The obvious reading of the deception would be to explain it in terms of a confusion of sign (signifier and signified combined) and referent. Thus, Proteus would be fooled because his concept of a seal is disrupted by Menelaus' disguise: he counts as seals people who are not really seals.[16] However, in my interpretation, this disguise functions as a way to reveal that something more basic is at stake: the relation between signifier and signified.[17]

The protean Proteus is evidently a figure who upholds the possibility of one more signified: but insofar as he is perfectly protean, a figure of pure change, Proteus does not recognize the internal limit of the symbolic, which is the only way of ensuring the possibility of meaning. Eidothea's trick stages the moment when his system of counting fails, when a gap emerges between signifier and signified. But how does this trick affect Proteus? The first significant moment arrives when Proteus counts his seals: οὐδέ τι θυμῶι / ὠίσθη δόλον εἶναι· ἔπειτα δὲ λέκτο καὶ αὐτός. When he realizes a seal is missing,[18] when he finds a signifier with no signified corresponding to it, he tries to close up the gap with another signified. But the only signified available is himself; Proteus thus counts himself for the first time.[19]

It is tempting to see this as his first moment of self-consciousness. But the text emphasizes that he remains unaware that this is a trick at all: οὐδέ τι θυμῶι / ὠίσθη δόλον εἶ ναι. Proteus' belief in his infallibility continues; he goes about with business as usual and lies down among his seals: λέκτο καὶ αὐτός.[20] This is at the conscious level. But unbeknownst to him, behind his back, something has changed. One seal has disappeared, and he himself has moved into the void where that seal once was. Proteus counts himself;

but he does not do so consciously. The ambiguity of the signifier λέκτο reflects the splitting of Proteus between what he does consciously and what he does unconsciously; he consciously "lies down," and he unconsciously becomes self-aware, "counts himself." Freud argued that slips of the tongue and punning jokes provide evidence of the workings of "another place" that undermines our conscious universes.[21] In Lacan's rewriting of Freud, the gap between signifier and signified (which in turn opens up the gaps between signifiers) allows us to locate this "other place." Puns and wordplays point toward the unconscious as they continually affirm that we, as conscious subjects, are never fully in control of what we say. For Proteus, this other place is opened up by the loss of a seal, a logical place that guarantees that there is a constitutive gap between signifier and signified. The ambiguity of the signifier λέκτο is evidence for the gap. Proteus' action of "lying down" no longer means what it used to mean, because his subjectivity will now be at stake through his "self-counting." Proteus acts out a pun, and as he does so he becomes a human subject.

Let us now turn to the second significant moment in Proteus' development. For though Proteus continues with business as usual by lying down with his seals, his unreflective existence does not last much longer. There is evidence of his failure of nerve in his struggle with Menelaus. On a simple reading of the tale, we have another puzzling aspect of Eidothea's trick. Just because Menelaus now has access to the sea god, there seems no clear reason why this should help him. For if Proteus remained protean, upholder of a symbolic without limit, representative of an infinite series of masks, there would surely be no need for him ever to give in to Menelaus. Menelaus would merely have been given access to an ever-changing god only to find out that his ever-changing masks were enough to defy capture endlessly. Yet, of course, Proteus does yield. Why?

Rather than see the delay in giving in to Menelaus as a problem, we should perhaps see it as the entire point of the episode. For it is in effect a temporal confirmation of the gap opened up between what happens to Proteus (the traumatic trick, the self-counting) and his ability to register that trick consciously. Proteus belatedly comes to terms with Eidothea's trick (and the pun he unwittingly acted out) and is now in some way aware of the possibility of a world outside his own, which in turn forces him to recognize the limits of his own world. Before the trick with the seals, Proteus would never have thought of giving in, because he had no reason to doubt his own status as perfectly, infinitely polytropic. But conscious doubt has now crept into his universe, in confirmation of the earlier self-counting that occurred unconsciously. Only at this moment does Proteus become self-conscious, insofar as he consciously doubts himself. His self-doubt in the struggle against Menelaus is a belated recognition of the fact that his seals were not naturally assigned numbers, that their enumeration depended on a counter. He knows that signifier is attached to signified because someone—that is, Proteus—made the attachment, and this self-objectification heralds the possibility of Proteus developing an ego—an objectified, definitive version of the self. Before this moment, we must assume that Proteus always counted correctly but had no idea who was doing the counting. The emergence of Proteus as subject is thus correlative to the loss of the seal. The seal causes (for Proteus) a gap to emerge in the universe; his doubt functions as a belated recognition of that gap; his future ability to count seals will depend on a projection of a self into that gap. The tale therefore suggests that self-consciousness arrives late on the scene. Proteus begins to suspect (but too late) what he himself was unconsciously doing all along; he is now conscious of an agency that has undermined his conscious existence and was thus prior to it. His self-consciousness is parasitic on his unconscious, and his objectified self (his ego) can never be the whole story.

### In the Beginning Was a First Name

But we have not yet finished with Proteus' problematic relation to language. For the story provides us with a series of puns on Proteus' name. Indeed, the episode is replete with beginnings. Eidothea claims that Proteus will first count his seals (πρῶτον ἀριθμήσει, 4.411) and, later, that he will first count Menelaus' men disguised as seals (πρώτους λέγε, 4.452). She encourages Menelaus to capture him when he <u>first</u> goes to sleep (πρῶτον κατευνηθέντα, 4.414), and Proteus himself will begin his transformations by turning into a lion <u>first</u> (πρώτιστα λέων γένετ᾽, 4.456). What is the significance of this further punning? At the very least, the problem of counting and inclusion is now written into the name of our protagonist. This might alert us to the possibility that the wider narrative pattern, involving a shift from infallible certainty to doubt, might have repercussions for how we conceive of our elementary symbolic link to the world of language: our proper names.

The simplest explanation would involve adhering to the split between human and god as a meaningful framework for this episode, reading the tale as the depiction of Proteus' arrival as a human named subject in *Odyssey* 4. For insofar as he is an infallible god, he is not a creature subject to language and the necessary possibility of deception that language brings with it. His arrival as a mortal would thus coincide with his subjection to language. There is a good deal of circumstantial evidence for this. Proteus' appearance, as a god, from the unknown realms of the sea occurs in the middle of the day (*Od.* 4.400 ff.), the time for epiphany.[22] In this liminal time and space, the realms of the human and divine can encounter one another. If this is a time when gods can be seen, Eidothea's gift of ambrosia, the "immortal" liquid, allows the human companions of Menelaus to enter, temporarily, the realm of the god.[23] These narrative details thus provide hints that Proteus is on display at a moment of vulnerability, when he is on a level footing with mortals who have been artificially strengthened. Eidothea's trick takes advantage of this moment of vulnerability to drag him into the realm of mortals; once he has been tricked and there is a gap in the universe for Proteus, he is no longer a god.

If this is the case, then Proteus' name must have been ironic; to borrow the terms of John Peradotto, it was an example of a significant name "motivated by its contrary or contradictory [meaning]."[24] For if, before the trick, Proteus represented a language without closure, a world without a gap, this must mean the positing of no end or beginning to the signifying chain. Compare Lacan's comment on the way the sense of a sentence is retroactively constructed: "It's quite clear, for example, that if I start a sentence you won't understand its meaning until I've finished it, since it's really quite necessary for me to have spoken the last word of the sentence if you are to understand where its first one was."[25] Before the trick, this retroactive construction of a beginning of a sentence never occurred within Proteus' universe. Proteus indulged in an impossible counting, a counting without a beginning or end; and because the symbolic can only create meaning by imposing limits and boundaries on reality—indeed, what we call "reality" is itself a product of these socially constructed, defined spaces—Proteus had no symbolic existence at all. He was a being of the Lacanian Real, the seamless world prior to language, which has no symbolic limit written upon it and which constantly resists the efforts of the symbolic to categorize it completely. The trick stages the first time that Proteus truly counts. *Odyssey* 4 narrates the moment when Proteus finally lives up to his name by creating a limit, a beginning, to the signifying chain. Proteus now allows the last signifier to determine retroactively the first, and he therefore creates meaning. This interpretation also helps us make more sense of the emphasis the tale places on Proteus' speech. For Eidothea's trick ends (and her victory is complete) the moment her father speaks to Menelaus. It is his words that signify that he has lost.

> And he will try you by taking the form of all creatures that come
>     forth
> and move on the earth; he will be water and magical fire.
> You must hold stiffly on to him and squeeze him the harder.
> But when at last he himself, *speaking in words, questions you,*

being now in the same form he was when you saw him sleeping,
then, hero, you must give over your force and let the old man
go free, and ask him which one of the gods is angry with you,
and ask him how to make your way home on the sea where the fish
    swarm.
(*Od.* 4.417–24)
(translation modified)

If we see Proteus as divine prior to the trick, then we can understand these
words as his first words, his first proper speech act. This would help us
make sense out of another interesting aspect of the tale. For until Menelaus
captures him, forcing him to speak, Proteus maintains a total silence within
the narrative.[26]

This also suggests a further irony in Proteus' supposed infallibility.
Proteus was indeed an unerring, ever truthful prophet; but his ability to
maintain such a status depended on his rejection of speech. Eidothea's
trick is thus completed when Proteus speaks, because the act of speech
itself is enough to guarantee that he can no longer be infallible. To enter
language is to admit the possibility that one can be in error or deceived.
Eidothea's trick provided Proteus with a truly representational language;
it allowed him to continue counting his seals, but this counting is of a
fundamentally different sort because it occurs against the background
of the loss of a seal. A fundamental Lacanian maxim is that a thing
must be lost in order for it to be represented—a maxim that seems to
be luridly realized in the *Apologoi*, where it is only by their death that
the companions of Odysseus are allowed inclusion in the poem. For
Proteus, his number system is no longer equivalent to the seals (as was
the case before the trick) but represents them. The loss of the seal now
makes sense to Proteus because of the system of counting up to five that
determines it as lost. This loss opens up a space for Proteus to come to
be as a desiring subject: he desires because there is now a lack within his
universe. But this desire means that he no longer has all the answers and
therefore is not unerring.

The story ends with one further development, which can help us see
the properly traumatic encounter, for Proteus, with the enigma of what the
other wants. For insofar as Proteus himself holds out the hope of a truthful,
unerring prophecy (access to the realm of a complete, all-knowing other
of knowledge), his awareness of his own fallibility is also a puncturing of
that hope. He himself becomes a living witness to the way the Other lacks.
Eidothea's suggestion that Menelaus should hold on to Proteus until he
asks him a question also sets up a basic narrative expectation for us. What

will be the first question the old man ever articulates in language? Let us turn to the text.

> "Which of the gods now, son of Atreus, has been advising you
> to capture me from ambush against my will. What do you want?"
> So he spoke, and I in turn spoke up and made answer:
> "You know, Old Man. Why try to put me off with your answer?"
> (*Od.* 4.462–65)

The remarkable thing about this question is the way Menelaus refuses to answer it. Menelaus acts as if Proteus is still infallible and therefore impossible to deceive. Though Menelaus was, in some sense, the direct agent of the trick, he appears to misunderstand the significance of the trick completely. He acts as if Proteus is an all-knowing being impervious to deception, when Menelaus' recent ability to pin him down proves the exact reverse: Proteus has just been fooled and wants to know why. In short, Menelaus quite misses the performative dimension of the trick itself, which changes Proteus. If the episode at first seems to end in a successful act of communication because Menelaus obtains the information he needs to get home from Proteus, the failure of Menelaus to answer Proteus' question suggests that there is also a more profound failure of communication. Not only is Proteus' question not answered, but Menelaus' refusal to answer suggests that he does not even trust Proteus' sincerity. Ironically, it is as if Menelaus takes the place of the divine Proteus before the trick, trusting in language's ability simply to describe the world outside of itself, rather than taking some part in constructing the universe of symbols.[27]

We can understand the failure of Proteus' counting system as his first encounter with the Other as a symbolic system. In turn, we can understand his perplexed question to Menelaus as his own first encounter with the Other as a system that is not whole but lacking—with the other as desire. Proteus has been wrested out of a complacent existence in a coherent, whole universe into a new one he does not yet understand. His question signifies both an effort to find out what has happened to him and a desire to find out what his place in this world will be. To ask, "What do you want?" [τέο σε χρή] (4.463), is also to ask, "What do you want from me?" His encounter with language has resulted in a loss (the lost seal) and thus a desire to heal that loss. He then turns to the first person he encounters in order to find an answer to his desire. He hopes that finding out what Menelaus desires can provide an answer to what he himself desires—return to a time before desire, when he lacked nothing. The roles of prophet and seeker of prophecy are reversed, even if Menelaus is quite oblivious to this shift. For Proteus' hope is that if he could answer the question of Menelaus' desire, of why he dragged him into the mortal world, the god could plug the gap that generates his own desire. From now on, Proteus will desire through others, gaining access to what he wants through the desires of others. Proteus thus asks the most basic, childlike kind of question to the being he believed produced him. What do you want from me? Why have you brought me into the world?

Let us now turn to a second possible interpretation of Proteus by testing out the possibility that he has been a doubter from the start of the episode, if we had but paid close enough attention; that is, we can read the narrative symptomatically, looking back for the signs of Proteus' infallibility that our interpretation might suggest. This might be more unsettling for us, as it more directly involves our desire. As I suggested earlier, the tragedy of Proteus depends on the way we, as readers, can make sense of the signifier *Proteus*. It thus implicates us through our abilities to make sense of language, even as it depicts Proteus' own failure to understand himself. With this in mind, it is worth paying closer attention to what I added to the tale in order to make sense of it.

There is clearly a delay necessary before we can make sense of Proteus' name; the story provides an "etymology" of a name, making retroactive sense of something that appeared senseless. But in trying to make retroactive sense of the tale, I had to forge a connection between the sense of Proteus as "first" and the sea god. This link turned Proteus into a figure not unlike the famed messenger-slave of antiquity who is completely unaware of the tattoo, engraved on his skull, that tells of his impending doom—a story Lacan himself used to illustrate the alien nature of the human unconscious.

> But in Freud it [the unconscious] is a question of something quite different, which is a *savoir*, certainly, but one that involves not the least *connaissance*, in that it is inscribed in a discourse, of which, like the "messenger-slave" of ancient usage, the subject who carries under his hair the codicil that condemns him to death knows neither the meaning nor the text, nor in what language it is written, nor even that it had been tattooed on his shaven scalp as he slept.[28]

The tragedy comes from our belated recognition that this was always an accident waiting to happen to Proteus. There is added irony in that what Proteus remained unaware of—and what necessitated his doom— was not something distant from him, but, rather, something too close to him for him to see: he fails to understand something that promises to constitute his essence, his own proper name as Proteus. This failure to see exactly what constitutes him is correlative to the message engraved on the slave's head.[29]

But here we need pause to doubt. For rather than take his behavior of counting seals at face value, we might use our awareness of his foolishness to ask a question. Why was he counting his seals so obsessively in the first place?[30] We might compare Proteus to the neurotic, who constantly thinks, counts, and recounts. This pseudo intellectual activity functions as a defense against his unconscious desire. If he can convince himself that he is consciously in control at all times, he would be able to forget the way he is ruled by unconscious desires. His constant conscious activity allows him to keep thinking and thus ignore the unconscious thought processes that nevertheless continue to govern him. He engages in a futile effort to deny the way he is split by language. This suggests a different way of understanding Proteus' actions; for surely he, too, in his obsessional devotion to counting his seals endlessly, seems to be much more neurotic than mad. If so, then the gap previously posited between his limitless counting and his name (signifying "first" and thus imposing a limit) is partially bridged. Proteus' incessant counting is an ongoing attempt to postpone something that he unconsciously knows: that he is a finite, living being, defined by language's limits. His name, Proteus, rules him in ways he refuses to acknowledge; he is ruled by it because he constantly tries to flee its truth, to avoid the necessary limit of the counting sequence by a constant counting of an indefinite sequence. In Proteus' case, we can now see a different motivation for his constant counting: for why else would he do it unless he was—in some way—aware of the possibility of failure?

Here the tale becomes more disturbing for us. For up until now, it seemed possible to take a certain amount of intellectual pleasure in the way we understand Eidothea's trick while Proteus does not. We make sense of the tale (if my reading of the significance of Proteus' counting is correct) by identifying with Eidothea's cleverness in tricking her father. But the final twist in this tale is that Proteus' ultimate error may be not in counting incorrectly but, rather, in the way he places so much effort on the process of counting, of making sense itself. The tale allows us, for a moment, to occupy a relatively secure position of knowledge in contrast to Proteus; we understand what is happening to him in ways that he fails to understand. But the tale pulls the rug out from under our feet by illustrating how the obsessional attachment to certain knowledge systems may itself prove to be a source of error and denial. Our pleasure in making sense out of the story of the deception of Proteus leaves us with a worry: what are we denying or ignoring as we make sense of the text; and what is at stake in such an obsessive desire to make sense out of the poem, to be caught up in its own obsession with numbers?[31]

### FROM COUNTER TO COUNTED

Let us now turn to the seals. For Proteus' counting clearly has consequences for the objects of his counting, his herd of seals. Given that the Homeric poems are obsessed with the problems of classification,[32] this topic is worthy of closer attention. Crucial here is the way that groups are formed through their common allegiance to a master, a master who holds the place of a master signifier. A master is someone whose power can only function while it is unchallenged, because the mastery itself is inherently senseless. If the subjectivization of Proteus takes us to the very brink of the logic of the master signifier, this subjectivization has consequences for those who are mastered.

It is perhaps simplest to examine this by comparing the problems with personal identity faced by both Proteus and the seals. Before the trick, Proteus never questioned his identity as master of his seals. If we are told that he is an unerring god, nevertheless his failure to question his own role suggests that he may only be a human fool who thinks he is a god. He is thus foolish in Lacanian terms. For Lacan, a fool is someone who believes that the role he or she plays is an actual property of himself or herself. He uses the example of a king who believes he is a king, rather than a contingent individual playing out the socially mandated role of king.[33] Proteus' self-counting allows him to establish a distance between the roles he plays and the subject who plays them. He thus experiences an emptying out of his invulnerable identity as counter of seals and of his identity as their natural master. But what is crucial here is that a similar process can be imagined for the seals.

Let us take as our starting point the way that the narrative questions the border between humans, gods, and animals. What happens if we anthropomorphize the seals?[34] Before the trick, Proteus' seals were grouped together as seals because of the performative nature of Proteus' counting. His counting of the seals coincided with the attribution to them of an identity (the ego identity of being Proteus' seals). But the emptying out of the identity of Proteus also leaves a question mark over the identity of the seals. What will happen to them if their counter, Proteus, no longer counts them? For if Proteus falls "down" from immortality into mortal status (or a more explicit confrontation with his mortal status), is it not possible that these animals too will fall "up" into the status of human mortals? If so, they will do so in and through a confrontation with a choice. They can either confront the contingency of their identity (realize that they are only playing out the role of Proteus' seals—that they are not really his seals but only his seals insofar as he counts them as his) or try to return to the safety of a fixed identity, the (now false) knowledge of being his seals. If Proteus is a human who unsuccessfully fantasizes that he is a god, perhaps the seals are humans who prefer to act as a herd of seals. If we read this tale as an allegory for ideological strategies, we can see it opening up the question of the fear that confronts subjects who realize the contingency of their socially mandated roles. Such roles offer an alternative to doubt in the form of a fixed identity, hoping that this fixed identity is preferable to the abyss of doubt.[35]

## FROM PROTEUS TO ODYSSEUS

We can now tentatively explore how the tale of Proteus raises questions about the *Odyssey* as a whole and, in particular, about its central character, Odysseus. For the duplicity in Proteus' own name can be related to the notorious riddles concerning the way the narrative fails to speak Odysseus' proper name in the proem. Goldhill has suggested that the lack of a proper name identifying *andra* (and the replacement instead with *polytropon*) functions as a *griphos*.

The surprising lack of a proper name in the first line(s) of the epic, then, prompts the question not simply of *to whom* does the opening expression refer, but of *what* is (to be) recognized in such a periphrastic reference. Indeed, the withholding of the name invests the proem with the structure of a *griphos*, a riddle, an enigma, where a series of expressions (of which *polutropon* is the first) successively qualifies the term *andra* as the name "Odysseus" is approached.[36]

A crucial problem suggested by the *griphos* is the problem of closure.[37] How can one ever fully define what a "man" is when there is always one more predicate that can be attached to him, retroactively changing any essence? As I have tried to show, this is the crucial problem of language itself, and it is explored in the tale of Proteus. By refusing to name Odysseus, the poem opens up a space where the identity of its major character can be constructed and reconstructed. It allows the hero to experiment with different masks, alternative options for being in the world. The person who is *not* named Odysseus is temporarily free from the constraints and obligations imposed by a social identity; the seductive illusion entertained is that he can be who he wants to be.

The nameless subject of the *Odyssey* thus seems to have a certain freedom within language, a freedom that is correlative to the storyteller's freedom to tell different tales. But the Proteus tale forces us to reevaluate this freedom. Just as Proteus is, at first, a being who is nothing more than an endless series of masks, so, too, the plot of the *Odyssey* is notoriously endless. The anticipated reunion of Penelope and Odysseus, the longed-for *nostos*, does not end the poem; the poem instead points beyond itself to an enigmatic further journey for Odysseus, prophesied by Teiresias. The poem thus seems to perpetuate this fantasy of an endlessly changing and plural self. But the problem with this fantasy is that it runs the risk of destroying any possibility of making sense of the self at all. In psychoanalytic terms, it flirts with psychosis: if there are no limits to the self, then the self seems to run the risk of total dissolution into senselessness: For sense itself depends on the stability and definition that limits provide. Rather than achieving a utopian, plural self, we run the risk of losing the self entirely as it becomes fundamentally ripped up in pieces and dissolved because of its lack of an anchoring point. The Proteus tale suggests that some limit is necessary for language to make any sense at all and that this limit brings with it a necessary loss, a prohibition of whatever is beyond the limit. This sets up parallel questions for the wider narrative of the poem: Are there any limits to Odysseus' polytropy? If so, what is Odysseus' relationship to the loss that created those limits?

We might start to answer these questions by returning to Odysseus' use of *metis* in his encounters with the Cyclops and the Phaeacians. In both cases, his *metis* succeeds. He manages to escape the clutches of the Cyclops, and he also procures his ride home from the Phaeacians. But the success of his trickery has its darker side. Odysseus succeeds, but both the Cyclops and the Phaeacians lose spectacularly. The Cyclops loses his eye; the Phaeacians lose their ability to transport strangers anywhere without a care. It is well known (and much discussed) that Odysseus' success against the Cyclops is dependent on an identification with a paradoxical identity that signifies absence and loss: the identity of "No one."[38] I suggest that this paradoxical identity should also influence how we understand the fate of the Phaeacians and Cyclops. Proteus moved into a truly human realm when he was forced to recognize the loss of one of his seals. I suggest that Odysseus, in his encounter with the Phaeacians and Cyclops, performed a similar role to the lost seal. He forces the Phaeacians and Cyclops to come to terms with the possibility of loss. If this interpretation is correct, then Odysseus' paradoxical identity as "No one" becomes more significant. If human identity is contingent, it can only be so against a background of the loss of belief in any fixed identity. Odysseus' role as *Outis*, "No one," signifies this loss. It is precisely this loss of belief in themselves that Odysseus forces the Cyclops and Phaeacians to undergo. In turn, this suggests that we need to reevaluate Odysseus' role in the entire poem. He is not simply a human survivor; he is someone who brings the concept of loss to others.[39]

NOTES

1. For some preliminary work on counting and classification, see the suggestive article of Henderson (1997).

2. The translation is Muellner's (1996, 14).

3. Muellner 1996, 16.

4. See, e.g., Vidal-Naquet 1986, chap. 1.

5. *Od.* 9.334 ff.

6. In the specification of Proteus as Aegyptian (*Od.* 4.385), it is tempting to see a connection, at the level of the signifier, to Aegyptius, the father obsessed with his fifth son.

7. Note how the simile νομεὺς ὣς πώοεσι μήλων signposts the connection to the tricking of Polyphemus in *Odyssey* 9, where a real shepherd will be deprived of his flocks. I discuss the similarity of the two tricks in greater detail in chap. 7.

8. πέμπε is Aeolic for πέντε. See Stanford 1965, ad loc. The meaning of the word is obscure enough to merit comment by the scholiasts: He measures, counts in fives. For πεμπάζειν means to measure in fives. For the Dorians call πέμπε "five" (A); He counts in fives. For the Aeolians call πέμπε "five"] (P.Q.) The definition in LSJ (sx.) strengthens the likelihood that πεμπάσσεται means "count in fives" by appealing to "counting on one's fingers"—of which there are, for most people, five. There is no verb τεσσαράζω for "counting in fours," though there is a verb τριάζω for counting in threes, which seems to be associated with wrestling, in which "three falls" are required for victory. This suggests that πεμπάσσεται does not mean "number every fifth one." I am grateful to Ann Hanson for pointing this out to me and just as grateful to Sally Humphreys for raising it as an objection. That Homer's characters might count on their fingers, in multiples of five, has actually long been recognized. See Wood 1775, 255–56 for a discussion of πεμπάσσεται.

9. See West's commentary in Heubeck, West, and Hainsworth 1988, 221. Though the pun is noted, it is not interpreted. This follows the scholiasts, who merely note that Horner uses the same word to signify different things: ὅτι τῆι αὐτῆι λέξει παραλλήλως οὐκ ἐπὶ τοῦ αὐτοῦ σημαινομένου κέχρηται (P.Q.).

10. Cf. another Egyptian tale with the same structure, the story of how Psammetichus came to power (Herodotus 2.147.4 ff). At a time when Egypt was divided up evenly between twelve kings, an oracle declared that the one who should pour a libation from a bronze cup in the temple of Hephaestus would become master of the entire country. When, later, all the kings were about to pour a libation in the temple, it so happened that the priest brought one cup too few. Psammetichus, because he lacked a cup, having no idea what he was doing, took his own helmet off to serve as a cup, and the oracle was fulfilled. Something goes missing, and someone (unwittingly) moves into the void opened up by the missing object.

11. On the manner in which Saussure grappled with the problem, see Porter 1986.

12. Copjec 1994, 174. Copjec is emphasizing the points made by Jacques-Alain Miller (1978) in his important article "Suture (Elements of the Logic of the Signifier)."

13. Cf. Zizek 1989, 87 ff, for a discussion of the Lacanian concept of the master signifier.

14. Fink 1995, 52.

15. The problem of counting and accounting is replayed in the sheep trick of *Odyssey*

9, where Odysseus undermines Polyphemus' control over his sheep and his ability to account for them, even as he submerges the remainder of his own men into the sheep of Polyphemus. This vocabulary of herding for men will reappear in the group killing of another set of men—the suitors, later in the poem. The politics of closeness to an animal acted out on the physical level in both these tricks (Menelaus and his men wrapped in sealskins, Odysseus' men attached to sheep) raises questions about the difference between humans and animals.

16. Cf. Detienne and Vernant 1991, 264: "The fact is that Proteus was deceived by the seal-disguise Menelaus and his companions adopted when they dressed up in the freshly flayed skins of these sea monsters; and the reason he was deceived is undoubtedly that the distance between man and seal is one that is easily crossed." Though there is a great deal of interest in the overall discussion of the similarity of humans to seals—in particular, in the question of the shared five fingers of both creatures—I maintain that these authors have alighted on a kind of alluring red herring in this story.

17. It is possible to understand this episode in the simpler way, as depending on the confusion of sign and referent. If it was possible for πεμπάσσεται to mean "number every fifth one," then the problem of "four seals" could be resolved if we were to presume that Eidothea killed four of Proteus' seals in order to get the skins for Menelaus and his men. This interpretation was initially suggested to me by Professor H. D. Cameron and underpins the suggestion of Professor Humphreys. The interpretation I offer seems more powerful, however, because it explains aspects of the text that otherwise remain puzzling, in particular the punning on λέγω and the emphasis on counting. There is no obvious reason why the tale (if interpreted in the simpler manner) needs to involve four people. One dead seal and Menelaus alone in a sealskin would be sufficient for it to work.

18. Of course, it is a "logical" seal that is missing. In reality, the number of Proteus' seals may well remain the same.

19. The endlessness of Proteus' system of counting, its lack of limits, might remind us of the endless series of guests who arrived at Phaeacia. Proteus had no idea of who was counting (a figure of pure sense) until he lost one of his seals. His counting was in an important sense automatic; it went on without any doubt on the part of any subject. It thus resembles the relationship between the Phaeacians and their ships, which pass people onto their destination automatically.

20. I here read λέκτο as from λέχομαι.

21. The classic text is "Jokes and Their Relation to the Unconscious."

22. On the time of epiphany, see Hinds 1988.

23. The immortalizing aspect of ambrosia is clear in its etymology as "immortal." See Chantraine 1984–90, s.v. "ambrosia."

24. Peradotto 1990, 113. Peradotto provides the example of Odysseus' dog, Argus—motionless, dying, yet called "Flash."

25. Lacan, Seminar X, 1957–58, Nov. 6. Quoted in Dor 1997, 197.

26. This would give a novel spin to Eidothea's formulaic phrase at 4.387: "And *they* say also he is my father, that he begot me." Others need to tell Eidothea that Proteus is her father, because he remains silent. This also gives more retroactive significance to the pun on λέγω and λέχομαι. For λέγω is also the most common verb used to mean "to speak."

27. As such, this miscommunication—between a human who believes a god still to be divine and a god who has just become human—previews the difficulty of recognition that Telemachus will encounter with Odysseus in book 16; for there, too, Telemachus clings to the belief that his shape-shifting father is a god. The problem Odysseus faces with Telemachus is itself of broader significance. In the first half of the poem, his tricks are

responsible for opening up the divides between gods and mortals by introducing them to loss. In the second half, he not only falls victim to the failings of his own power but seems unaware of the lessons he has taught others.

28. Lacan 1997, 302.

29. Here there is an obvious similarity to Oedipus, so crucial to Freud not because he slept with his mother but because he did not know who he was.

30. See Fink 1977, chap. 8.

31. See Henderson 1997 for the most sublimely obsessive attempt yet made to come to terms with counting in the *Odyssey*. I have learned a great deal from this attempt.

32. For some obvious examples that are central to the narratives of both poems, consider the catalog of ships in *Iliad* 2, which follows Odysseus' ordering and counting of each division of troops earlier in the book. Also, Odysseus is careful to chart in some detail the gradual loss of his own soldiers in the story of his wanderings to the Phaeacians; the loss of his men leads to ongoing restructuring of the group. In both cases, the way humans become part of a social group is put under the microscope. I take up this problem at length in chaps. 6–7.

33. For a discussion of this Lacanian point, also well understood by Marx, see Zizek 1989, 46 ff.

34. For this "experiment," I beg the reader's indulgence; whether it is viable for the poem will ultimately depend on the extent to which one believes that the *Odyssey* is constantly engaged in questioning the limits that separate humans from animals. In chap. 7, I explore the ways in which human and animal life are strangely intertwined; see esp. my discussion of the transformation of men into animals on Circe's island. At any rate, the metaphor of animal herding for people is central to the epic idea of what constitutes a people. Haubold (2000, 17 ff.) argues for the centrality of "shepherding," embedded in the phrase ποιμὴν λαῶν, to the epic construction of the "people." Crucial for me is less the specificity of shepherding than the general principle of "herding" as a metaphor for the control of a human population—a metaphor that can slip from sheep to other animals, such as seals. This centrality of the metaphor has an important consequence—and here I part company with Haubold. When we move into actual descriptions of the herding of animals, the epic poems may well be literalizing (and thus redefining) the nature of the metaphor itself, telling us more about its underlying dynamics; that is, the metaphorical use of "shepherding" can allow us to see, in any act of real herding, a redefinition of the problem of what a leader of the people is doing.

35. The dilemma I have traced for the seals is structurally similar to the problem faced by Odysseus' men as they consider the possibility of rebellion from Odysseus, a rebellion suggested by Eurylochus in book 10.

36. Goldhill 1991, 4.

37. On the allures and dangers of a teleological criticism, see Porter 1990.

38. This is one of the central issues examined by Peradotto (1990).

39. Here, we might see a connection with the traditional phrase ὤλεσε λαόν. It is certainly true that much of the second half of the *Odyssey* will play with the possibility that Odysseus is just such a people-destroyer. But in these tales, he does something more profound: he introduces the possibility of absolute loss, the utter contingency of any communal identity, to a species that had not encountered such a possibility before. On the importance of this dynamic, see Haubold 2000.

RICHARD HEITMAN

# The Stakes of the Plot

In *On The Sublime*, Longinus judges the *Odyssey* to be clearly inferior to the *Iliad*, on the grounds that the former appears less dramatic and vivid. The 1996 edition of the *Oxford Classical Dictionary* seems to agree: "The *Odyssey* is a romance, enjoyable at a more superficial level than the heroic/tragic *Iliad*" (718). Longinus rejects plot unity in the *Odyssey* out of hand: he thinks that the aging Homer not only loses his edge but his direction as well. "Henceforth we see the ebbing tide of Homer's greatness, as he wanders in the incredible regions of romance" (9.13). The *OCD* echoes, "For many readers the adventures are the high point" (719). In fact, many school editions of the epic (e.g., Herbert Bates's otherwise admirable 1969 translation) altogether exclude the Telemachy and other "slow" parts and begin with Odysseus weeping on the Ogygian shore. This approach is not restricted to editors of school editions. Peter Brooks, in his 1992 *Reading for the Plot: Design and Intention in Narrative*, writes, "The *Iliad* opens with Agamemnon and Achilles locked in passionate quarrel over the girl Briseis, and the *Odyssey* with Odysseus, detained on Calypso's island, expressing the longing of his *nostos*, the drive to return home" (38). Of course, the *Odyssey* does not open on the Ogygian shore; the tale takes us first to Olympus and then to Ithaca. Moreover, it does not open at a moment particularly significant in the tale of Odysseus's *nostos*.

From *Taking Her Seriously: Penelope & the Plot of Homer's* Odyssey: 11–33 © 2005 by the University of Michigan.

Why does the *Odyssey* begin when and where it does, in Ithaca, in the twentieth year after the beginning of the Trojan campaign? One who takes the *Odyssey* primarily as a *nostos* story might conceivably answer that since Ithaca is Odysseus's abiding goal, the audience ought to have an image of it to keep in mind as he journeys homeward. This is far from a satisfying answer, however, since what is currently happening in Ithaca is so unpleasant that it is more likely to undermine the goal of homecoming. Better for emphasizing the *nostos* story, I should think, would be to let the audience experience the adventures with the same idealized view of the goal that Odysseus has. This is probably why *nostos* tales, as Uvo Hölscher has shown in his analysis of folktale (1978, 1989), invariably begin with the earliest adventures of the returning hero and continue in a strict chronological order until the hero is home.

We have to put aside the idea that Homer's *Odyssey* is a traditional *nostos* story. As fatuous as the sea-tales that Odysseus recounts, they constitute a minor part of the poem compared to the struggles in Ithaca. Ithaca, after all, is where considerably more than half of the action takes place; Ithaca gets at least four times more attention than Scheria, the next most featured place. Furthermore, Athene elects to go to Ithaca to help Telemachos rather than to Ogygia to aid Odysseus. In fact, Athene's decision has the effect of delaying Odysseus's return. Apparently, her chief worries concern Ithaca.

As Hölscher has shown, rather than the *nostos* pattern, the beginning of the *Odyssey* conforms better to a folktale pattern sometimes called the "nick-of-time," which proceeds something like this: a departing husband specifies to his wife a limit to the time that she is supposed to wait for him before she is to consider him dead and remarry; the appointed time comes without the husband; the wedding takes its course, but the husband comes home (perhaps in disguise) just in time to prevent (or reverse) it. In the *Odyssey*, the appointed time is when the beard grows on Telemachos's chin.

Hölscher's studies have shown that Homer chose to begin the *Odyssey* in Ithaca for reasons that do not directly bear on Odysseus's *nostos*. But unfortunately, Hölscher has not solved the logical difficulties of the narrative that I discussed in my introduction. Furthermore, whereas the *Odyssey* employs the "nick-of-time" motif in the Telemachy, it distances itself from that pattern in the presentation of Penelope's weaving. As an excuse for not remarrying, the weaving of a shroud for Laertes makes very little sense. Penelope's father-in-law is old and feeble and may be near death, but the imminence of his death is emphasized only here and could easily be ignored for the purposes of the plot: no other element of the drama relies on his being moribund. A much more appropriate excuse than making a shroud for Laertes would have been making something for the impending wedding—a bridal gown, for example. The unceasing weaving and unweaving of a wedding dress ought to have been an irresistible device for a "nick-of-time" folktale. The substitution of the shroud more likely implies the hand of the poet eager to avoid, as far as possible, association with the "nick-of-time" motif and therefore with hopes for Odysseus's return. In short, the dramatic situation in Ithaca is designed not to concentrate the focus on the promise of Odysseus's return.

The question remains why the *Odyssey* begins where and when it does. Once again, Hölscher is a pioneer in the pursuit of a meaningful answer. In a 1976 lecture at the University of Cincinnati, entitled "The Transformation from Folk-Tale to Epic," he argued: "It means that the *Odyssey* starts with a crisis. Every scene of the first book is saying one thing: that the state of affairs is not to be endured any longer; that the moment has come when a decision has to be taken" (Hölscher 1978, 57). *Crisis* may be a strong word for those who hold the traditional view and insist that the basic situation in Ithaca has remained the same for many years. (This tradition is so ingrained that the entry on Penelope in the third edition of the *Oxford Classical Dictionary* mistakenly asserts that Penelope holds off the suitors by weaving and unweaving Laertes' shroud for ten years.) But crisis it is.

I part ways with Hölscher over the nature of the "state" that "is not to be endured any longer." Still looking for the folktale core, Hölscher emphasizes the romantic pressure placed on Penelope to marry, ignoring, for the most part, the struggle over the future of the House of Odysseus—a struggle without which the *Odyssey* remains the mere romance that Longinus disdained, not the agonistic drama that it might be. I agree with Agathe Thornton, who writes:

> But ... we have to change our view of the *Odyssey*: it is not a fairy story of princes competing for the hand of a beautiful queen, but it is a tale from times in which power based on wealth and brute force was little hampered by law, a tale of greedy and ambitious aristocrats trying under a thin veneer of courtliness to seize the absent king's wife, wealth and position. (1970, 67)

To know what is really going on in Ithaca and what counts in the structure of the plot, we must take a careful look at the epic's generally neglected second book. It delineates a power struggle in which the principal agents are the Ithacans, the suitors, Telemachos, and Penelope.

## TELEMACHOS: *Odyssey* 2.1–14

As book 2 begins, Telemachos awakens and prepares himself to address the Ithacan assembly that he has called. To describe Telemachos, Homer here uses the same three lines that he employs to describe Menelaos in book 4. Like that triumphant hero, the young man cuts a godlike figure.

> [He] put on his clothes, and slung a sharp sword over his
>     shoulder.
> Underneath his shining feet he bound the fair sandals
> and went on his way from the chamber, like a god in presence.
>     (*Od.* 2.3–5)

Telemachos will cut a very different figure by the end of book 2, but here the Ithacan people "marvel at the young hero" as he strides into the assembly, spear in hand, with a couple of fine hounds at his side and with Athene's enchanting grace glowing forth from his whole person. The elders make room for him, and the epic audience is set to expect great and noble words.

## AIGYPTIOS: *Odyssey* 2.15–34

The first to speak is not Telemachos but one of the Ithacan citizens, "the hero Aigyptios, who was bent over with age, and had seen things beyond number" (*Od.* 2.15–16). His first words reveal that there has been no official assembly in Ithaca for twenty years—that is, since Odysseus left. "Never has there been an assembly of us or any session since great Odysseus went away in the hollow vessels" (2.26–27). This means that Telemachos has never before convened a public assembly. In fact, Telemachos's public life has been so slight that Aigyptios cannot even guess that Telemachos might be behind the call.

So who has been ruling Ithaca? The answer is no one. Odysseus did once, as "king," when he was in Ithaca, but since then, apparently no one has taken his place. There has not even been any official public discussion of the matter. Ithaca has therefore been more or less in anarchy for twenty years, a system that seems to have worked tolerably well for everyone. I think we can figure that each Ithacan household has reverted to the ancient practice of taking care of itself. Aigyptios's own family, consisting of his four sons, reflects a balance of interests in regard to the House of Odysseus. Two of his sons have involvement with it, one as a friend and one as an enemy. Antiphos sailed with Odysseus to Troy; Eurynomos is a suitor. The other two sons (unnamed, as are all of the unaffiliated Ithacans except Aigyptios) are at home, minding their familial estates (2.22). If we take Aigyptios's family as representative of the interests of the Ithacan populace, we see that Telemachos is about to address an assembly of men with complex, balanced affiliations that are dominated by private pursuits. Most of them have been doing just fine and will continue to do so if nothing changes.

Aigyptios assumes that this rare public assembly has been called because of some public emergency. He proclaims goodwill for anyone ready to shoulder public concerns and aid the community at large. Even before he knows the identity of the one who has convened the assembly, he offers his approval and endorsement: "I think he is a good man and useful. So may Zeus grant him good accomplishment for whatever it is his mind desires" (2.33–34). This enthusiastic endorsement is highly ironic within the context of the *Odyssey*. The accomplishment of Telemachos's desires will prove a curse to Aigyptios, who still grieves over the loss of his first son: "he could not forget the lost one. He grieved and mourned for him, and it was in tears for him, now, that he stood forth and addressed [the assembly]" (2.23–24). Aigyptios's second son will die along with the other suitors.[1]

Telemachos takes Aigyptios's words as support and encouragement but immediately acts in a way to render them inapplicable. Aigyptios has praise and appreciation for anyone who warns against invasion "or has some other public matter to set forth and argue" (2.32), but not for one like Telemachos, who has come to request help, not to offer it. Though urgent, Telemachos's business is a private matter, a mere personal need. Mutatis mutandis, Telemachos's line is an echo of Aigyptios's, but in the negative: "nor have I some other public matter to set forth and argue" (2.44). Aigyptios's hopes are doomed to be frustrated.

## THE TWO EVILS: *ODYSSEY* 2.46–61

Telemachos begins to present his case. Two evils (*kaka doia*) have struck his household. First, he explains, "I have lost a noble father, one who was king once over you here, and was kind to you like a father" (*Od.* 2.46–47).[2] The statement of the first evil is bound to be surprising to the audience, who has witnessed, not long before, the opening scene on Olympus and therefore knows that Odysseus is not lost. But Telemachos's statement admits no equivocation. He offers no hope, warning, or threat that Odysseus might someday return home, though such a threat might have greatly aided his case against the suitors and, considering the lack of a corpse, might plausibly have been believed by the assembly.

Can Telemachos possibly believe that his father will never return? The answer is, simply, yes: he can and does. He has already announced this belief in book 1, no fewer than three times. As he first gushes out his complaints about the household to Athene, he says: "As it is, [Odysseus] has died by an evil fate, and there is no comfort left for us, not even though some one among mortals tells us he will come back. His day of homecoming has perished" (1.166–68). A little later, he says to his mother: "Odysseus is not the only one who lost his homecoming day at Troy. There were many others who perished, besides him" (1.354–55). Sixty lines later, he declares, "Eurymachos, there is no more hope of my father's homecoming" (1.413). Though Athene sends Telemachos on a long voyage to inquire about his father, she never tells him unequivocally that Odysseus is still alive. Fourteen books later, after he has absorbed many stories about his father, Telemachos levels with Theoklymenos:

> Friend, I will accurately answer all that you ask me.
> Ithaka is my country, and Odysseus is my father,
> if ever he lived; but by now he must have died by a dismal death.
>      (15.266–68)

Telemachos's standard response to the several omens that predict his father's return is disbelief. There is no way around it: Telemachos doubts that his father is alive up until the very moment, in book 16, that the two come face-to-face.[3]

The first evil, then, is old news and is accepted as such by Telemachos and the Ithacans. (Telemachos would probably never have bothered to mention it if the second evil had not recently befallen him.) The second evil, the real cause for alarm, is the damage being done to the household by the suitors.

> [A]nd now here is a greater evil, one which presently
> will break up the whole house and destroy all my livelihood.
> For my mother, against her will, is beset by suitors.
>      (2.48–50)

Telemachos does not deny the suitors the right to court his mother. His complaint is only that they are courting her improperly. A proper courtship would leave his inheritance intact. If the suitors are serious in their courtship, he argues, they ought to petition Ikarios, Penelope's father, for her hand. The import of these lines can hardly be exaggerated. Telemachos tacitly justifies the legitimacy of the suitors' right to court his mother. Their suit is not prima facie illegal, irreverent, or contrary to custom.

The suitors do not think that they are doing anything blamable by courting Penelope. Athene condemns them often for courting the wife of a living man, but this is an unfair charge to level at them. No one, aside from gods and prophets, claims that Odysseus is still alive. The suitors' clear conscience on this matter is most strikingly shown in the desperate defense that Eurymachos offers to Odysseus in book 22, as "each man looked about him for a way to escape sheer death" (22.43). Eurymachos does not deny that he courted Penelope, but for all that is punishable, he puts the blame on Antinoös, who, he claims, was not interested in Penelope but had other intentions.

> It was he who pushed for this action,
> not so much that he wanted the marriage, or cared for it,
> but with other things in mind, which the son of Kronos would
>     not
> grant him: to lie in wait for your son and kill him, and then
> be king himself in the district of strong-founded Ithaka.
>     (22.49–53)

So, Telemachos claims that his mother "against her will, is beset by suitors" (2.50), but he does not claim the stronger case that the suitors have no right to court her, as they would if Odysseus were still alive. On the contrary, Telemachos wants his mother to remarry, as do Penelope's own parents (and Penelope knows that they do). Telemachos actually encourages the courtship, going so far as to reproach the suitors for laxity in their efforts. If they want Penelope so much, why have they not simply gone to her father with gifts as is customary?

> These shrink from making the journey to the house of her
>     father
> Ikarios, so that he might take bride gifts for his daughter
> and bestow her on the one he wished, who came as his
>     favorite.
>     (2.52–54)

Telemachos apparently assumes that Penelope's father has the authority to give away his daughter (which the father would hardly have if the husband were generally still considered alive). For their part, the suitors offer to bring their suit to Penelope's father if Telemachos will send her home, which in itself assumes that she is no longer legally bound by her marriage to Odysseus.

What peeves Telemachos the most is that the suitors' means of courtship
is destroying the estate that he is due to inherit. But whose responsibility is
it to protect the property? Obviously, the responsibility is Telemachos's own,
in the absence of his father. Telemachos recognizes this but admits himself
to be woefully inadequate to the task.

> We have no man here
> such as Odysseus was, to drive this curse from the household.
> We ourselves are not the men to do it; we must be
> weaklings in such a case, not men well seasoned in battle.
> I would defend myself if the power were in me.
>     (2.58–62)

## TELEMACHOS'S PLEA FOR HELP: *ODYSSEY* 2.63–84

Telemachos can only get what he wants if the Ithacans lend him the muscle
to take it. But why should they? Like Aigyptios, they have as much fealty
to the suitors as they do to Telemachos. In an attempt to win them over,
Telemachos serves up a gallimaufry of pleas, which become progressively less
savory. I discern at least seven separate appeals, beginning with an appeal to
altruism and ending with one to greed. First, Telemachos begs for help on the
grounds that his situation is no longer endurable to him (*Od.* 2.63). Second,
he attempts to arouse indignation over the abuse—"beyond all decency"—of
his estate (2.63–64). Third, in an attempt to shame the Ithacans into action,
he says, "Even you must be scandalized and ashamed before the neighboring
men about us, the people who live around our land" (2.64–66). Fourth, as
if giving up on the Ithacans' sense of fair play, Telemachos attempts to tap
their fear: "Fear also the god's anger lest they, astonished by evil actions,
turn against you" (2.66–67). Fifth, he offers himself as a suppliant and pleads
pathetically, "leave me alone with my bitter sorrow to waste away" (2.70–71).
He thereby methodically undercuts his own best argument for the intensity
of the evil that has befallen him and for the urgency of his need.

As if this were not enough, Telemachos's sixth strategy involves insulting
the Ithacans. He implies that they have gone well beyond mere toleration
of the suitors, that they, in fact, are the very ones who incited the suitors
and instigated the attack on his property (2.73–74). Finally, Telemachos
follows this up with a cynical appeal to greed (2.74–79). He suggests that
the Ithacans cut out the suitors as middlemen and snatch all his property for
themselves. That way, he says, he might one day have some chance of getting
it back. Better to be robbed by thieves that cannot run too far. If anything,
Telemachos has now sunk below the low moral standards of which he has

just been accusing the Ithacans themselves. That the Ithacans do not take him up on his offer or race each other to loot the palace becomes a tribute to their basic honesty and reminds us that they are not as Telemachos portrays them.

The fall from the heroic opening lines is precipitous. Telemachos ends up presenting himself as an extremely callow and pathetic character, reduced to ineffectual and adolescent anger: "So he spoke in anger, and dashed to the ground the scepter in a stormburst of tears" (2.80–81). The Ithacans are silent, like those who hear a riveting story with a bad turn. They are unsure how to react. They seem to feel that the most proper response to the implicit insults and attacks would be angry words of their own. But no one dares. It is not, of course, that they are afraid of Telemachos but that he seems too fragile, too near the breaking point.

## THE SUITORS' COUNTERSUIT: *ODYSSEY* 2.85–128

Antinoös, the ringleader of the suitors, takes the floor to present their case. He admits that the courtship has gone awry, but he puts the blame squarely and solely on Penelope. Pieced together from Antinoös's account, the chronicle of events seems to run as follows. For nearly four years, at least, the suitors have had a desire for Penelope to marry one of them.[4] The trouble began early on, when Penelope began "denying the desires of the Achaians" (2.90), who began to feel cheated. At or about this time, she made clear her intentions. She admitted Odysseus's death and promised—tacitly, if not explicitly—to remarry. She sent out—or continued to send out—secret messages of encouragement to all the suitors individually: "For she holds out hope to all, and makes promises to each man" (2.91). Nevertheless, she requested a delay before she chose the man—enough time, she contended, to do her duty by her father-in-law, who would need a burial shroud when he dies. This is the famous weaving trick that is recounted three times in the *Odyssey*. The suitors consented and considered themselves rather gallant for doing so: "and the proud heart in us was persuaded" (2.103). The weaving went on for more than three years before the suitors discovered that Penelope had been cheating them, unweaving at night whatever she had woven by day. When the suitors eventually caught her, they compelled her to finish the shroud. They were not, however, able to compel her to choose a husband.

The question of how much actual power the suitors have over Penelope is complex and is fundamental to understanding the structure of the conflicts in the *Odyssey*. Telemachos says that his mother is beset by suitors "against her will" and that the suitors can and will force her to marry. Yet we must confront complaints, like those from Denys Page, that the suitors do not exercise the power that they have. Page accuses Homer of a serious lapse of narrative competency when the suitors neglect to force Penelope to marry once she has finished the shroud.

> [F]or it would surely be a sad story-teller, who told us that Penelope was caught unpicking the web and compelled to finish it, and yet that nothing whatever happened as a consequence— that the Suitors generously regarded the incident as closed, and allowed affairs to continue exactly as they were before the story of the web began. But that is what actually happens in the *Odyssey*.... (1955, 120–21)

The suitors are not acting generously. Rather, they are applying as much pressure as they can manage. If they do not go farther, it is because their power is checked by the power that the Ithacan populace itself wields.

It is an overlooked—if strange—fact that the structure of power between the protagonists and the mass of unnamed common people is more significant in the *Odyssey* than in the *Iliad*. Though the setting of the *Iliad* is either the crowded Greek camp, bustling Troy, or the battlefield, the Greek or Trojan populace has little or no influence on the direction of the plot, and their leaders do not expect them to claim any. The poet gives them flighty emotions and no backbone. Thersites, thoroughly dominated and humiliated by Odysseus, is the symbol of their role. In the *Odyssey*, in contrast, each party thinks that having the populace on its side would ensure its success; but the populace is sternly independent. Each party is also afraid that a mistake on its part will push the populace over to the other side. Furthermore, it seems that solid moral standards guide Ithacan opinion. Telemachos is afraid of popular resentment if he sends his mother away. The suitors are afraid of popular retaliation if they are caught hurting Telemachos. Once home, Odysseus also assumes that the Ithacan populace will be a force to reckon with. He asks Athene how he will escape even if he kills all the suitors. The implication is that the Ithacans will not tolerate his action. From book 24, we know that this is a fact. No one seems to have any confusion about the popular Ithacan response. The people are not to be easily manipulated. Theirs is a solid and primal sense of justice. They would rise up equally against the killers of Telemachos as against the murderer of the suitors.

Telemachos's claim that Penelope is being courted against her will is not in any way a moral accusation. How unwilling can Penelope be and still hold out hope to the suitors? Anything to which she does not consent would probably be much resented by her own parents and would certainly not be sanctioned by the Ithacans. Furthermore, the suitors need Penelope to choose one of them. If the choice is not hers, I think it would be impossible for the suitors to decide among themselves who would carry her away and who would go home disappointed. If it were possible simply to carry off an unwilling Penelope, as if by the hair, someone probably would have already done so.

Like Telemachos, Antinoös ends by implicating the Ithacans. Unlike Telemachos, he makes a point that the Ithacans cannot deny: Penelope is increasing her *kleos*, and the Ithacans are helping her. The townspeople esteem Penelope in direct proportion to her obstinate fidelity to the memory of Odysseus (as many modern readers of the epic do as well). Several sources reveal that this is the opinion of the Ithacan populace. In his very next speech in book 2, when he gives the culminating reason not to send Penelope home to her father, Ikarios, Telemachos cites the fact that the Ithacans would resent him for it (*Od.* 2.136–37). Penelope, in book 19, reveals Ithacan expectations when she wonders whether she should continue to live in a way that would please the people or whether she should remarry and leave her house (19.524–29). Finally, the Ithacans speak for themselves in book 23. We overhear them speculating, outside the barred doors of the palace, that Penelope has disappointed them by accepting a new husband (23.148–51). To them, Penelope is most admirable if she resists marriage. Antinoös seems to know this, since he does not ask for direct intervention from the Ithacans: he merely asks them to stay out of the way.

What is left to the suitors if they cannot or will not use direct force against the person of Penelope? They seem to believe that they have but one alternative. If Penelope cannot be directly pressured as a woman, she can be indirectly pressured as a mother. Therefore, the suitors have quite consciously resolved to do just what Telemachos is complaining about. They intend to waste the estate until either there is nothing left of it or Penelope chooses a new husband. Their hope is that the mother will capitulate to pressure from her son or will buckle under the weight of her own guilt over depriving her son of his rightful inheritance and destroying his future prospects. "So long, I say, will your livelihood and possessions be eaten away, as long as she keeps this purpose, one which the very gods, I think, put into her heart" (2.123–25). This is a united front. Later, Eurymachos, in his speech, echoes the strategy: "there will not be compensation, ever, while she makes the Achaians put off marriage with her" (2.203–5).

One of the most important implications of this sequence is that the suitors have only recently begun their war of attrition against the House of Odysseus. There are many reasons for thinking so. Before Penelope began to frustrate their marital hopes, the suitors had no incentive for squandering an estate that they hoped to acquire themselves. (In fact, the suitors seem mainly to have offered hospitality to Telemachos in their own homes.)[5] It is unlikely that they were pursuing this strategy during the three years that Penelope resorted to the trick of the web. Until the suitors caught Penelope at her trick, they had no reason to antagonize the woman whom each hoped would choose him to wed and from whom each was getting secret, personal encouragements. Besides, Penelope's trick of the web becomes much less effective—if not self-destructive—with the suitors in residence. Even if we assume that Odysseus's wealth (poor, compared to that of the kings of the mainland cities) could have supported the suitors for so long, what good would Penelope draw from giving them carte blanche to waste it? Also, what good would the suitors' strategy of attrition do them if Penelope has already proved impervious to it? One would even expect Telemachos, far from giving up his cause just after Eurymachos complains about having been forced to waste so much time on false promises, to have simply reminded Eurymachos that he had been paid well for those years. Furthermore, Telemachos says that he was alerted to the threat to his property only some little time before Athene's epiphany. If he had ignored that fact for three years, he would perhaps be as culpable as the suitors—and much more stupid. In short, the only sequence of events that involves no logical or narratological contradictions is one in which the suitors' strategy of attrition is started after Penelope is caught cheating and still refuses to pick a husband, even though the shroud is complete.

## TELEMACHOS'S ANSWER: *Odyssey* 2.129–45

The suitors' strategy is aimed at Penelope. It is never intended to force Telemachos's hand directly or even to get him to do what it claims to ask of him. Though Antinoös pretends to urge Telemachos to return Penelope to her father, the suitors apparently neither want nor expect Telemachos to do anything of the kind. They seem as reluctant as Telemachos to involve Ikarios. After all, as Telemachos points out, the suitors could ask Ikarios for his daughter's hand on their own account, even in Penelope's absence. Thus, Antinoös seems to make his demand knowing full well how unthinkable it is for Telemachos, who, in fact, rejects it promptly in his next speech: "Antinoös, I cannot thrust the mother who bore me, who raised me, out of the house against her will" (*Od.* 2.130–31).

His reasons are not very high-minded and mainly involve concern for his own personal and financial security. Sending Penelope away, he worries, would incur a great expense (presumably because her dowry would go back with her) as well as retaliation from the wronged parties—Penelope's father, Penelope herself, and the Ithacan people.

> It will be hard
> to pay back Ikarios, if willingly I dismiss my mother.
> I will suffer some evil from her father, and the spirit will give
>     me
> more yet, for my mother will call down her furies upon me
> as she goes out of the house, and I shall have the people's
>     resentment.
> (2.132–37)

Telemachos ends by saying, "I will not be the one to say that word to her" (2.137). He thus leaves open the possibility that he would not oppose the one who did. For their part, however, the suitors have no intention of playing that role, and they do not blink when Telemachos effetely insists that if they are not happy with his demands, they can just go home. Telemachos lacks the heart to brave either of his options—repatriate his mother or fight the suitors. He is reduced to threatening to call on Zeus for aid, though his threat seems pathetically weakened by the word somehow: "I will cry out to the gods everlasting in the hope that Zeus might somehow grant a reversal of fortunes" (2.143–44).

## THE SPEECHES OF HALITHERSES AND EURYMACHOS: *ODYSSEY* 2.146–223

To everyone's surprise, two eagles suddenly appear in the sky. They fly companionably together until they reach the assembly. Then,

> they turned on each other suddenly in a thick shudder
> of wings, and swooped over the heads of all, with eyes glaring
> and deadly, and tore each other by neck and cheek with their
>     talons.
> (*Od.* 2.151–53)

"This," says West, "is the commonest type of omen in Homer, and the interpretation is invariably easy" (1988, 141). The Ithacans, however, are less sure of its meaning: "Then all were astounded at the birds, when their eyes saw them, and they pondered in their hearts over what might come of it" (*Od.* 2.155–56).

Taking the floor, Halitherses offers his interpretation, construing the omen in a way that is congenial and not at all surprising to us, the external audience, who have been privy to the Olympian council described in book 1. Halitherses prophesies that Odysseus is still alive and will soon be on his way home (2.163–66). The prophecy does not impress the Ithacans. Nor should it, really. After all, as fictional characters and members of the audience internal to the narrative, they do not enjoy the advantage of knowing what we, the external audience, know. The narrator, who endorses Halitherses' skill to us, does not speak to them. They are left merely with Halitherses' self-promotional claim: "I who foretell this am not untried, I know what I am saying" (2.170). Halitherses offers no recent or conclusive examples of his skill. He gives only one old and wholly inadequate example.

> Concerning [Odysseus], I say that everything was accomplished
> in the way I said it would be at the time the Argives took ship
> for Ilion, and with them went resourceful Odysseus.
> I said that after much suffering, with all his companions
> lost, in the twentieth year, not recognized by any,
> he would come home. And now all this is being accomplished.
>   (2.171–76)

His argument is essentially this: "The fact that I so clearly foresaw an event through the gloom of twenty long years ought to prove to you that I can easily discern this same event when it is just around the corner."

The force of the narrative is to pull the audience in two directions. We who know of the council on Olympus know that Halitherses' prediction is substantially right, if not entirely accurate.[6] At the same time, we cannot reasonably expect any levelheaded Ithacan to accept Halitherses' specious logic.

Eurymachos, the next suitor to speak, impugns the prophet's motive and method. First, he makes a cogent, general point about the interpretation of natural signs. Not all things, he argues, are meaningful simply because we wish them to be: "Many are the birds who under the sun's rays wander the sky; not all of them mean anything" (2.181–82). Next, he attacks Halitherses for offering his accommodating prophecy with an eye to personal profit. Eurymachos then offers his own prediction, which, given Telemachos's psychology and the hostility that his current demands have aroused in the suitors, has a certain ring of wisdom.

> But I will tell you straight out, and it will be a thing
>   accomplished:

if you, who know much and have known it long, stir up a
   younger
man, and by talking him round with words encourage his
   anger,
then first of all, it will be the worse for him; he will not
on account of all these sayings be able to accomplish anything.
   (2.187–91)

Though less prophecy, perhaps, than threat, Eurymachos's words constitute a more plausible account of future facts. Kindling the impotent anger of Telemachos will only ignite the potent wrath of the suitors. Eurymachos would fain portray the suitors as Telemachos's real protectors: "And on you, old sir, we shall lay a penalty, and it will grieve your mind as you pay it, and that for you will be a great sorrow" (2.192–93). Eurymachos's advice that Telemachos obey the suitors, though, is quickly backed up by more unconditional demands and threats of force. He then restates the grim purpose of their strategy of attrition: "[Telemachos's] possessions will be wretchedly eaten away, there will not be compensation, ever, while [Penelope] makes the Achaians put off marriage with her" (2.203–5).

    Like Antinoös, Eurymachos ends his speech with the insistence that the suitors are really Penelope's victims, and he even adds more plausibility to the argument. By stringing the suitors along with her delays and tricks, he claims, Penelope has wasted their valuable time and prevented them from wooing other desirable young women as their brides.

... while we, awaiting this, all our days
quarrel for the sake of her excellence, nor ever go after
others, whom any one of us might properly marry.
   (2.205–7)

By implication, private Ithacan families with daughters of marriageable age are also paying the price of Penelope's dilatory tactics.

    Howard Clarke's judgment intended to describe Telemachos in book 1 rings true here as well: "Athena's encouragement is not without its effect, but Telemachus' adolescent attempts to take charge are a fiasco" (1969, 29). All of a sudden, Telemachos drops his plea, as if finally recognizing that he can make no headway in this manner without the support of the Ithacans. He contents himself with announcing that he wants to go away on a voyage to Sparta and Pylos to learn what has happened to his father. Even here, the young man's essential resourcelessness is painfully evident: he must petition the suitors to provide him with a ship and a crew.

## THE SPEECHES OF MENTOR AND LEOKRITOS:
### *ODYSSEY* 2.224–59

Mentor, an old and close friend to Odysseus, intercedes in an attempt to shame the Ithacans into defending the House of Odysseus. He lays directly on the Ithacans' shoulders the blame for the suitors' excesses.

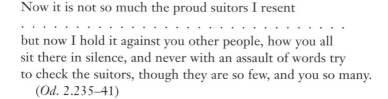

> Now it is not so much the proud suitors I resent
> . . . . . . . . . . . . . . . . . . . . . . . . . . . . . .
> but now I hold it against you other people, how you all
> sit there in silence, and never with an assault of words try
> to check the suitors, though they are so few, and you so many.
>      (*Od.* 2.235–41)

Mentor's rebuke is caustic. He implies that the Ithacans are cowards. He says that they are unworthy of decent, fair, or benign rule, since obviously they respond only to force and shun the imperatives of justice. He claims that they have forgotten the legacy of Odysseus.

Mentor, of course, as an appointed caretaker of the House of Odysseus wrongly assumes that Ithacan interest corresponds to his. As we have seen, the Ithacans have other interests as well. Even the invocation of Odysseus as the gentle and benevolent leader is called into question by the text, since Odysseus proved to be a disaster for many of these families. Aigyptios's son, for example, was one of those eaten alive by the Cyclops. Nevertheless, the violence of the next speaker's response indicates a fear that Mentor's argument may have touched too close to home. Mentor was making a good point.

Leokritos now brazenly threatens brute force against any Ithacans who might think about taking up Telemachos's cause. He emphasizes that the suitors' strength and determination know no bounds and that none would scruple to apply brute force. Telemachos, he says, may have a couple of old men on his side, but the boy lacks all resolve and will accomplish nothing. When Leokritos abruptly cuts the assembly short, the suitors are in full control.

## TELEMACHOS'S BREAK WITH THE SUITORS:
### *ODYSSEY* 2.260–320

Walking along the beach, alone and despondent, Telemachos betrays his tendency to give up altogether too easily. In his prayer to Athene, he claims that the plans she had sketched in book 1 are now thwarted by both the

Achaians and the suitors. He knows himself incapable of taking the initiative in planning his own trip. Without divine intervention, he would have presumably abandoned it. But Athene, disguised now as Mentor, takes over, assuaging the young man's deepest worry by twice insisting that Telemachos is no coward.

While Athene goes off to secure a ship for the trip to the Peloponnese, Telemachos returns to his house, though still shaken. He now has a private confrontation with Antinoös, who attempts to make peace and, amazingly, removes every obstacle to Telemachos's voyage.

> Antinoös, with a smile, came straight up to Telemachos,
> and took him by the hand and spoke and named him, saying:
> "High-spoken intemperate Telemachos, now let no other
> evil be considered in your heart, neither action
> nor word, but eat and drink with me, as you did in past time.
> The Achaians will see to it that all these things are
>     accomplished,
> the ship, and chosen companions, so that you may the more
>     quickly
> reach sacred Pylos, after news about your proud father."
>     (*Od.* 2.301–8)

It is important to understand that Antinoös is offering to reinstate a former friendliness. This means that at some time—and from Antinoös's point of view, probably to this very day—Telemachos was more or less one of the group and thought of himself that way. Antikleia, in Hades, gives independent confirmation that Telemachos and the young lords of Ithaca used to get on well (11.184–87).

Telemachos now wholly rejects the help of the suitors and all association with them. He scalds them with the anger that is "steaming up" inside him (2.315). "I will endeavor to visit evil destructions upon you, either by going to Pylos, or remaining here in the district" (2.316–17).

Is announcing an irreconcilable animus toward these desperate men a foolish move on Telemachos's part? Is Telemachos being reckless and shortsighted? I shall have more to say about these issues in chapter 3, when I investigate Telemachos's character. In any case, Telemachos never again fraternizes with the suitors except as is called for in the plan of revenge that he and Odysseus implement in the later books. I see no reason to accept George Devereux's psychoanalytic claim that an Oedipus complex renders Telemachos ambivalent about what the suitors deserve.[7]

## THE SUITORS' TRUE INTENTIONS:
### ODYSSEY 2.321–36

Once Telemachos is off the scene, the suitors express their unguarded thoughts. We learn of the falseness of Antinoös's offer of friendship. These men have no tenderness whatsoever for Telemachos. As they prepare their dinner and move freely about the house, they mock and insult Telemachos behind his back. They maintain that as long as Telemachos is in Ithaca and under their control, he is harmless. They are aware, however, that Telemachos's intended trip to Pylos and Sparta could change everything. There, on the mainland, he might recruit reinforcements. Worse, he might obtain poison and return to kill them all by treachery.

By highlighting the threat of poison (or reinforcement), Homer preserves a delicate balance in the plot. Telemachos remains a personally undaunting figure and becomes an outsized threat only when he is allowed to leave the island. The suitors are not wrong to worry about poison. This could easily have been Athene's plan, since she describes a similar tactic used by Odysseus: "Odysseus, you see, had gone there also in his swift ship in search of a poison to kill men" (*Od.* 1.260–61). Had the thought occurred to him in Sparta, of course, Telemachos might have easily gotten the means to overpower the suitors. Menelaos declares that he had been ready to drive out the dwellers of a whole city for Odysseus (4.176), and Helen displays her pharmacological skill.

The suitors now boldly confess what they call their work. They intend to divide up all of Telemachos's possessions among themselves (though whoever succeeds in marrying Penelope will also become owner of the palace, presumably because that is something that cannot be easily divided). In short, their method is deceit, and their actual purpose is not love but theft.[8]

## EURYKLEIA'S WARNING AND TELEMACHOS'S
### DEPARTURE: ODYSSEY 2.337–434

The scene abruptly shifts to the wide storeroom of the palace, where lie the treasures that the suitors aim to plunder.

> [Telemachos] went down into his father's high-roofed
> and wide storeroom, where gold and bronze were lying piled
>     up,
> and abundant clothing in the bins, and fragrant olive oil,
> and in it jars of wine, sweet to drink, aged,
> were standing.
>     (*Od.* 2.337–41)

Telemachos has his nurse, Eurykleia, the incontestably loyal servant and guardian of the house, prepare his traveling provisions for him. When he confides his plans to her, she is appalled at the foolishness of the risk and aggressively tries to dissuade him from the voyage. She seems to know quite well just what the suitors intend. "And these men will devise evils against you, on your returning, so you shall die by guile, and they divide all that is yours" (2.367–68).

The final fifty-two lines of the book are devoted to the arrangements that Athene makes for the voyage. She borrows a ship and drugs the suitors into a sweet slumber. Finally, after everything is ready, she calls Telemachos to board the ship. Slipping it out of the harbor, they set sail for Pylos.

## FURTHER CRISES: BEYOND BOOK 2

The first major crisis in the *Odyssey*, then, is precipitated by the suitors' change of strategy in their struggle with Penelope and places Telemachos squarely in the middle of the conflict. From this moment, the danger to Telemachos steadily intensifies. Two more crises mark its significant stages.

In book 4, as they amuse themselves nonchalantly "with discs and with light spears for throwing" (4.626), the suitors get a shock. Noëmon, the Ithacan citizen from whom Athene borrowed a ship, casually asks Antinoös whether he thinks Telemachos might have returned from Pylos yet. The suitors, who had no idea that Telemachos ever sailed, are stunned. Antinoös is beside himself with anger, as the true seriousness of the threat to his interests suddenly dawns on him. He is described as "raging, the heart within filled black to the brim with anger from beneath, but his two eyes showed like fire in their blazing" (*Od.* 4.661–62). These lines were athetized by Aristarchus because they are identical to *Iliad* 1.103–4. But reference to the *Iliad* nicely brings out the tone of this passage. Antinoös and Agamemnon feel the same way. In the *Iliad*, Calchas has just indicted Agamemnon as the cause of the devastating plague, and Agamemnon realizes that he will have to surrender Chryseis, the concubine that he loves as much as—if not more than—his lawful wife, Clytemnestra. Calchas threatens, and the Atreidean eagle prepares for attack, eyes blazing like fire.[9] One is reminded of the boar in the hunt in book 19 of the *Odyssey*.

> The thudding made by the feet of men and dogs came to him
> as they closed on him in the hunt, and against them he from his
>      woodlair
> bristled strongly his nape, and with fire from his eyes glaring
> stood up to face them close.
>      (19.444–47)

Telemachos has brought Antinoös, the man in power, to bay—like a wild boar.

In fear that Telemachos might now topple his greedy plans, Antinoös furiously decides to ambush the boy on his way home from Pylos and to kill him.

> But come now, give me a fast ship and twenty companions,
> so that I can watch his return and lie in wait for him
> in the narrow strait between Ithaka and towering Samos,
> and make him sorry for this sea-going in search of his father.
>     (4.669–72)

The third crisis in the conflict between Telemachos and the suitors is forced by the failure of this ambush. In book 16, the suitors call a secret assembly and impel the next move.

> We who are here must make our plans for the grim destruction
> of Telemachos, so he cannot escape us; since I have no thought
> we can get our present purpose accomplished while he is living.
>     (16.371–73)

Antinoös fears that Telemachos will report to the Ithacans and that they will be sufficiently scandalized and enraged to attack the suitors. Once again, the Ithacans are a factor in the balance of power. Antinoös has no doubt that they would be sufficient to drive him and his fellow suitors into exile.

> But come now, before he can gather the Achaians and bring
>     them
> to assembly; for I think he will not let us go, but work out
> his anger, and stand up before them all and tell them
> how we designed his sudden murder, but we could not catch
>     him;
> and they will have no praise for us when they hear of our evil
> deeds, and I fear they will work some evil on us, and drive us
> from our own country, so we must make for another
> community.
>     (16.376–82)

Antinoös, whether sincerely or not, presents the suitors with an alternative to the assassination of Telemachos. If they are not seriously ready, he explains, to kill Telemachos and to continue with their plan to rob the boy of what he has and divide it among themselves (a plan that Antinoös reiterates here), the suitors can disband and go each to his own home, courting Penelope from there with whatever expensive gifts each might manage. None of the suitors embraces this alternative except Amphinomos, who only wants to delay long enough to query the gods' will.

> We should first have to ask the gods for their counsel.
> Then, if the ordinances from great Zeus approve of it,
> I myself would kill him and tell all others to do so.
>    (16.402–4)

Homer's plot necessitates the delay. Without it, Telemachos would be dead before he could set foot inside the palace again.

But the suitors have no intention of renouncing their plans, a fact that the poet makes emphatically clear some fifty lines later, when Eurymachos lies to Penelope, who has just heard of the plot against Telemachos's life and is demanding that the suitors give it up. Eurymachos says that "of all men Telemachos is the dearest to me by far" (16.445–46)—and there is ample evidence that of all the suitors, Eurymachos is, at least, the most friendly to Telemachos. However, after Eurymachos claims that he would never allow any harm to come to the boy, the poet adds, "So he spoke, encouraging her, but himself was planning the murder" (16.448–49).

From here on out, the death of Telemachos is merely a matter of time; that is, unless the suitors are checked by some potent force outside themselves, they will murder Penelope's son. In fact, they are on the brink of assassinating him in book 20, on the very morning that Penelope announces the bow contest—that is, on the last day of their own lives.[10]

## NOTES

1. Curiously, Eurynomos is the only named suitor whose death is not accounted for by Homer. A metrical replacement, Eurydamas, otherwise unmentioned in book 22, dies in what seems to be his stead. In two key manuscripts (Marcianus and Caesenas), the name is Euryalos, which appears in a list of Trojans cited by Demodokos (*Od.* 8.115). The pattern of the deaths of the fourteen named suitors who die is highly structured. The anomaly of 22.283 is therefore striking. If, indeed, Odysseus kills Eurynomos (not Eurydamas or Euryalos) in this line, the irony of *Odyssey* 2.34 is all the greater.

2. R. D. Dawe finds this passage disturbing. He questions the purpose of announcing an event that took place "at some unspecified time during the last twenty years" (1993, 95). Dawe is surely right that this first evil (or, rather, the acceptance of it) occurred much earlier and is, in this sense, old news. What is new, however, is the public announcement. Without it, most of what follows would be incomprehensible, especially Telemachos's attitude toward the courtship of his mother by the suitors.

3. Telemachos daydreams about his father's return, but even he recognizes this as no more than a daydream, and his journey to the mainland is not motivated by belief in Odysseus's return. I will return to these points in chapter 3, when I investigate Telemachos's character and psychology.

4. We do not know whether the suitors were actively courting Penelope before this. If they were, she was somehow not denying their desires; perhaps she was tolerating their amorous interests.

5. See *Od.* 11.187.

6. Halitherses' prediction is not entirely accurate even from the audience's point of view. We know that Odysseus is in fact not "already somewhere nearby" (*Od.* 2.164–65). Nor is he "working out the death and destruction of all these men" (2.165–66).

7. Devereux writes of Telemachos, "Like Hamlet, he is incapable of punishing the suitors, because he unconsciously identifies himself with them" (1957, 381).

8. Do the suitors feel shame about their real intentions? I find the best evidence that they do in the report that Amphimedon makes to the shades in Hades: "At that time [i.e., as soon as Penelope had finished the shroud under duress] an evil spirit, coming from somewhere, brought back Odysseus to the remote part of his estate, where his swineherd was living" (*Od.* 24.149–50). Amphimedon ignores the interval of time between the completion of the shroud and the arrival of Odysseus. This is the time of the suitors' shameful waste of Telemachos's estate. Though he does not totally avoid responsibility for his actions as a suitor, he may be (understandably) eager to minimize them. Why should he make himself seem worse to his fellow shades than he has to? Page calls this passage "among the most perplexing of all mysteries in the *Odyssey*" (1955, 120).

9. Dawe discounts the lines of the *Odyssey*, taking as the original the *Iliad*, "where Agamemnon may reasonably be said to be feeling sorrow" and "where flashing eyes belong more to the outraged field marshal than to the *primus inter pares* domestic villain Antinoös" (1993, 203). Such criticism seems to flow from the commonplace discounting of the domestic situation at Ithaca. Is the purpose of the supposed interpolation meant to unfairly (melodramatically) augment the stature of Antinoös, making him as noble as Agamemnon? One could quibble about the nobility of Agamemnon or to what degree he is held in honor by Homer. More important, the lines do not heighten (or even lower) the moral status of Agamemnon; they are primarily used in the *Iliad* to intensify a sense of danger and threatening power.

10. Contrary to Longinus, I find that the construction of the conflict in the *Odyssey* bears a family resemblance to that of the *Iliad*. In the broadest strokes, the success of character A (Penelope/Chryseis) forces character B (the suitors/Agamemnon) to exert power over character C (Telemachos/Achilles), whose dilemma fuels the plot. Thus, the *Odyssey*—no less than the *Iliad*—opens at a moment of crisis. This initial crisis reveals the major conflict of the plot, which in the *Odyssey*, as in any satisfying story, establishes an anxiety about the outcome.

# Chronology

| | |
|---|---|
| 1400–200 BC | What is today known as Greece exists as Balkan Peninsula, composed of many small kingdoms. |
| 1250–1200 BC | Troy destroyed. Some historians believe Trojan War did occur; yet Homer's writings are not to be construed as an accounting of that occurrence. |
| 8th century BC | Homer born and lived in Eastern Greece or Asia Minor. |
| 8th or 7th century BC | Homer composes *Iliad* and *Odyssey*. |
| 776 BC | Panathenaic games, models for modern-day Olympics, first occur. Homer's works recited at such Greek festivals. |
| 6th or 7th century BC | Written manuscripts of Homer's work available. |
| 1488 | First printed works of Homer appear in Florence. Prepared by Chalcondyles of Athens, who taught Greek in Italy. |

# Contributors

HAROLD BLOOM is Sterling Professor of the Humanities at Yale University. He is the author of 30 books, including *Shelley's Mythmaking, The Visionary Company, Blake's Apocalypse, Yeats, A Map of Misreading, Kabbalah and Criticism, Agon: Toward a Theory of Revisionism, The American Religion, The Western Canon,* and *Omens of Millennium: The Gnosis of Angels, Dreams, and Resurrection. The Anxiety of Influence* sets forth Professor Bloom's provocative theory of the literary relationships between the great writers and their predecessors. His most recent books include *Shakespeare: The Invention of the Human,* a 1998 National Book Award finalist, *How to Read and Why, Genius: A Mosaic of One Hundred Exemplary Creative Minds, Hamlet: Poem Unlimited, Where Shall Wisdom Be Found?,* and *Jesus and Yahweh: The Names Divine.* In 1999, Professor Bloom received the prestigious American Academy of Arts and Letters Gold Medal for Criticism. He has also received the International Prize of Catalonia, the Alfonso Reyes Prize of Mexico, and the Hans Christian Andersen Bicentennial Prize of Denmark.

CHARLES SEGAL, now deceased, was Professor of Classics at Harvard University. He wrote many books on ancient Greek literature, including *Euripides and the Poetics of Sorrow* and *Sophocles' Tragic World.* He also edited volume seventy-six of *Harvard Studies in Classical Philology* and contributed to other volumes in that series.

MARGALIT FINKELBERG has been Professor and Chair of Classics at Tel Aviv University. She has written extensively on ancient Greek literature

247

and is the author or coauthor of titles such as *Homer, the Bible and Beyond* and *The Birth of Literary Fiction in Ancient Greece*.

S. DOUGLAS OLSON teaches classics at the University of Minnesota. He is the author of *Euripides' Cylcops* and the editor of books by or about Aristophanes.

LILLIAN EILEEN DOHERTY teaches classics at the University of Maryland, College Park. She has published *Gender and the Interpretation of Classical Myth* and also translated Jacqueline de Romilly's *Short History of Greek Literature*.

HELENE P. FOLEY is Professor of Classics at Barnard College, Columbia University. Among her publications are *Female Acts in Greek Tragedy* and *Homeric Hymn to Demeter*. She also coauthored *Women in the Classical World: Image and Text* and has edited or translated titles.

FREDERICK AHL teaches classics at Cornell University. He published a book on *Oedipus* and also *Metaformations: Soundplay and Wordplay in Ovid and Other Classical Poets*. Additionally, he has translated texts.

HANNA M. ROISMAN teaches classics at Colby College. She published *Nothing Is as It Seems: The Tragedy of the Implicit in Euripides' "Hippolytus."*

NANCY FELSON-RUBIN has been Professor of Classics at the University of Georgia and has published *Regarding Penelope: From Character to Poetics*. Additionally, she has written many articles on early Greek epic and lyric poetry and literary theory.

STEPHEN V. TRACY has been Professor of Classics at Ohio State University. He authored *Athens and Macedon: Attic Letter-Cutters of 300 to 229 BC*.

BRUCE LOUDEN teaches in the languages and linguistics department at the University of Texas, El Paso. In addition to his book on the *Odyssey*, he authored *The* Iliad: *Structure, Myth, and Meaning*.

MARK BUCHAN teaches classics at Princeton University, where he specializes in Archaic and Classical Greek literature. He has published *The Limits of Heroism: Homer and the Ethics of Reading*. He is co-editor of a forthcoming collection of essays on Lacan.

RICHARD HEITMAN is Assistant Professor of Classics, Philosophy, and Great Ideas at Carthage College. He has also taught at the University of Chicago and in the CUNY system. His book *Taking Her Seriously: Penelope & the Plot of Homer's* Odyssey was published by the University of Michigan Press in 2005.

# Bibliography

Barnouw, Jeffrey. *Odysseus, Hero of Practical Intelligence: Deliberation and Signs in Homer's* Odyssey. Lanham, Md.: University Press of America, 2004.

Benardete, Seth. *The Bow and the Lyre: A Platonic Reading of the* Odyssey. Lanham, Md.; London: Rowman & Littlefield Publishers, 1997.

Brann, Eva T. H. *Homeric Moments: Clues to Delight in Reading the* Odyssey *and the* Iliad. Philadelphia: Paul Dry Books, 2002.

Cook, Erwin F. *The* Odyssey *in Athens: Myths of Cultural Origins*. Ithaca, N.Y.: Cornell University Press, 1995.

Crotty, Kevin. *The Poetics of Supplication: Homer's* Iliad *and* Odyssey. Ithaca, N.Y.: Cornell University Press, 1994.

Curry, Neil. *The Bending of the Bow: A Version of the Closing Books of Homer's* Odyssey. London: Enitharmon Press; Chester Springs, Pa.: U.S. distributor, Dufour Editions, 1993.

Dimock, George. *The Unity of the* Odyssey. Amherst: University of Massachusetts Press, 1989.

Doherty, Lillian Eileen. "Contemporary Feminist Readings of Homer's Penelope." From *Classic Joyce*, edited by Franca Ruggieri: 229–243. Rome, Italy: Bulzoni, 1999.

———. *Siren Songs: Gender, Audiences, and Narrators in the* Odyssey. Ann Arbor: University of Michigan Press, 1995.

Dougherty, Carol. *The Raft of Odysseus: The Ethnographic Imagination of Homer's* Odyssey. Oxford; New York: Oxford University Press, 2001.

Edwards, Mark W. "Homer and Oral Tradition: The Formula, II." *Oral

*Tradition* 3, nos. 1–2 (January–May 1988): 11–60. (Journal article)

———. "Philology and the Oral Theory." *Pacific Coast Philology* 17, nos. 1–2 (November 1982): 1–8.

Fajardo-Acosta, Fidel. *The Hero's Failure in the Tragedy of Odysseus: A Revisionist Analysis.* Lewiston, N.Y.: E. Mellen Press, 1990.

Felson-Rubin, Nancy. *Regarding Penelope; From Character to* Poetics. Princeton, N.J.: Princeton University Press, 1994.

Finley, M. I. "The World of *Odysseus.*" New York: New York Review of Books, 2002.

Foley, John Miles. *Traditional Oral Epic: The* Odyssey, Beowulf, *and the Serbo-Croatian Return Song.* Berkeley: University of California Press, 1990.

Fowler, Robert. *The Cambridge Companion to Homer.* Cambridge: Cambridge University Press, 2004.

Griffin, Jasper. *Homer.* London: Bristol Classical, 2001.

Harrison, S. J. *Texts, Ideas, and the Classics: Scholarship, Theory, and Classical Literature.* Oxford; New York: Oxford University Press, 2001.

Helldén, Jan. "The Homeric Epics: Collective Memory or Collective Fantasy." From *Inclinate Aurem: Oral Perspectives on Early European Verbal Culture: A Symposium,* edited by Jan Helldén, Minna Skafte Jensen, and Thomas Pettitt: 21–53. Odense, Denmark: Odense University Press, 2001.

Jong, Irene J. F. de. *A Narratological Commentary on the* Odyssey. Cambridge; New York: Cambridge University Press, 2001.

———. "The Subjective Style in Odysseus' Wanderings." *The Classical Quarterly* 42, no. 1 (1992): 1–11.

Katz, Marylin A. *Penelope's Renown: Meaning and Indeterminacy in the* Odyssey. Princeton, N.J.: Princeton University Press, 1991.

Komar, Kathleen L. and Ross Shideler. *Lyrical Symbols and Narrative Transformations: Essays in Honor of Ralph Freedman.* Columbia, S.C.: Camden House, 1998.

MacDonald, Dennis Ronald. *Christianizing Homer: The* Odyssey, Plato, *and the Acts of Andrew.* New York: Oxford University Press, 1994.

———. *The Homeric Epics and the Gospel of Mark.* New Haven: Yale University Press, 2000.

Mackie, C. J. *Oral Performance and Its Context.* Leiden; Boston: Brill, 2004.

Malkin, Irad. *The Returns of Odysseus: Colonization and Ethnicity.* Berkeley; London: University of California Press, 1998.

Martin, Richard P. "Homer's *Iliad* and *Odyssey.*" From *Teaching Oral Traditions,* edited by John Miles Foley: 339–350. New York, N.Y.: Modern Language Association of America, 1998.

Martindale, Colin and Paul Tuffin. "If Homer Is the Poet of the *Iliad*, Then He May Not Be the Poet of the *Odyssey*." *Literary and Linguistic Computing: Journal of the Association for Literary and Linguistic Computing* 11, no. 3 (September 1996): 109–120.

Mifsud, Mari Lee. "On the Idea of Reflexive Rhetoric in Homer." *Philosophy and Rhetoric* 31, no. 1 (1998): 41–54.

Mills, Donald H. and James G. Keenan. *The Hero and the Sea: Patterns of Chaos in Ancient Myth*. Wauconda, Ill.: Bolchazy-Carducci, 2002.

Minchin, Elizabeth. *Homer and the Resources of Memory: Some Applications of Cognitive Theory to the* Iliad *and the* Odyssey. Oxford; New York: Oxford University Press, 2001.

Morrison, James V. *A Companion to Homer's* Odyssey. Westport, Conn.; London: Greenwood Press, 2003.

Peradotto, John. *Man in the Middle Voice: Name and Narration in the* Odyssey. Princeton, N.J.: Princeton University Press, 1990.

———. "The Social Control of Sexuality: Odyssean Dialogics." *Arethusa* 26, no. 2 (Spring 1993): 173–82.

Rutherford, Richard. *Homer*. Oxford: Published for the Classical Association, Oxford University Press, 1996.

Shear, Ione Mylonas. *Tales of Heroes: The Origins of the Homeric Texts*. New York: A.D. Caratzas, 2000.

Skafte Jansen, Minna. "The Fairy Tale Pattern of the *Odyssey*." *Telling Reality: Folklore Studies in Memory of Bengt Holbek*, edited by Michael Chesnutt: 169–193. Turku: Nordic Inst. of Folklore, 1993.

Thalmann, William G. *The* Odyssey: *An Epic of Return*. New York: Twayne Publishers; Toronto: Maxwell Macmillan Canada; New York : Maxwell Macmillan International, 1992.

———. *The Swineherd and the Bow: Representations of Class in the* Odyssey. Ithaca, N.Y.; London: Cornell University Press, 1998.

Tracy, Stephen V. *The Story of the* Odyssey. Princeton, N.J.: Princeton University Press, 1990.

Van Duzer, Chet. "Duality and Homeric Saving Devices." *Midwestern Folklore* 23, no. 1 (Spring 1997): 5–12.

———. *Duality and Structure in the* Iliad *and* Odyssey. New York: P. Lang, 1996.

Walsh, Thomas R. *Fighting Words and Feuding Words: Anger and the Homeric Poems*. Lanham, Md.: Lexington Books, 2005.

Weinbaum, Batya. "Lament Ritual Transformed into Literature: Positing Women's Prayer as Cournerstone in Western Classical Literature." *Journal of American Folklore* 114, no. 451 (Winter 2001): 20–39.

# Acknowledgments

"Transition and Ritual in Odysseus' Return" by Charles Segal. From *Singers, Heroes, and Gods in the* Odyssey: 65–84. © 1994 by Cornell University. Reprinted by permission.

"Odysseus and the Genus 'Hero'" by Margalit Finkelberg. From *Greece & Rome* 42, no. 1 (April 1995): 1–14. © 1995 by Oxford University Press. Reprinted by permission.

"The Wanderings" by S. Douglas Olson. From *Blood and Iron: Stories and Storytelling in Homer's* Odyssey: 43–64. © 1995 by E.J. Brill. Reprinted by permission.

"Internal Narrators, Female and Male" by Lillian Eileen Doherty. From *Siren Songs: Gender, Audiences, and Narrators in the* Odyssey: 127–160. © 1995 by the University of Michigan. Reprinted by permission.

"Penelope as Moral Agent" by Helene P. Foley. From *The Distaff Side: Representing the Female in Homer's* Odyssesy, edited by Beth Cohen: 93–115. © 1995 by Oxford University Press. Reprinted by permission.

"Rival Homecomings" by Frederick Ahl and Hanna M. Roisman. From *The* Odyssey *Re-Formed*: 27–42. © 1996 by Cornell University. Reprinted by permission.

"Penelope's Perspective: Character from Plot" by Nancy Felson-Rubin. From *Reading the* Odyssey: *Selected Interpretive Essays*, edited by Seth L. Schein: 163–183. © 1996 by Princeton University Press. Reprinted by permission.

"The Structures of the *Odyssey*" by Stephen V. Tracy. From *A New Companion to Homer*, edited by Ian Morris and Barry Powell: 360–379. © 1997 by Koninklijke Brill. Reprinted by permission.

"Kalypso and the Function of Book Five" by Bruce Louden. From *The* Odyssey: *Structure, Narration, and Meaning*: 104–129. © 1999 Johns Hopkins University Press. Reprinted by permission.

"In the Beginning Was Proteus" by Mark Buchan. From *The Limits of Heroism: Homer and the Ethics of Reading*: 50–71. © 2004 by the University of Michigan. Reprinted by permission.

"The Stakes of the Plot" by Richard Heitman. From *Taking Her Seriously: Penelope & the Plot of Homer's* Odyssey: 11–33. © 2005 by the University of Michigan. Reprinted by permission.

# Index